Nature's Wings

and

Their Passengers

B.H.Coles

First Published in the UK in 2018
by
Constant Copy
The Fort Offices
Artillery Business Park
Oswestry
SY11 4AD

www.constantcopy.co.uk/press

Constant Copy
A way with words

A catalogue record of this book is available from the British Library.

ISBN 9781729173961

ACKNOWLEDGEMENTS

A number of relatives and friends have helped in bringing this book to fruition by reading and advising on the text. Among these are Andrea Burton and her birdwatching friends, my daughter Helen Adderley, who has meticulously edited the manuscript, my niece Julie Fitzsimons, who has proofread the final manuscript, my friend and colleague Professor Maria Krautwald from Leipzig University and my son, Nigel Coles. I am particularly grateful to John Drakeley for providing the jacket photographs. In addition, many professional colleagues and fellow birdwatchers and staff at the North of England Zoological Society, and the Liverpool Ornithological Society have often unknowingly contributed to this book by triggering off my thoughts on particular aspects of the subject.

ANY MISTAKES OR FALSE CONCLUSIONS ARE ENTIRELY THE FAULT OF THE AUTHOR.

ABOUT THE AUTHOR

Dr. Brian Coles has practised as a veterinary surgeon since qualifying from Liverpool University in 1956. He has had links with Chester Zoo since his student days and remains an external advisor to their Animal Health, Welfare and Husbandry Sub-Committee. Having run his own practice on the Wirral for over thirty years, he has treated countless pets of all kinds, zoo and farm animals, numerous varied wildlife casualties and thousands of birds from hundreds of different species.

In 1985, Brian published his first book "Avian Medicine and Surgery" which remains a staple text for both veterinary students and practitioners, and which has been translated into Japanese. He has also contributed to numerous academic publications, presented papers and lectures, been interviewed on radio and appeared on the

BBC and ITV. In 1999, in recognition of his work, Brian became an Honorary Fellow of the Royal College of Veterinary Surgeons and his work also led to him being made Emeritus Specialist in Zoo and Wildlife Medicine of the R.C.V.S. in 2010, a very rare honour for practitioners.

He was a founder member of the European College of Avian Medicine and Surgery, which merged to become the European College of Zoological Medicine, of which Brian was made an Honorary Diplomat in 2015.

Since his early teens, when his family was evacuated to North Wales during the Second World War, Brian has had an endless fascination with animals of all kinds. By the time he sold his practice in 1994 Brian was working solely with birds and was being consulted by colleagues as far afield as Belgium, Canada, Sweden and Finland. Brian continued to work as a specialist consultant in his former practice for many years.

Now in his ninety-first year, Brian is widowed, lives in Chester, has two grown up children and four grandchildren, and remains active both in his leisure time when he enjoys opera and travelling, and professionally.

DEDICATION

To my ever patient and understanding
late wife, Daphne.

CONTENTS

NATURE'S WINGS AND THEIR PASSENGERS

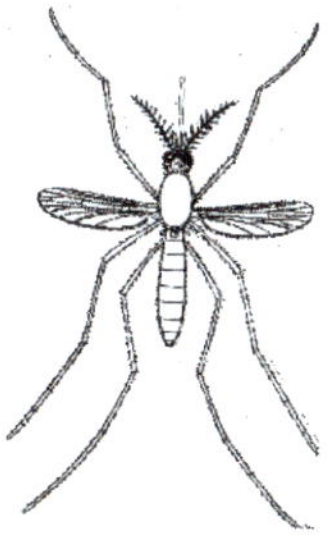

The story of the ultimate origin and evolution of infectious disease in humans, in birds and other winged creatures and in all living creatures.
An intelligent person's guide to the ultimate origin of infectious diseases.

"The important thing in science is not so much to obtain new facts as to discover new ways of thinking about them."

Sir William Bragg *1862-1942*

FOREWORD

On a warm summer's day, you may be alerted by the harsh screaming "sweeree" sounds above your head and gazing upward, you see the swifts wheeling and circling expertly in the sky. You note in admiration that they hardly ever seem to close their wings like a swallow, but glide effortlessly on outstretched wings most of the time.

How high they fly will depend on how hot is the day, because they glide in the warmed layer of rising air where their prey is to be found. With their mouths agape they are expertly trawling the air to catch their dinner from amongst the multitude of tiny insects and other creatures forming the aerial plankton occupying the layer of warm summer air.

The swifts are particularly noticeable and noisy in summer above the hot city streets of a southern European town such as Zaragoza in Spain or even in North Africa. Alternatively, if weather conditions are right, the swifts may be seen hawking low over green pastureland or over an expanse of water.

Plate No.1 swifts in summer sky

Again, how many birdwatchers will know that all types of birds are carrying within and on the surface of their bodies quite a large passenger list of other living creatures? A few of these fellow travellers may have the potential to cause infectious disease, whilst others are mostly just relatively harmless travellers, or even helpers, in the battle for life of the bird carrying them.

Plate No.2 A skein of Hooper Swans in V-formation flight

We might also gaze in wonder at the Hooper swans flying in the characteristic energy saving V-formation, typical of many groups of larger birds. These Hooper swans were travelling from their overnight roosting site to their early morning feeding ground in southern Scotland during early March, before migrating north to their breeding grounds in Iceland later in the year.

Coming closer to ground level and observing the starlings or blackbirds on the lawn, how many of those birdwatchers gazing with interest will know that there may be tiny insect passengers on these birds which are themselves carrying other minute living organisms?

Some people's reaction to this knowledge might be "How horrible, I shall never again look on these beautiful creatures in quite the same way". Nevertheless, this is all part of the intricate web of life, forming the natural world in which we, and all other living creatures, live.

Over the last 30 years or so, birds have become ever more prominent in the public eye. Birdwatching has grown increasingly popular and been encouraged by societies such as the RSPB in the UK and the Audubon society in the USA. Furthermore, the BBC wildlife programmes presented by David Attenborough and other naturalists have encouraged the general public to become much more aware of wildlife and particularly the birds around them.

We are constantly being warned about the effects of human activity, such as changes in farming practices, including the excessive use of fertilisers and pesticides, the use of antibiotics as growth promoters, all combined with contamination of the environment with industrial chemicals such as phthalates and polychlorinated biphenyls (PCBs). All these factors, together with global warming, are threatening the continued existence of many familiar birds and other wildlife as well as our own human survival.

From what we hear and see in the media, particularly if the facts can be made to appear dramatic, we get the impression that all bugs, bacteria, viruses and fungi are bad news. We hear quite a lot about human infectious disease such as emergent antibiotic resistant strains of bacteria like MRSA and *Clostridium difficile,* and also particularly, at the time of writing, of the Ebola and Zika viruses.

Also, we are alerted to news of dangerous new types of bird and swine flu viruses which may also be infectious to humans. Only then perhaps do we realise that birds and other creatures do carry some infectious diseases similar to those occurring in humans. In fact, many of the infectious disease-producing agents, the so-called pathogens, affecting birds and other animals are related to, or even the same as, those infecting humans.

The agents of infectious disease are living organisms themselves. Furthermore, like all other living things, they have evolved with us and the birds from a single original common ancestor. They haven't just occurred; they have been with the birds, with us, and all other living creatures from the beginning of life on earth.

However, in contrast to humans, in general, wild birds and other wild animals, have tended to adjust to the pathogens, enabling them to live with many of these fellow time travelers in relative harmony. Only comparatively few of these minute living transmissible disease producing agents have become directly harmful to birds or even to humans and even then, often only under certain conditions, often provoked by human activity.

The unaided human eye is not able to view the multiplicity of bacteria, of fungal spores, of viruses and many other microscopic organisms, all of which represent the greatest diversity of all life on earth. These microscopic organisms are everywhere, in the air we breathe, on the ground on which we tread, and in the surroundings which we touch. They are far greater in number than all of the life forms which we can see with our normal unaided eyes.

We sometimes hear about so-called "emerging" diseases as if they, figuratively speaking, have suddenly crawled out of the woodwork. These often turn out to be caused by a previously unrecognised microscopic organism which has been in the environment all the time but only recently been identified as the cause of a particular disease.

Looking back to the time when we were at secondary school and first starting to learn about biology, we may have been taught about such creatures as the amoeba and hydra and perhaps even bacteria. Maybe we were encouraged to read about such diseases as smallpox and how Lady Mary Wortley Montagu, wife of the British ambassador to Turkey in the early 1700's when George I was on the throne, who, although not medically qualified, defied medical convention and encouraged a type of vaccination (variolation) against smallpox. Dr Edward Jenner didn't introduce the safer method of vaccination until 1796. It might also have been suggested that we glance at Charles Darwin's book "The Origin of Species."

On entering university, a choice must be made. You study either veterinary or human medicine or biology, as distinct sciences, in much greater detail than that which you were taught at school. Your thoughts and learning are guided by your professors and lecturers, all of whom will have developed their own ideas, which

are to their students perhaps, less open to challenge. After you have left university and try to put into practice what you have been taught you may discover that things, as you may come to see them, are sometimes rather different.
I would now like to invite you to come on a journey with me to share my thoughts which have developed from my observations and study since I started out as a vet in the 1950's.

The purpose of this book is an attempt to illustrate the principles and the ultimate origin and evolution of all infectious diseases, primarily through the eyes and interest of the naturalist and birdwatcher. I want to put forward the idea that infectious disease is not just a bird disease or a disease of other animals or even just a human disease but is caused by an infectious agent which may or may not be infectious to one, two or indeed many different types of animals including humans. Furthermore, many infectious diseases are spread by winged flying creatures and are not just passed from one individual to another by direct contact, that is, by contagion (like the Ebola or HIV viruses) between infected individuals. Moreover, I want to illustrate that some infectious agents have close relatives which are sometimes beneficial and even essential to their hosts, often other living creatures.

In today's world, discussion about infectious disease particularly in the popular media is mostly anthropocentric, considering only those infectious diseases in humans, or in our domesticated animals. However, infectious disease affects all living organisms, from the very smallest to the largest, whether domesticated or wild. We could include plants but the situation is complicated enough when just considering the animals! Moreover, the pathogenic organisms causing infectious disease didn't just occur, they have been gradually evolving from the very beginning, from the time when all life on earth first began.

Although this book is entitled *NATURE'S WINGS AND THEIR PASSENGERS*, it will be seen that although birds can become infected with and carry many diseases, it isn't just birds that act as the carriers of infectious disease. Many other flying creatures, particularly bats and flying insects such as mosquitoes, Tsetse flies, sand flies, even the common housefly, may carry disease producing organisms.

CHAPTER 1

The author's growing interest in the evolution of the infectious disease producing organisms; the Pathogens.

Since the 1950's I have had a connection with zoo kept animals when, during my training as a veterinary student, I saw practice (a type of apprenticeship) with the veterinary surgeon Bill Jordon, dealing with the treatment of sick animals at Chester Zoo.

It was during this time that I noticed that the mortality rate amongst zoo kept animals was sometimes quite high. Why should this be so? These zoo animals are in a protected environment and fed on the best diet.

If an animal died in the Zoo you just went out and arranged to get a replacement from an animal importer. In fact, at that time it was said of the well-known department store in London, Harrods, that they 'would be able to order any wild animal you required - even an elephant'. Only in January 2014 did Harrods announce the closure of their department selling exotic animals.

Nowadays sourcing animals for the more advanced zoos is very different. Mostly, replacement animals often come from other zoos where they have been bred.

Also, much more attention is now being paid to why a zoo kept animal dies. A lot of investigation using detailed microscopic pathology and other laboratory techniques is used to find out why an animal has died and, perhaps more importantly, could anything have been done to prevent the death and therefore any other animals from suffering the same fate.

This is an activity with which I, now in my early 90's, am still involved. Also, as the database of which diseases affect zoo kept animals is gradually building, this knowledge can be applied to the same species of wild animals and can serve to help in their conservation.

Great attention is now given to making sure the diet and the environment in which the zoo animal is kept is of the highest standard. At Chester Zoo, a scientific dietician works out the best diet for all types of zoo kept animals, and this knowledge is made available to other zoos. At one time, many animals in zoos were kept as singletons of their species. Now a lot of international effort is made to at least keep animals in breeding pairs or in groups of their own species.

If a replacement is required it is often obtained from another zoo, sometimes from the other side of the world. Moreover, many countries which are not as wealthy as the western nations, are being helped and encouraged to protect and conserve their remaining wildlife together with their habitats, and also to educate their children in this very important aspect of their own country's heritage. Many children in third world countries do not know of, or have never seen some of the indigenous species of their own countries.

My particular veterinary interest in birds was stimulated by a client, the late Mrs. Jane Radcliffe, a skilled and knowledgeable naturalist who rescued injured wild owls and then attempted to rehabilitate them.

When she first brought them to my surgery and I told her I knew nothing about wild birds, she replied, "*Well you should shouldn't you? You are a Vet aren't you*"? I then thought to myself; *"You are quite right*", so I started to learn more about wild birds and their diseases.

I soon found that a bird's response to infectious disease was sometimes somewhat different to how humans and other animals responded. In the 1960's, unlike today there were no courses, lectures or even many textbooks on the subject, and there was no internet. It was a matter of learning on the job and digging out information where it could be found.

I lived quite close to Liverpool University's veterinary field station, so I had the opportunity to use this valuable resource, researching in their library and exchanging ideas with some of the lecturers. I also learned by talking to those people who did know something about birds because of their working experiences with birds, such as falconers, naturalists, game or aviary keepers and the like. However, they did not necessarily know how to diagnose the ultimate cause of a disease, nor how to effectively treat the condition.

Today, with the multiplicity of textbooks, the specialist organisations, such as the American Association of Avian Veterinarians, the European college of Zoological Medicine and Surgery, (which I helped to found), the British Veterinary Zoological Society, and many other international organisations, all interconnected by the internet, acquiring such knowledge is very much easier.

In the early days, I was also encouraged and helped by a local G.P., the late Dr David Cook who was a keen birdwatcher, a conservationist and a very good wildlife photographer. He had been trying to treat injured wild birds himself, and in order to do this, to anaesthetise them (but unfortunately not very successfully). He soon discovered that I was a more successful bird anaesthetist, and so we learned from each other.

At university, I had been taught about the anatomy of the chicken and about poultry diseases in general. However, I soon realised that poultry were not typical of birds as a whole. The farmyard chicken has evolved from the wild Red Jungle fowl of Asia which many breeds of chicken still resemble.

Plate No.3 The Red Jungle fowl

Although this bird can fly sufficiently well to be able to perch above ground in a tree, it spends much of its time scratching for food on the ground and not flying. In addition, the diseases to which poultry are subject, are often due to them being confined and concentrated together on poultry farms or on smallholdings. Furthermore, the diseases of poultry tend to be somewhat different from those which affect wild birds. Domestic poultry do not get some of those infections which occur in free living wild birds, or even those birds kept as pets or in zoos such as the parrots, mynah birds, budgerigars, canaries or even penguins.

When you start to consider the subject of the evolution of infectious disease in animals and humans as a whole, you soon realise that the vast majority of the research has been, and is still, naturally enough, being carried out on human disease. Nevertheless, much of the research carried out specifically regarding humans is still applicable to all animals because the basic biological processes of combating infectious disease are similar in all animal species.

In addition, the human species is just one species, whereas birds comprise about 10,000 species. It should also be remembered that our own human species, the *Homo sapiens,* came into existence on this planet about 160,000 years ago. Even the earliest members of the genus *Homo habilis,* died out about two million years ago, whereas the earliest birds started to evolve from a group of feathered dinosaurs about 115 **million** years ago, which is a timespan over 50 times as long.

Not all types of birds evolved at the same time, and not all wild birds get the same kinds of infectious diseases, the subject is almost limitless. In addition, humans evolved from a common ancestor together with the monkeys and apes, also known as the primates. Some of the primates, including the old-world baboons, the macaques and some of the apes, inhabited the tropical and semitropical regions of Africa and it is from this area that the ancestors of modern man are believed to have emerged some 5-7 million years ago. Consequently, the study of the infectious diseases in today's human species (*Homo sapiens*) covers a much shorter time-period, and also a more restricted field of infectious disease affecting just one animal species, when compared with the situation in birds, or even more so when considering that of all the other animals.

It follows then, that the birds have had a very much longer timespan to adapt to the organisms causing infectious disease. In fact, at least 16 times as long as modern man. It is true that many human diseases still infect the monkeys and apes, and in fact that is where some of todays' human emerging viruses have originated.

Consequently, interested parties of 'eco' tourists, being taken to view the gorillas in central Africa, must be kept some distance from these animals, lest the humans pass on their infectious diseases, such as influenza, to the apes.

Health and Safety officials often worry about human visitors to the zoo picking up diseases from the animals, but sometimes the more serious risk is the other way around. The captive apes in the zoo face a greater danger of catching diseases from human visitors such as the Human Respiratory Syncytial virus.

What is more, much of today's human infectious disease has been fostered by a change in lifestyle from the original humans who lived in small groups of hunter gatherers. In general, these hunter gatherers, gradually grouped together to become pastoralists rather like some of today's Bakhtiari people of south western Iran.

The pastoralists gradually mixed together and became more settled, to form groups of village farmers. All such people began living in closer association with the animals, including poultry, which they had captured and then domesticated and which they then concentrated in ever more dense holdings.

The growth of human populations has led to people living in increasingly more concentrated groups. These communities have evolved from a collection of a few dwellings into hamlets. The hamlets then progressed to become villages which are often, in the UK at least, today governed as parishes. These then merged into towns with the original parishes still retaining their names as districts of the larger towns. The towns themselves often then evolved into much larger conurbations or cities. In biblical times Babylon was the first city to have over 200,000 inhabitants and historically was known for its succession of 'plagues'. This was arguably the beginning of the age of epidemics.

Today such mega cities as the London metropolis, Tokyo, Mexico City and Dhaka each have around 10 million inhabitants and all are still fast expanding. Until comparatively recently some of these towns and cities, although not as large as they are today, had inadequate sanitation and sewage disposal, so some infectious diseases such as Typhoid and Cholera were easily transmitted between individuals.

The foregoing is only a very rough guide to the evolution and the gradual development of the modern mega city and it should be remembered that this description applies principally to the Western world, although it is beginning to take place in other regions, such as China.

The whole process originally started in the 'cradle of civilisation' – that is to say, in the fertile crescent at the head waters of the Tigris and Euphrates valleys of Mesopotamia. Why it is thought to have initially started in this geographical region was due, by chance, to a number of factors simultaneously occurring in this region of the world. First, there was a mild Mediterranean climate, secondly there occurred several wild species of annual plants (the grasses), producing a yearly crop of edible cereal grain (Emmer wheat, Einkorn wheat and Barley are examples), as well as the pulses (lentil, pea and chickpea.) Lastly, there occurred several wild mammals which could be domesticated such as sheep, goats and cattle.

This combination of factors did not simultaneously occur in other parts of the globe at the same time, and indeed some of the world's human populations have still not advanced much from the hunter gatherer stage. For instance, the San people of the Kalahari Desert are still hunter gatherers, as are several of the tribes living in the Amazonian rainforest. Also, the Aboriginal people of Australia and some tribes of New Guinea are still very much hunter gatherers. About 30% of Mongolians are nomadic pastoralists, as are the Tuareg people of Mali.

Birds have also, to some extent, been affected by the changes man has brought to this planet such as the destruction or pollution of some of the birds' habitats. However, apart from the poultry industry, humans have had comparatively little effect on the relationship between wild birds and their infectious diseases. This is notwithstanding the effects that man has had, and is continuing to have, on the wild birds' environment.

In comparison with humans, some species of birds, such as penguins, do collect together in closely packed rookeries of 2 million or more individuals. Roosts of gannets and other sea birds may be as large as several thousand individuals. Also, there are the flamingos, some colonies of the Lesser Flamingo in Kenya are recorded as having 100,000 individuals. These groups of birds form large numbers of relatively closely packed nesting birds. Nevertheless, in these large densely packed colonies of birds the nests are usually evenly spaced out with just enough distance between individual nests so that the threat of aggression is not too much of a problem.

There is of course no sanitation, and there is the potential for the easy transmission of infectious organisms, especially if insects, such as flat flies, act as vectors. Moreover, birds do carry lice, which in humans can transmit bacterial organisms such as the Rickettsia causing Typhus or *Trench fever.* This organism was common both in the Nazi concentration camps of the Second World War and in the prisons of the Middle Ages. It is recorded that from such places as the notorious Newgate prison in London the disease spread to the Old Bailey, the Central Criminal Court situated next door, and so spread to infect not only the prisoners but the court officials as well.

It is estimated by Robert Burton that about one tenth of the world's bird species breed in colonies. Nevertheless, these colonies are not usually affected with large 'die offs' caused by infectious disease. Why should this be?

Plate No.4 Little Stint [Calidris minuta] searching in the muddy shallow water at low tide.

Have you ever wondered, whilst watching the many varieties of wading birds seen on the coastal mudflats and marshes, such as curlew, redshank, oystercatcher, knot, dunlin or egrets, each digging for invertebrates in the mud, which itself is teaming with bacteria, why these birds never get bacterial infectious disease? Again, you may see a water rail or spotted crake slowly picking its way through the almost repulsive glutinous mud of a reed bed searching for its food. All these different types of birds are different species, each of which will be reacting to their environment in their own individual way. Some of these birds are regularly seen on human sewage farms.

Multiple mortality among the wading birds, when it takes place, is often due to chemical pollution caused by human activity. Birds have, over eons of time, evolved to become resistant to most of the bacterial pathogens, always provided that humans do not make sudden and important changes to the avian environment. Geographical position may well be important too. It is possible that because gannet and tern colonies are situated in windy, well ventilated sites, or flamingo colonies are situated in the middle of large areas of water of high salinity, this may have an impact on disease resistance. It is arguably also possible, that the overriding common condition with all of these species is that birds have had very much longer than humans to develop an effective innate immune response to the microorganisms which thrive in the birds' excreta. This book focuses on just a few infectious diseases to illustrate the author's ideas, developed since qualifying as a veterinary surgeon in 1956.

CHAPTER 2

In the very beginning, the start of all life, including the agents of infectious disease.

To consider how all life, including that which is responsible for infectious disease, from the smallest bacteria to the largest elephant and man, is related, we need to look at how all life on earth is believed to have originated from the scientific point of view. It is thought that all living things started from a single last universal ancestor (LUA), also known as the last universal common ancestor (LUCA). Charles Darwin wrote in his Origin of Species;

> *"Therefore, I should infer from analogy that probably all the organic beings which have ever lived on this earth have descended from some one primordial form, into which life was first breathed".*

He includes within this all those creatures, of which some have become disease producing organisms, or parasites of other living organisms. Furthermore, in 1871 Charles Darwin wrote in a private letter to a friend

> *"life possibly arose in some warm little pond, with all sorts of ammonia and phosphoric salts, light, heat, electricity etc."* and he continued *"perhaps a protein molecule was chemically formed, ready to undergo still more complex changes."*

This idea was regenerated in the 1920s by both J. B. S. Haldane and A. I. Oparin. They predicted that simple organic molecules were formed in the primeval seas from the dissolved gases: carbon dioxide, ammonia, methane and hydrogen, these gases having been originally formed in the primitive atmosphere when planet earth first came into existence from its parent star, the Sun.

Darwin's original hypothesis was later partly confirmed experimentally in the laboratory in 1953 by Stanley L. Miller and Harold C. Urey (1) working at the University of Chicago. Their experiment was more recently repeated in October 2008 by Adam P. Johnson and his colleagues. These last researchers designed their experimental conditions to mimic those environmental conditions near a hot submarine volcanic vent. This is the environment in which it is now thought, where the actual synthesis of LUCA is more likely to have taken place.

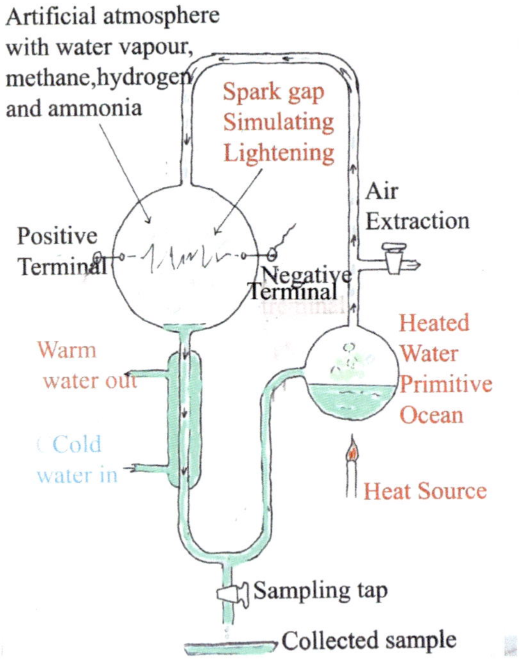

Fig No. 1 An illustration of the Miller and Urey laboratory apparatus

It is thought that some of the relatively simple organic molecules so formed, possibly reacted together, so that the product of their chemical reaction became the catalyst for a repeated chemical reaction between these same primeval molecules, that is, they formed their own, auto-catalyst and so a self-replicating process was started. There is in fact a lot of scientific evidence that major volcanic eruption was taking place on earth about 4,000,000,000 years ago, and most evolutionary biologists now believe that the precursor of all life forms started at about the same time, around 4,000,000,000 years ago.

Stuart Kauffman (4) believes that at some point in time, as the diversity of the chemical components increased, a complex interconnected web of self-catalysed chemical reactions came into existence, ultimately resulting in an early LIVING ENTITY, i.e. 'Life'. It is suggested that all these chemical mechanisms have gradually evolved over possibly three billion years so that ultimately Carl Woese and Norman Pace (5) believe that an interconnected web formed a sort of continuous living slime. This then possibly formed a kind of microbial mat covering large areas of the floor in the depths of a murky sea.

Recent research by Victor Gallardo of the University of Concepcion in Chile, who has taken part in a Census of Marine life, has discovered vast areas of the oceans' floors are in fact covered by giant bacterial mats where some of the bacteria are still deriving energy via the breakdown of the hydrogen sulphide, (the gas that smells like rotten eggs), in the black ooze in the depths of the ocean. Within this microbial mat, some controlling lengths of the web-like system possibly formed the first genes. Other sections of the web may have broken free to form the early viruses.

Several differing hypotheses on the actual site of the origin of life have been put forward by other scientists and some are listed below.

Darwin's idea of a warm little pond was more likely to be either a hot submarine volcanic vent or even a hot spring like those in Yellowstone National Park in the USA.

File:Grand prismatic spring.jpg
From Wikipedia, the free encyclopedia

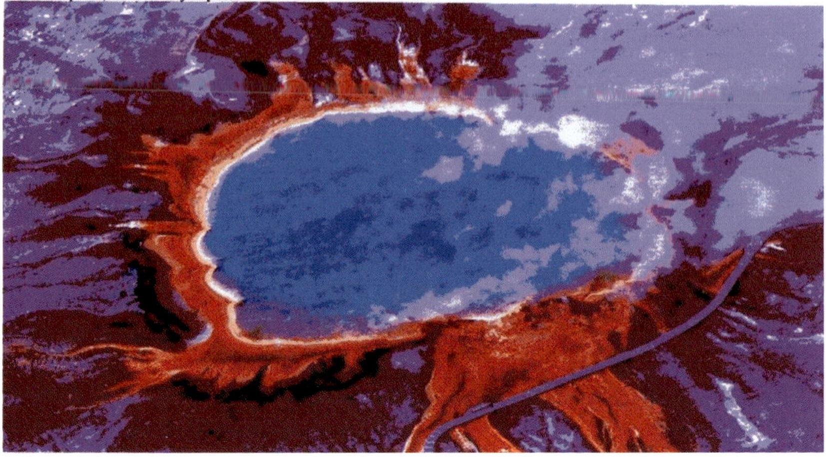

Plate No.5 Hot Spring in Yellowstone National Park USA.

In this breathtaking aerial view of the geyser the Grand Prismatic Spring, taken by Jim Peaco of the U.S. National Park Service, you can see the vivid colours which are produced by heat tolerant, early evolved bacteria which can thrive in temperatures of 50 to 70°C (122 to 158°F).

In this area, any surface water collecting in a pool from rainwater, drains down through fissures in the surface rock to a depth of 4 kilometres, where it meets molten lava. In fact, studies by David Deamer (80), working at Bumpass Hell on the bubbling mud pools of the volcanic area of North California, in a similar environment to Yellowstone, indicate a similar process could still be continuing even today. Also, recent studies in 2010 by Olivia U. Mason et al (93) using deep rock drilling techniques developed by the oil industry have demonstrated bacteria thriving deep in the earth's crust.

Similar hypotheses have been put forward by other scientists such as Martin and Müller (68). They believe that life possibly started in a similar environment at the bottom of the ocean, in muddy black ooze at a depth of 3.5 kilometres, where there was no oxygen but only the toxic gas hydrogen sulphide.

Again, in 2009, the biochemist and evolutionary biologist, Nick Lane highlighting the ideas put forward by Peter Mitchell, Bill Martin and Mike Russell has suggested, that life possibly started in an alkaline hydrothermal vent. Here the sea water seeped down in cracks in rock on the ocean bed. As the water seeped further down it got hotter and expanded to still more fractionate the rock. At the same time, the water chemically reacted with the rocky mineral Olivine. Eventually the hot water reached the underlying magma to boil and mix with the gases hydrogen, methane, ammonia and hydrogen sulphide. These gases then helped to form bubble permeated rocks riddled with a labyrinth of tiny pores, the size of which are not dissimilar to the dimensions of today's living cells. They may even have formed a template for the early cells, Nick Lane (92).

As the bubbling rocks pierced the surface of the sea bed they formed rocky pinnacles, almost like cathedral towers and when first discovered in the mid-Atlantic were thought to be the lost city of Atlantis.

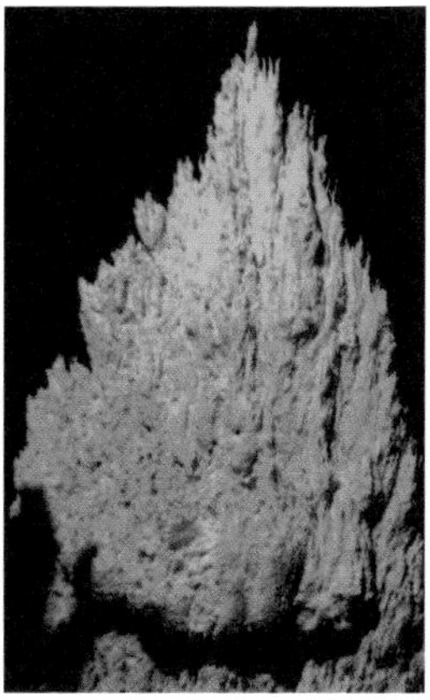

Plate No. 6 Bubbling rocks piecing the sea bed to form rocky pinnacles like cathedral towers in the mid -Atlantic

A similar idea has been put forward by Professor Martin Brasier, a palaeobiologist from Oxford University who suggests that pumice stone may have provided the medium in which life was first formed. Pumice is of course well known to many people who use it as a mild skin abrasive. It is of volcanic origin and is formed when lava, a superheated semi solid rock, flowing from a volcanic vent is rapidly cooled when it meets water and starts to solidify. The process results in a rock filled with numerous tiny pores. These make the pumice unusual amongst rocks in that it floats in water. The minute pores in the pumice were also lined with titanium oxide.

Today pumice is used by industrial chemists as a catalyst to manufacture ammonium fertilisers from atmospheric nitrogen. Professor Brasier presented his ideas to a meeting of the European Geosciences Union in April 2011.

However, despite all of these theories, it is almost certain that life probably only started once, in just one of these locations.

The first living organisms (the anaerobic bacteria) to evolve did not live in or on other creatures which had not yet evolved, and neither did they derive their energy from the sun's rays like today's plants. They absorbed their essential chemical constituents and their energy by the chemical reactions taking place in the volcanic seas in which they originated.

The Gene and the double stranded molecular helix.

After studying the X-ray diffraction images produced in the laboratory of the crystallographer and biophysicist Rosalind Franklin, James Watson and Francis Crick in 1953, formulated their hypothesis of the double stranded molecular helix forming DNA.

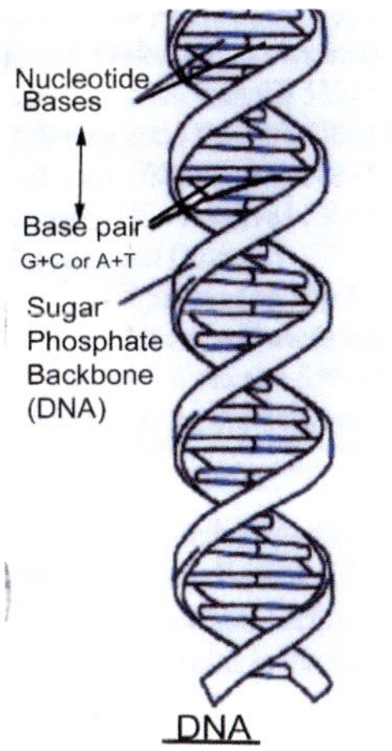

Fig.No 2 the double helix.
Schematic representation of a very short length of the basic structure of DNA

Often a length of DNA is very much longer than that illustrated.

Although Watson and Crick were working at Cambridge University, Rosalind Jackson was at Kings College London together with Maurice Wilkins and others such as Raymond Gosling all of whom provided the theoretical calculations which gave a clue to Watson and Crick in the interpretation of 'Photograph 51' the important image of the structure of DNA.

DNA forms the genetic code for **all** living things, be they bacteria, elephants, birds or humans. However, DNA has now become an expression which has entered our language to be used in a rather woolly manner, when describing the basic structure of all sorts of organisations not necessarily biological.

DNA is comprised of a long double chain of molecules (much longer than illustrated in fig No 2) which are twisted into a spiral. Each twist of this spiral is made of pairs of molecules (called nucleotides). Each member of the pair is linked to its partner by a hydrogen atom. The backbone holding the chain together and forming the twist of the helix is composed of a chain of sugar phosphate molecules composed of Deoxyribonucleic acid (DNA).

Thc four bases (the nucleotides) involved in this many times repeated structure are Adenine(A), Cytosine(C), Guanine(G) and Thymine(T). There is a pair bond rule, so that G is always paired with C and A is always paired with T. This is because each of the bases of a pair have slightly different shapes and must interlock together. Thus, the two sides (of the chain) of paired bases fit together rather like the two sides of a zip-fastener. Moreover, it is the constantly repeated, exact sequencing of these "base pairs" along the chain which acts rather like the bar code on packaging and which is important in the formation of a particular gene's structure and the gene's influence in the living body.

For instance, one individual gene can have TAGC at a certain position along its length, whilst another may have CGTA This very, very large linear molecule (of DNA) forms the basis of the gene that preserves genetic information of all individual living organisms be they bacteria, tigers, owls, insects or humans. Today this is the foundation of the generally accepted gene theory of evolution.

Each complete set of genes for an individual is called the genome of that organism. The number of genes in a genome may be very large indeed. In the human genome, this is 3,200,000,000 bytes of information (3.2 GB) whilst even the smallest virus, a pig circovirus has 1,759 bytes (1.8KB).

Sequencing of the genome of a particular organism using modern automated analysis, combined with fluorescent dyes, is now rapid, a matter of hours instead of days. It is widely used in many disciplines particularly in medicine to compare two pathogenic organisms, in biology to work out how closely related two similarly looking species actually are, and also in forensics when investigating crimes, to determine whether a specimen is related to other biological material at the scene of a crime. DNA analysis is also increasingly being used in archaeology to date biological items not only of skeletal remains but also wood and leather items revealed when glacial ice melts, due to global warming.

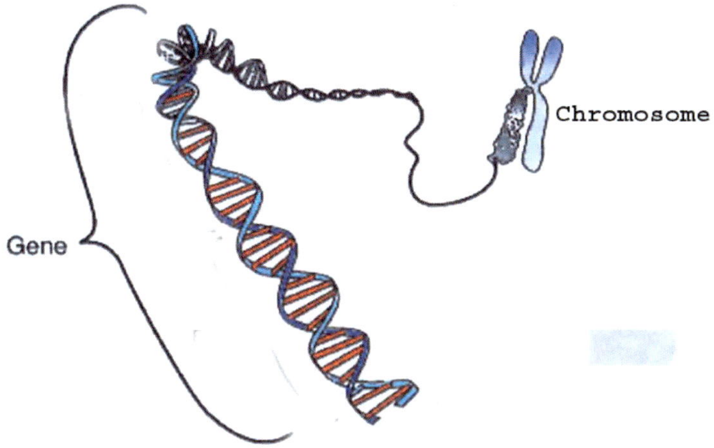

Fig No 3 The basic concept of the Gene and how this fits in with other genes to make up the chromosomes dwelling in the nucleus of each of the body's cells.

Mitosis

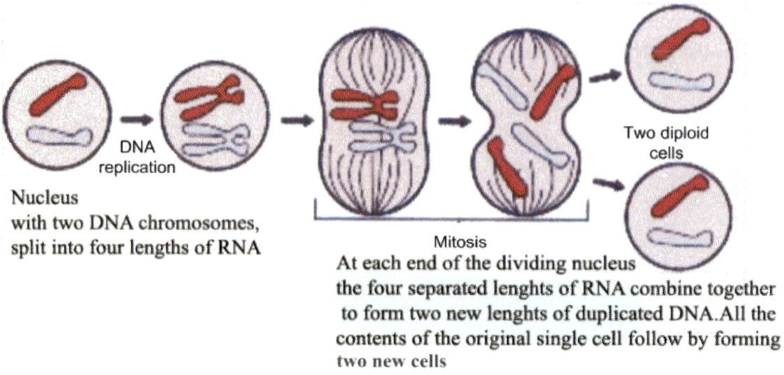
DNA
replication
Nucleus
with two DNA chromosomes,
split into four lengths of RNA
Two diploid
cells
Mitosis
At each end of the dividing nucleus
the four separated lenghts of RNA combine together
to form two new lenghts of duplicated DNA.All the
contents of the original single cell follow by forming
two new cells

Fig No 3a An outline of Mitosis illustrating how the chromosomes and their contained DNA are duplicated.

A further advance in understanding how the DNA could be read and interpreted was made by Marshall Nirenberg and J. Heinrich Matthaei in 1962. They showed that during the normal growth of each creature's body, there is replication of each body cell, including copying of the nucleus with its contained DNA. The double helix of DNA is zipped open, (similar to the workings of a zip fastener), along its length into two halves by the enzyme (a chemical catalyst) RNA polymerase. The enzyme runs along the edge of the DNA helix zipping open the spiral of DNA into two halves. At the same time this RNA polymerase reads and transcribes the genetic code onto two lengths of Ribonucleic acid (RNA).

RNA is a single stranded molecule and similar to one longitudinal half of DNA.

After the initial DNA has been split into its two halves and converted into two lengths of RNA, the whole process is then reversed. Using a similar series of biochemical reactions, the two new lengths of RNA, each made from one half of the original DNA, are used as a template and are transcribed into two new lengths of double stranded DNA.

The net result is that the separated two lengths of RNA formed from the original length of DNA have now been formed into two new lengths of DNA. Division of the whole body cell follows suit and the original single cell has now multiplied into two cells. As this is simultaneously happening in all the adjacent tissue cells, growth of the body organs continues.

Also, the same researchers showed how, in the formation of new germ cells in the sex organs (the ova/eggs of the female and the sperm of the male), the combined DNA of the parents is passed on to their offspring.

The result is that **each** cell in the body of the newly formed offspring will have in its nucleus a copy of the combined DNA of its parents. Half of the DNA will have been contributed by the male parent, and half by the female parent.

Meiosis

In contrast, during meiosis, that is, those body cells going to form the gametes, (the ova or egg of the female, or the sperm of the male), each of these will only contain just half (the haploid) of the number of genes as are contained in all the parent's mature body cells, (each of which contain the diploid (double) number of genes.)

During this rather complex copying process to form the genes in the nucleus of each new germ cell, a slight change in the sequence of the nucleotides forming the chain of DNA may 'accidentally' occur. For instance, the sequence of the nucleotides CCTA may be changed to CCAT. The same nucleotides are in use but a slip has occurred in their sequence.

Such a change in sequence during the copying process to form the gametes is called a "mutation."

Since each gene controls the formation of different proteins, each mutation will influence the composition of the variously formed different body proteins. Such proteins form enzymes, (biological catalysts), involved in the creation of the newly forming cell. These mechanisms form the complex chemistry of all life and this process is carried out in the same way by all living organisms including plants, fungi, animals and even bacteria.

A mutation can similarly also occur in viruses, although most biologists do not consider viruses to be living organisms.

A *mutation* may ultimately contribute to a change in body form such as the thickness of the skin or feather colour.

Alternatively, a mutation could result in the formation of a cancerous growth. In the bacteria, a mutation may result in an increase in toxicity to other living creatures which the bacterium may invade, to cause disease, or a mutation may result by the bacterium developing an increased resistance to antibiotics. Furthermore, any of these mutations in an animal, may have been triggered by an environmental chemical or a natural fungal toxin such as an aflatoxin, or by ultraviolet light or high energy radiation from a nuclear reactor.

In animals, a beneficial mutation may result in a slight increase or decrease in overall body size or perhaps in longer or shorter legs. This may ultimately result in Darwinian "natural selection" and in a better adaption to the environment which the creature inhabits, so resulting in the evolution of a new species. Alternatively, the mutation may be neither beneficial nor harmful to the animal, as it is in many cases. The mutation could just spread through the species as each member of that species reproduces, when the result is just known as *genetic drift*.

The genes are said to express themselves by directing a particular biochemical reaction, which in turn will trigger another biochemical reaction and so starting a cascade of such reactions or biochemical pathways within the particular cell.

The expression of the genes result in the formation of particular proteins and some of these may become enzymes. Other proteins are involved in the formation of bone, of skin or muscle and other parts of the body such as liver or kidney.

Enzymes have the ability to fold themselves up like a three-dimensional jigsaw puzzle. The folding results in complex spaces into which fit specific amino acids. The amino acids may be found 'floating' freely in the cytoplasm of the cell. When the amino acids are held temporarily in close association with each other, in their allotted spaces in their particular-matching enzyme, they react and join together to form the larger molecules of peptides.

The peptides then ultimately connect to each other to produce even larger protein molecules. In some cases, the protein will become another type of enzyme, which then catalyses a further biochemical reaction. This type of enzyme may be involved in the digestion of a food, or alternatively, in neutralizing a toxin (a poison) which could have been produced by a pathogen such as the bacterium causing Typhoid fever, or even by a species of plant (e.g. *Digitalis* or Foxglove used in treating heart conditions in the higher animals.)

However, some proteins are produced under the influence of so called "master genes" which serve only to activate or inhibit other genes. In these cases, these particular proteins are then called *transcription factors.* These are the main players in the regulatory networks, or cascades, of the vast number of biochemical reactions taking place within each individual cell.

In 1990 James Watson, one of the original discoverers of DNA, some time later initiated the Human Genome project. His proposal was to sequence the whole of the human genome. It was thought, at the time, that this project would identify the causes of many inherited diseases, and also the risk factors involved in some cases of cancer. In a few instances this has turned out to be the case, but it has also been found that very often a single gene is not linked specifically to a single trait in the body. A trait is often under the influence of multiple genes working in concert, and although the whole of the human genome project has now been completed, with the sequencing of an estimated 100,000 coding genes, it has been found that the body only makes *direct* use of about one quarter of these genes.

It is becoming increasingly evident, that it is not so much how the body makes use of each individual gene, but rather how the genes are reshuffled, in a manner rather like a pack of cards, that is important. As a follow up to The Human Genome project the ENCODE project was set up by the US National Human Genome Research Institute (NHGRI) in September 2003. The idea behind this was to provide an encyclopaedia of DNA. By 2012 the majority of the results had been released.

However, time moves on and it is becoming increasingly evident the more we learn about the human genome, the more we realise we don't know, and of course, this will apply to other living creatures as well as humans.

As creatures evolve, each living organism contains very nearly the same genes as its ancestor. A well-researched group of these genes are the HOX genes, which control how the organs and body parts of a multicellular creature develop in a regulated sequence. The HOX genes were first found in fruit flies, *Drosophila melanogaster*, in 1995 by Nüsslein-Volhard and Wieschaus, and in fact are found in all animals. It is only by the *gradual* mutation of the controlling genes that different animals, (and all life forms), have evolved. This can be seen in the various species of the cat family such as lions, tigers and leopards, together with the many races or breeds of domestic cats, for instance, all of which are genetically related and have gradually evolved from a common ancestor.

Arhat Abzhanov an evolutionary biologist from Harvard University, has demonstrated this in the laboratory. First, he drilled a small hole in the shell of a chicken egg in which the developing embryo had reached a certain stage of its development. Next, through the hole was inserted a small drop of gel containing certain laboratory produced protein signalling molecules. The signalling molecules are produced by the master genes to switch selected genes on and off. By this means, Abzhanov was able to "switch" the genes controlling the developing beak of a bird, to those that control the development of a snout similar to that in a crocodile. Both birds and crocodiles, in the distant past descended from a common ancestor, and their embryos in the developing egg go through similar stages of development, Sujata Gupta (110).

Epigenetics

This is the study of genetic effects not encoded in the DNA sequence of an organism, (hence the prefix epi- meaning over, outside of, around.) Such effects may result from external or environmental factors that switch genes on and off and affect how cells express genes.

It is becoming increasingly evident that how the genes are expressed is often under the influence of "epigenetic" markers. These epigenetic markers or "tags" which bind to the gene are mainly methyl groups (carbon hydrogen radicals, CH3, or one atom of carbon with three atoms of hydrogen). They are attached separately to each gene and act rather like an on/off switch and indicate to the gene whether to ignore or exaggerate the specific trait the gene expresses.

This biological mechanism is the same for all living creatures and the effect is simply illustrated by honeybees (*Apis Mellifera*). The queen honeybee mates with many male bees (drones) during the time of more than one mating flight. The sperm donated by the males is stored for future use by the queen in her spermatheca (a small sac in the reproductive tract.)

The queen bee will choose not to fertilise some of the eggs she has laid and these will develop into sterile males (drones.) These unfertilised eggs will carry only half the number of chromosomes, (the haploid number), as described above.

The remaining eggs (the ova produced by the queen herself), the queen will choose to fertilise with some of the stored sperm and, consequently, these will carry a full set (the diploid number) of chromosomes. These fertilised eggs have the potential to turn into either worker bees or queen bees and all are genetically true sisters; that is, they are all true clones, genetically identical to each other.

However, only a few of these fertilised female bees will turn into queen bees. This is because it is only the larvae that are continually fed throughout their growing period on royal jelly which will become queens. Feeding is carried out by so-called nurse bees, a specialised group of worker bees.

Royal jelly is a particularly nutritious food, being a mixture of special proteins, amino acids and unusual fats. It is secreted from special glands on the head of the nurse bees and it is fed continuously to the queen throughout her life, enabling her to go on laying eggs, sometimes up to 1000 a day. The rest of the larvae will turn into worker bees, and these are only fed on royal jelly for the first three days.

For female bees therefore, it is their diet during development rather than their genetic make-up as females which is important, and which decides whether the larvae eventually turn into sterile female workers or into another fertile queen bee.

Royal jelly enables the ovaries of the queen bee to develop, which doesn't happen in the worker bees. Also, the queen bee grows much larger than the workers. Worker bees have a life span of a few weeks, whereas a queen bee may live for several years.

Among the female bee population, a very few (fed on royal jelly) will develop into reproductive queen bees. These may mate with some of the males and then all these bees will quickly leave the hive, together with a swarm of workers to start a new colony.

Another experiment illustrating the influence of diet on how living creatures develop was discovered by feeding an unusually coloured type of mouse called the *Agouti*.

In normal coloured mice, the hairs are banded in colour, being black at the tip, yellow in the middle then black again at the base of the hair, and the hair colour is controlled by the *agouti gene*. However, if pregnant female *Agouti* mice were fed a diet rich in certain vitamins and amino acids, both of which constituents have a high level of methyl (CH3) chemical radicals, these females gave birth to normal brown coloured offspring, in contrast to those females not so fed, because the *Agouti* gene had been switched off.

In the *Agouti* mouse, when each single embryo is formed after the union of the ovum and the sperm, so creating the zygote, this gradually develops into the adult animal. At this initial stage, each cell in the developing embryo will have exactly the same active genes in its genome. However, very soon some genes (such as those controlling hair colour), will be tagged (with Methyl chemical radicals from the mother's diet for example), so that those genes involved in hair colour are switched off. This results in the normal, fully formed, adult mouse with a whole host of body cells, but with each individual cell having changed their genome from those in the initial embryo. This "switching on or off" of a particular gene or group of genes occurs throughout life.

Another illustration of the effects of **epigenesis** is the case of human identical twins. When born, these individuals start life with identical genomes in all their body cells but as the children get older they gradually develop different characteristics which were not caused by genetic mutation. This was illustrated by a study which included 80 sets of identical twins with an age range of 3-74 years. These types of differences were most marked in those pairs of twins with different lifestyles and little contact with each other whilst growing up, thus illustrating the effect of the different environments in which the individuals had developed into adults.

Any complete story of epigenesis is much more complicated than has been indicated here, but the essential difference between epigenetic factors in the environment, and the effects of a toxin or poison on an individual, is that toxins affect only the one *individual* animal which has taken the poison. In contrast, epigenetic factors have an influence on a gene's expression which is then usually passed on from one generation to the next.

Although this phenomenon has only been recognized relatively recently, Jablonka and Raz (94) have listed over one hundred cases of inherited epigenetic variations in bacteria, in other single celled organisms, in fungi, plants and a few higher animals. In their opinion they consider the phenomenon may be ubiquitous.

To make things even more complicated, lengths of DNA are far too long to fit into the nucleus of a cell. In humans, this length is approximately two metres, and all this could not be squeezed into the nucleus of a cell of approximately 0.01 (i.e.1/100th) of a millimetre in size. In consequence, the length of DNA is wrapped around globular clusters of folded proteins called **Histones**. These are rather like a length of knitting wool rolled into a ball to make it more manageable before being knitted together to make a garment.

Histones themselves can also be affected by epigenetic changes brought about by the attachment of Methyl and Acetyl radicals and can also influence specific genes being switched on or off.

Biological knowledge is continually and rapidly advancing in the new field of Epigenesis and a group of biologists are in the process of producing an **Epigenomic map** which will enable diagnosticians to discover which specific cells in the body are responsible for different diseases.

The USA Environmental Protection Agency estimates there are at least 60,000 commercially produced *toxic* chemicals in the environment. Toxic chemicals may not just affect one individual, but could affect a whole group of creatures which come into contact, either directly or indirectly, with that toxin. Such a toxic chemical may impact future generations because of its epigenetic influence on a variety of creatures. Many of these toxins could have hidden epigenetic effects on the expression of genes, and this is happening not only in humans, but in all living species, including birds and bacteria.

As we are continually learning more about the epigenetic influences in the environment, it is becoming increasingly apparent (as the evolutionary biologist, Stephen Jay Gould has pointed out in his book *Wonderful life* published in 1989), that if we were to turn the evolutionary clock back to any point in the past and start again, the outcome would be quite different.

Some of the basic explanations of all the mechanisms involved in gene expression will only come after studying what happens in simpler organisms such as bacteria or insects.

Looking into the future, with regard to specific genetic change, since 2013, work has been done to develop a laboratory technique to 'cut out' (using "***chemical scissors***"), particular non-desirable genes and replace them with a more advantageous gene using the so called CRISPR/Cas9 method, resulting in a type of precise genetic modification.

We should now look at how some groups of organisms have gradually changed over time to become infectious pathogens.

CHAPTER 3

The classification of all living organisms.

Why is this important when considering disease caused by microorganisms? Because we need to know which organism is involved and where it has originated. Some microorganisms may be relatively non-harmful, whilst a related organism could be toxic. An organism such as that causing The Great European Plague or "Black Death", may well have evolved from a much less deadly organism.

In the past, traditional Taxonomy (the science of classification of both living and dead biological organisms) has relied on the system devised by the Swedish naturalist Carolus Linnaeus (1707-1778), who classified individual animals and plants into species according to shared physical characteristics, or what they looked like, according to their so called "phenotype."

This method relies heavily on the comparison of observable characteristics, such as in the body plan: looking at the individual elements of the skeleton and noting the differences or similarities of the skull of some vertebrates, for example. Today, much more reliance is being placed on molecular (DNA) taxonomy, and the comparison of how the DNA is sequentially arranged along the length of all the genes extracted from the nuclei of the body cells. Recent research into their DNA, has shown that there are now more subspecies of giraffe than was originally thought.

It is important to be aware that only individuals of a living species can successfully mate and reproduce members of their own species. This contrasts with the situation where two individuals, not of the same species, mate, and produce offspring that are usually infertile.

This is because the genes of each of the parents have changed (mutated) so much over generations from their original common ancestor, that their gametes (e g. sperm and Ova) are no longer able to match up and produce a viable embryo able to develop into an adult of that species. Mating between individuals of similar, related, but different species produces *hybrids* which are usually infertile in mammals, but not always in birds.

A cross between a horse and a donkey produces the infertile mule. Crosses between lions and tigers produce ligons, (the offspring from a male lion and a female tiger), or tigons (the offspring from a male tiger and a lioness), both of which are infertile.

Amongst birds, interbreeding between similar species is not uncommon and the hybrids are often **not** infertile. The Eurasian Siskin (Carduelis spinus), which is found in Britain and northern and eastern Europe, can produce hybrids with some other finches such as the Canary (Serinus canaria). The wild Canary naturally breeds only in Madeira and parts of the Canary Isles.

Plate No.7 The Siskin (Carduelis spinus)

The American Black Duck (*Anas rubripes*) can mate with the common Mallard Duck (*Anas platyrhynchos*). In fact, many of the 'wild ducks' seen on the waterways in many parts of the more temperate climatic regions of the world, are not true representatives of the species of wild Mallard Duck but are often fertile crosses with domesticated breeds of duck. All of these ducks, both domesticated and wild, evolved from the original Wild Mallard Duck of Southeast Asia and Siberia.

The Mallard Duck can also mate with the Northern Pintail Duck (*Anas acuta),* producing fertile hybrids, as indeed it can with some other close relatives (in the same genus), but these hybrids are not always fertile. Because of this interbreeding with many close relatives, the Mallard Duck is a worldwide problem for many conservationists trying to conserve pure species of ducks.

Problems with the American Ruddy Duck.

The importation into Europe of the American Ruddy Duck (*Oxyura jamaicensis*), by the naturalist Sir Peter Scott, has resulted in this species thriving in its non-natural habitat.

Plate No.8 A male American Ruddy Duck (Oxyura jamaicensis)

This American duck has spread widely into western Europe and the male's aggressive courting behaviour and willingness to interbreed with the endangered native White-headed Duck, (*Oxyura leucocephala),* is causing problems in the White-headed Duck's native habitat.

Plate No.9 A male White-headed Duck, (Oxyura leucocephala)

This species is native to southern Europe, and the introduction of the Ruddy Duck has resulted in hybrids, causing concern for the survival of the White-headed Duck as a pure species. There is now an international programme to eliminate the American Ruddy Duck from Europe.

Hybridisation amongst other species of birds is not all that uncommon. Within the group of birds of prey known as the Falcons, particularly the larger falcons, all included in the subgenus the *Hierofalcons,* are four closely related species of falcon; the Lanner Falcon *(falco biarmicus)*, the Laggar Falcon, *(falco jugger),* the Saker Falcon *(falco cherrug),* and the Gyrfalcon (*falco rusticolus*). These large falcons all hunt in level flight, as distinct from the diving hunt of a Peregrine Falcon. The author has seen the individual hybrids (for example a Saker falcon crossed with a Gyrfalcon), which were then mated again (producing a triple cross) by their falconer owners. A hybrid might be mated with one of the smaller common falcons, such as the European Kestrel, to produce a smaller bird with some of the characteristics of its larger relations.

The hybrid, while retaining *some* of the 'advantages' from the unaltered genome of each of the two parent pure-bred species, (which each will only be changed by *mutation*), may therefore have an advantage over the genes of the unaltered representative member of one or other of the two "parent" species.

Fairly recently, hybridisation has been confirmed as having taken place amongst some of the group of birds scientifically classified as

Birds of Paradise. Erwin Stresemann, a 19th century German naturalist and ornithologist from Dresden, put forward the theory that many of the rarer Birds of Paradise were in fact hybrids. This was confirmed by a DNA study in 2009. The family is now known to have forty-one species distributed through 14 genera.

Modern molecular taxonomists study how to classify living organisms using sophisticated laboratory techniques combined with computerised software programmes. They can produce printouts of the DNA sequences along the genes of an organism and thereby enable comparisons with the DNA of other organisms. These may show how the sequences of DNA in the two organisms have changed through mutation over time, so that the molecular changes in DNA now indicate the formation of two distinct species of living organisms.

Sometimes the different organisms are noticeably physically different (as in the ducks mentioned above), but for a much smaller living organism such as bacteria, the formation of a distinct species will not be so obvious until their DNA has been sequenced and comparisons made.

In the group known as bacteria, the length of DNA forms an un-packaged structure, not enclosed within the membrane of the cell's nucleus. This is known as the *nucleoid.*

As slightly more advanced creatures developed, the chromosomes were collected together into a "packet" to form the cell nucleus, which became surrounded by its own nuclear membrane. The nucleus is situated within, and separated from, the bulk of the cell, which is composed of the various chemical units forming the cytoplasm.

The first living organisms, the bacteria, not having their chromosomes enclosed within a nuclear membrane, are referred to as Prokaryotes, whilst all other living creatures, with their chromosomes surrounded with a nuclear membrane, are called Eukaryotes.

Slime Bacteria (*myxobacteria*.)

These formed a syncytium (mass created from multinucleated cells), of continuous slime, as envisaged by Carl Woese and Norman Pace, as mentioned in Chapter 2, in describing the early evolution of life on earth. There exist today the myxobacteria ("slime bacteria") (such as *Myxococcus xanthus*). These are found almost ubiquitously in soil, moving actively by gliding through their habitat. They typically travel in large groups like a wolf pack containing many millions of cells, kept together by intercellular molecular signals, using a system of so called "quorum sensing". Slime bacteria are predatory, feeding on other soil bacteria.

There are also the "slime moulds" which are types of primitive fungi. The *Myxomycota* and the similar but unrelated *Acrasiomycota* are types of slime moulds, which can also form a slime containing un-separated nuclei and from which can subsequently emerge single amoeboid cells, each with its own nucleus of packaged chromosomes.

The evolution of such life forms was all happening millions of years before the birds and humans evolved, but it was the beginning of all life on earth.

The first definitive *living* organisms to evolve were the bacteria.

Chapter 4

The Viruses - Possibly the first ever pathogens

The infectious agents which today occupy an increasingly prominent place in all our minds and particularly of those trained in all branches of medicine, are the viruses. It is important to be quite clear that the bacteria and other microorganisms causing disease, are quite different from the viruses. Sometimes this distinction gets mixed up in the minds of newspaper columnists and others in the media reporting on infectious disease.

Today, because of recent serious outbreaks, both the Ebola and Zika viruses occupy a prominent place in our thoughts. We are all also concerned about the Measles virus, and about the different kinds of Influenza viruses. Besides the common 'flu which many of us get each winter, there are Swine 'flu and bird, or Avian, 'flu all of which potentially make us feel quite ill. In addition, there are many different viruses causing the common cold. Sometimes the common cold may be severe enough to be mistaken for one of the 'flu viruses.

In fact, the initial signs and symptoms of many diseases, both those caused by viruses and bacterial infections, can be very similar. They all show the same signs of the body's defensive reaction. There is a lack of energy and tiredness, depression, loss of appetite and sleepiness (all of which indicates the infected person is instinctively conserving the body's resources), and there may be a raised body temperature. These are all clear signs of the body's defensive response to a pathogen. The skill of the physician is to identify the underlying cause. This may be easier for the human doctor, who can reach a conclusion by questioning the patient, but an experienced veterinarian, by careful observation and examination, will be able to detect these tell-tale signs in all types of animals.

Farmers worry about Foot and Mouth disease infecting their cattle and about Blue Tongue and Schmalemburg viruses in their cattle and sheep. The latter results in the miscarriage or malformation of new born offspring. This virus was first seen in the UK in 2011, where it was spread from mainland Europe by small windblown biting midges.

African Horse Sickness may similarly be transported in the future to the UK by minute biting midges.

Virus particles themselves are so small, being about 1/100th the size of bacteria, which themselves are extremely small. Viruses cannot even be seen with a light microscope, as distinct from bacteria which, when suitably stained with an appropriate dye, can be seen with the microscope.

So how do viruses differ from bacteria in their structure?

Viruses largely consist of their genome, the long string of genes which is balled up like a length of knitting wool. This is usually enclosed within a protein shell called the capsid.

The capsid is sometimes helical (like a compressed spring), or icosahedral in shape, with 20 or more equilateral triangular faces forming a structure rather like a sphere (fig 4). Sometimes, as in the case of the papilloma viruses, the capsid, although still spherical in shape, has up to 72 identical faces. The viral capsid is a complex structure composed of a wall of folded protein molecules. It is manufactured by the host cell under the direction of the viral genes. In effect, the viral genes are instructing the host cell's genes to "make a viral capsid in accordance with my instructions in which I can hide."

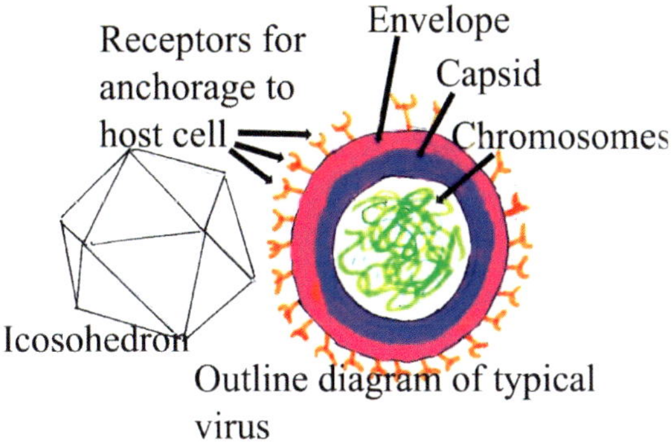

Fig. No.4 Basic structure of a typical icosahedral virus.

The colours in the diagram bear no relation to the colour of the virus, which in life is colourless.

The essential difference between bacteria and viruses is the place where they are usually found. Most bacteria don't enter the body cells of the animal or plant which they have invaded, most bacteria reproducing in the intercellular spaces *between* the body's cells. There are a few exceptions to this rule which are those bacteria causing human undulant fever (brucellosis), and those causing the disease babesiosis in humans and other mammals, as well as the bacterial pathogens, rickettsia and chlamydophila, all of which **do** enter the body cells of the infected host.

In contrast, **all** the viruses enter the host's cells and are dependent on the nucleus of such invaded cells of the infected living creature, and on the chromosomes of each invaded cell, to reproduce themselves.

Surrounding the viral capsid, many free-living viruses also have a fatty envelope derived from a host's cell wall. The virus acquires this envelope when exiting from a previously infected host cell, ready to infect another neighbouring body cell, as the disease progresses from cell to cell throughout the infected host, be it human or animal.

This viral envelope determines which cells of a host the virus particle will be able to invade. This is controlled by the protein receptor molecules formed on the viral envelope's surface, which must match precisely those receptors found on the surface membrane of the newly to be infected cell. Overall, various kinds of different viruses can infect the cells of all types of living organisms but *only* those cells for which their surface receptors match precisely those on the host's body cells, be they animals, plants or even bacteria.

Sir Peter Medawar (16) has described viruses as little more than "a piece of bad news wrapped up in a protein."

Viruses are considered by many scientists not to be truly living creatures, because they can only reproduce themselves with the aid of the cells of the animal or plant which they have invaded. Although they may persist in the environment, it is thought they cannot reproduce by themselves outside of a living host creature.

For those viruses which do have an envelope, and most do, after the virus has invaded the host cell, it is "un-coated", being stripped of both the envelope and its capsid, thus exposing the viral genes. Following this, the viral genes invade the host animal's own cellular nucleus and proceed to integrate, or squeeze themselves into selected spaces (or slots) in the host's genome (see fig. no. 2 in Chapter 2).

Having thus become part of the host's genome, the virus's genes make use of the host cell's enzymes to reproduce themselves. The viral genes are in fact 'taking over' their host's genome for the sole purpose of reproducing themselves. Like many species of bacteria, the individual particles of a virus can replicate rapidly, often in as little as 12 hours.

The whole sequence of viral gene replication exactly copies the same complex process as when the host's own cells themselves are duplicating. Duplication of body cells normally takes place during wound healing, or when growing the new body organs of a developing animal or a human fetus.

During infection by the virus, the host, having already produced the necessary enzymes for its own reproduction, is having these same enzymes “hijacked” by the viral invader, so that in effect, the host's cells carry out the work of replication for the invading virus.

After invading a host cell, the virus may go on to invade neighbouring cells, each time replicating itself to produce many more virus particles. This process may, and sometimes does, kill the host. Moreover, as the virus particles go on to invade and kill neighbouring host cells, the host becomes progressively sicker. If enough host cells are destroyed and the infected host cannot mount an effective defence, the human or animal will die.

Death of the host does not always happen. If it did, not only would the resulting epidemic wipe out all the individuals of the host species, but also that particular species of virus would become extinct. There would be no remaining animals of the host species to further replicate the virus.

Usually a compromise is reached. Either the host's immune system holds the virus in check, and the virus may take up permanent residence in some of the host’s cells (to become a latent infection), or the virus, during replication, mutates to become less virulent. The overall result is a ‘truce’ in the 'arms race' between the host and the parasitic virus.

Some viruses, such as the pox viruses, are able to carry out most of their replication within the host cell’s cytoplasm without all the virus actually invading the host cell's nucleus.

Other types of pathogenic viruses can remain dormant or latent within their host. A common example of a latent infection is the human herpes type chickenpox virus, scientifically known as the Varicella zoster virus. Chickenpox is an unfortunate name, since it has nothing to do with pox in chickens.

Overall, the genus (or related group) of herpes viruses in general have a characteristic ability to remain latent. In fact, their name is derived from the Greek word "herpein" meaning to creep or remain dormant.

The virus causing chickenpox in young children may alternatively lie dormant in humans from childhood through to adulthood. The latency occurs in some of the adult human host's special nerve cells. These are found in nodules lying along the spinal column, and form 'the dorsal root ganglia'. Later in the life of the adult person, the dormant virus may reactivate to cause the disease called Shingles. This disease can be quite a painful condition, as the author knows from personal experience. Shingles causes a red skin rash anywhere over the body surface, but most often around the waist, on the back, or on the face, and is accompanied by a fever, headache and sore throat. A vaccine is now available for suitable adults.

Another herpes virus which often becomes latent is Cytomegalovirus. This is so named because it causes a huge enlargement of the infected cell. It is common in humans, infecting between 50 and 80% of all persons in the USA, and by age 80 over 90% of individuals show that they carry a latent infection of the virus. However, it is only potentially fatal to very young children and immuno-compromised older individuals.

Cytomegalovirus has been found to infect some African and Australian finches, particularly the Australian Gouldian finch in which it can be fatal. The colourful Gouldian finch is an aviculturist's bird and can be difficult to breed outside its native habitat of the tropical savanna woodland of northern Australia. The virus is only recognised in captive birds when sick 'Gouldians' are taken to a veterinarian for treatment. Consequently, these birds were probably latent carriers of the virus, which is only exhibited when the bird becomes stressed during captivity. Moreover, in their native habitat, Gouldian finches often associate with other species of finches such as Long-tailed finches and Masked finches, which probably also carry the latent Cytomegalovirus, but which are not often kept as aviary birds.

Plate No.10 Gouldian finches (also called the Rainbow finch.)

Overall, there are over 130 species of herpes viruses, with some being identified in mammals, birds, fish, reptiles, amphibians, and molluscs. Since 1995 a group of about five distinct types of herpes virus have been identified in elephants. These mostly attack Asian Zoo kept animals, but the virus has been found in captive African elephants and also in both types of wild elephants. The mortality rate in young animals is about 80%. Death of young elephants, which are usually one to two years old, is caused by massive internal bleeding due to rupture of the internal blood vessels. In all probability, some adult elephants carry the virus in a latent condition.

Bovine malignant catarrhal fever.

This is another virus often carried in a latent condition, fatal to all species of cattle, together with deer, antelope and buffalo, and is carried by sheep without causing the sheep any harm or showing any signs of infection.

Mammalian herpes viruses are believed to have evolved between 180 and 220 million years ago, but it is probable that all latent viruses evolved long before then.

Amongst the many infectious pathogens of birds, some are latent viruses and only show themselves if the bird becomes stressed. The best known to the general public of a latent bird infection is that causing parrot fever or Psittacosis (due to Chlamydophila). This is not actually a virus, but in fact a type of bacterium.

The Nature of viruses and where have they come from? How have they evolved?

The current view among most medically trained persons, including human physicians, veterinarians, and microbiologists, is that viruses are the ultimate stripped down obligate intracellular parasites. They apparently contribute nothing to the cells which they have invaded, and as has already been pointed out, some viral infections eventually result in the death of the host.

However, the view amongst many evolutionary biologists is changing, as we shall see at the end of the following section.

It is likely that viruses have been around since the dawn of life, estimated to have been about 4,000 million years ago. However, Professor Anna Marie Shalka of the Fox Chase Cancer centre, has sequenced the genomes of 31 vertebrates for ssRNA viruses and has only been able to accurately assess their age to between 50-60 million years. Since today the viruses which have been identified require the RNA/DNA of living creatures to replicate, they must have been able to replicate by themselves, before living creatures had evolved.

In 2012 Jes Jǿrgensen, the lead astronomer of Denmark's Copenhagen University, was looking for signs of life in the universe beyond our planet. He discovered that there was evidence in the form of the molecules of a simple sugar called glycolaldehyde in the gas surrounding a star 400 light years away. Glycolaldehyde can be a precursor of RNA. Consequently, life may have started elsewhere than on planet earth.

Practically all living things, be they plant, animal or bacteria have viruses which have invaded them and which have evolved in conjunction with their hosts over millions of years.

The first virus to be identified was a plant virus, the Tobacco mosaic virus which causes mottling of the leaves of tobacco and related plants such as tomato plants, cucumbers and peppers. Although this infectious disease had been recognised since 1883, Dmitri Ivanovsky found evidence that the filtered sap of the infected plant could be passed through the finest Chamberland filters and still contain the infectious agent. This infectious agent was not isolated until Wendell Meredith Stanley crystallised the infectious sap of a plant in 1935.

Incidentally the crystallographer in Meredith Stanley's team was Rosalind Franklin, who later contributed to the discovery of the DNA double helix with Watson and Crick in 1953.

Unlike many life forms, viruses have left no typical fossils. Did the viruses travel over millions of years with the prokaryotes (the bacteria), as bacteriophages (small viruses invading bacteria), and then undergo gradual evolution to become more complex viruses, invading the archaebacteria (the fore runners of all other life forms)? Certainly, the adeno and herpes viruses resemble bacteriophages in several aspects of their replication and particle assembly, as is suggested by Ackermann, Berthiaume and Tremblay (17).

There are three main hypotheses regarding the origin of viruses.

1) They are “rogue” fragments of genetic material (either RNA or DNA), which have broken free of their chain of RNA or DNA within the cell and found a way, by using horizontal gene transfer, to locate in another cell.

So how did these 'rogue' pieces of DNA get out of the cell?
Plasmids are discrete, circular, small sections of DNA found in bacterial cells, and which are separated from the main mass of the bacterial cell's chromosomes (see fig. No. 6, Chapter 5). Plasmids are able to escape through the bacterial cell wall to enter a neighbouring cell. This can also happen in other simple life forms such as some worms. Therefore, why shouldn't these bits of an original genome not form a new virus in this same way? In this regard one might consider the relatively small circular genome of the circoviruses.

2) The second theory of viral origin, is that viruses evolved from proto, or simple, bacteria which have regressed from being free living organisms and, having discarded most of their cellular chemistry, have become obligate parasites. They have found it easier to hijack the essential cellular biochemistry used by their host, so that they can continue to propagate themselves and pass on their genes. Similarly, the types of bacteria called the Rickettsia and Chlamydophila are only able to replicate within the c*ytoplasm* of a host cell but not in the nucleus.

3) A third hypothesis for the origin of viruses, and the one which seems the most likely, is put forward by Ritchie, B.W(63). This is that both host and virus started out together from a common ancestor in the primeval sea. Recalling the hypotheses put forward by both Carl Woese & Norman Pace, and subsequently by Stuart Kauffman, the protists (an informal term for any eukaryotic organism that is not an animal, plant or fungus), and the early viruses, parted company to become separate self-replicating organisms. Later, the virus, having mutated during the course of many millions of years, invaded the original partner.

Colin Tudge (28) has suggested that possibly viruses have multiple origins, so that all three theories may have some truth in them. It is probable that those viruses which infect a broad range of species such as birds and many mammals including humans, such as influenza A virus and avian flu virus, are of more ancient origin than human smallpox virus, which only infects humans. Certainly, different types of viruses vary in the size of their genome and in the shape of their capsid, and so perhaps also in their life history.

Many viruses are single or double stranded RNA viruses. Others are single or double stranded DNA viruses.

Many viruses may also be classified according to the type of clinical disease they cause, such as the pox viruses or the 'flu viruses.

Some viruses are able to cross the species barrier, such as Cytomegalovirus, instanced above, infecting both birds and humans.

Another illustration of a viral disease which has crossed the species barrier is the economically important Gumboro disease, or infectious bursal disease, of growing chickens.

This was first discovered in Gumboro on the west coast of the state of Delaware in the USA in 1962. This virus has now spread worldwide. The cloacal bursa of Fabricius in birds, an organ in the rear gut junction of the bird, is an important site in young growing birds up to 8 weeks of age, producing the B-lymphocytes of its' immune system. The equivalent in humans is perhaps the tonsils or lymphoid tissue in the intestine. Inflammation of this organ in birds leads to a serious immune deficiency, and is often fatal. In some cases of Gumboro disease there is 60 to 100% mortality of young birds.

This type of virus is a birnavirus, which is believed to have been passed to young growing chickens from fish meal made from salmon-like (Salmoniformes) fish, Kannan Ganapathy (122). In fish, the virus causes a fatal infectious pancreatic necrosis._

Viruses are able to cross species barriers because the genome of *all vertebrates* is similarly constructed.
The virus is able to use the similar sections of DNA to integrate (or insert itself into the length of the host's genome), and so to replicate. In Chapter No.1 it was explained that when the double helix of DNA was split along its length into two halves to form two lengths of RNA, this was like opening a zip fastener. When an RNA virus inserts itself into the DNA of the parasitized host, it is using the length of RNA 'like the one side of the zip fastener' to fit into the host's DNA.

Other similar infectious agents to viruses are viroids, which are small molecules of RNA-like viruses but they have no capsid and they only infect plants. Also, the prions, which are not viruses but lengths of freely-existing infectious misfolded protein but which contain no nucleic acid, neither RNA nor DNA.

A type of prion infection in sheep, causes a disease called Scrapie, a fatal, degenerative disease that affects the nervous system, and which is so called because the intense itching of the skin causes the animal to rub or scrape itself on walls, fence posts and the like. In cattle, the same prion disease affects the brain and causes 'Mad Cow disease' and in humans it causes Kuru or Creutzfeldt-Jakob disease.

None of these infectious agents have been identified in any carnivorous birds, such as vultures, or any other carnivores, which is surprising since the prions are retained in some types of soil such as clays or kaolin, and infection in sheep, (Scrapie), takes place via the intestinal tract subsequently passing to the lymph glands. This does not mean the disease in pure carnivores does not take place, but only that it does not cause significant changes in the living carnivorous bird or animal to produce a recognisable disease. **However**, humans are omnivores and so partly carnivorous.

Because of the theoretical multiple origins of viruses and similar biological molecules, **it is certain** that new 'viral diseases' will emerge in the future. In fact, at the Los Alamos National laboratory in the USA, using modern bio-informatics computerised technology, specimens of blood or tissue can be subjected to a sophisticated DNA/RNA sequencing technique called GenBank, to search for new viruses which may be responsible for causing an unidentified illness in a human or animal.

In 2003 La Scola (18) reported finding a very large doubled stranded virus which he called Mimivirus.

Giant Virus compared with HIV virus and common bacteria

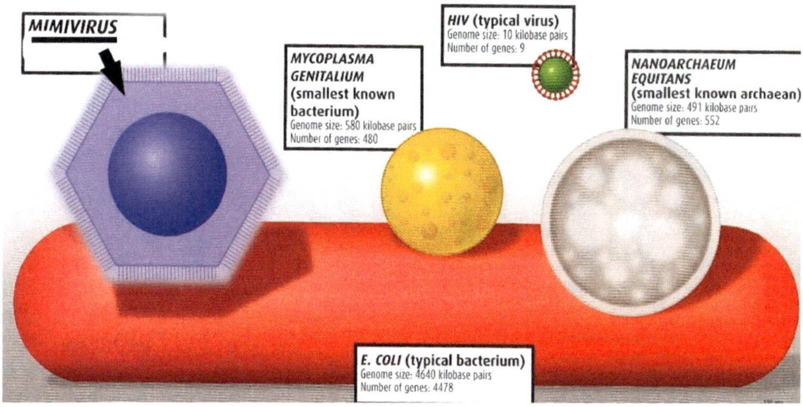

Plate No.11 Mimivirus

This organism had first been noticed by Dr. Timothy Rowbotham in 1992 when he had then called the organism, the *Bradford coccus*.

The organism was found residing inside a type of amoeba (see fig.6 in Chapter 6), inhabiting the inner wall of a water cooling tower in a power generating station. The amoeboid organism was Acanthamoeba, which is ubiquitous in nature, being found in freshwater lakes, rivers, salt water lakes, sea water, soils and even in the atmosphere. Moreover, like all amoebae this organism is able to engulf and encyst any suitable possible food substance that comes within its path.

Mimivirus has a hexagonal capsid and at the time of discovery contained the largest genome of any known virus. From this particular virus's genome, several protein enzyme molecules, (a DNA polymerase, mRNA, tRNA and also a synthesizing enzyme), all used for the replication of the virus, have been recovered. Altogether, over 1000 protein coding genes have been found in Mimivirus which have not been seen in other smaller viruses.

Since La Scola's original discovery, other similar large viruses have been found, such as Megavirus chilensis, found off the coast of Chile in 2010. Following the discovery of these two very large viruses, two other amoeba infecting viruses, (pandoraviruses), have been found. One in 2013 off the coast of Chile (Jean-michel Claverie), and another in a fresh water pond in Australia. These very large viruses have genomes with 1,181,404 base pairs.

Mimivirus was found by La Scola (19) to be tentatively involved in human pneumonia in Edmonton, Canada, where 376 hospital patients were found to have antibodies to this organism in their blood. Like the pox viruses, Mimivirus can replicate entirely in the host's cell's cytoplasm, and completely independently of the host cell's nucleus. Mimivirus constructs a virtual "virus factory" within the host cell's cytoplasm. Moreover, this very large virus also has a gene that codes for the protein which carries ATP, used like all biological cells in the production of energy, Jean-michel Claverie (73).

Since Mimivirus was first discovered, J. Craig Venter and his colleague Seshadri (20), searching the Sargasso Sea and the Gulf of Mexico with a privately funded ocean going laboratory, aboard a specially adapted ship, have found when using the techniques of 'metagenomics,' other large DNA viruses, together with a multitude of other previously undocumented life forms (such as Archaea), and 148 types of bacteria never found before and which are not thought to be pathogenic.

Metagenomics, or eco genomics, is the study of genetic material recovered directly from environmental samples such as the ocean, deep mines, hot volcanic vents and various geological sites.

Geologists working for the oil industry have found, in deep sedimentary rock, amongst the hydrocarbons produced from the breakdown of plant and animal material forming oil, that there are some long chain organic viral-like molecules, which could only have come from the breakdown of animal cellular membranes.

All these studies have indicated that viruses are universally in great abundance, not only in the sea but in acidic hot springs, in the desert, in Antarctic glaciers, in polar lakes and even in rocks 2000 meters below the ground's surface.

Viruses are now thought to be the most abundant genetic entities on earth, with perhaps as many as 100 million types of viral genomes, most of which have never been identified, Hamilton G (21).

To date, at least 2,000 species of viruses have been described infecting both plants and animals.

Geneticists have now discovered that the genomes of every living organism are laden with the remains of ancient viral infections.

It has been found that in the eukaryotes, (including birds and all the other complex animals including humans), the main source of unidentified DNA, (that which is not at present found to have any identifiable function and which at one time was called junk DNA), could be as much as 34%. These are the RNA retroviruses which have converted their own RNA by reverse transcription into the host's DNA. This 'parasitic DNA' is incorporated using an enzyme called integrase (manufactured by the virus itself) into the host's DNA.

In birds, some of these types of viruses can cause some types of cancer, such as the avian Rous sarcoma in chickens, and of which several strains have been identified.

This is also the case in some human diseases. It is estimated that at least 20% of all human cancers are virus based. Further, not only cancers but also some autoimmune diseases such as Lupus and possibly Multiple Sclerosis are ultimately caused by viruses.

Sometimes these retroviruses become a permanent addition to their host's genome, and so have become endogenous retroviruses. They are then inherited and passed on through to succeeding generations.

Frank Ryan (22), quoting several authors has suggested that some of these retroviruses, by becoming inserted in the genome of the host's reproductive cells, have become 'symbiotic' associates and have influenced the evolution of their hosts. Of course, Ryan is referring to research mainly in human genetics, but the case is gradually being revealed to be the same in all other animals, and even plants. The endogenous retroviruses are in fact the 'fossils' which the viruses have left from their early evolution.

Koonin, Senkevich and Dolja (23), propose the concept of an *ancient virus world* derived from the primordial pool of primitive genetic chemical strands which arose in the prehistoric seas. Patrick Forterre (24), and others, believe that early 'life' was a period of intense biochemical experimentation in which molecular systems were continually being invented, or in other words, formed anew. Genetic information was constantly being thrown together by viral gene transfer, resulting in numerous new and increasingly complex and alternative pro-life forms (that is, the 'RNA world' proposed by Carl Woese and others).

As already pointed out by Frank Ryan, who suggested endogenous retroviruses were probably one of the driving forces behind early evolution, such as the change from the rather unstable 'RNA world' into the more stable 'DNA world' of today.

As Koonin and colleagues have suggested, a world of increasing viral genome complexity took place: the very first evolution of life on earth probably didn't take place by a simple process of survival of the fittest individual organism, as Darwin had envisaged. More likely it came into existence by a continuous sharing and interchange of genetic material, until a stage was reached when the most successful method for the transmission of the genetic code was developed.

The very early viruses probably had no genes which encoded protein enzymes to produce their viral capsid proteins. Later in genome evolution, the development of a capsid helped to stabilize their viral genome.

From these early, probably short single stranded viruses, evolved today's longer single stranded RNA viruses, then the double stranded RNA viruses and then ultimately the more complex double stranded DNA viruses. So, the early viruses probably evolved in parallel with the first living organisms, that is why they have the same basic structure of nucleotides forming DNA and RNA

Because of their characteristics, the large viruses first found by La Scola can be placed at the boundary between "the true living and the non-living viral world."

Why haven't any more of these very large viruses like Mimivirus been found which are pathogenic? Probably because they are mostly not highly pathogenic, and medical and veterinary scientists haven't been looking for them. After all, the vast majority of micro-organisms are not in fact pathogenic.

So, in conclusion, although most biologists up to the present day do not consider viruses to be living organisms because they are not capable of reproducing themselves, considering the two theories of the *ancient RNA* and the *ancient virus* worlds, the viruses are very closely related to the origin of life on earth. Every living form of cellular life will have at least one virus, (and probably many more), associated with it, and viruses are the most abundant form of organism 'associated' with life on this planet.

Certainly, because of endogenous retroviruses, the viruses had a very profound effect on the evolution of all life on earth. At the

American Academy of Microbiology colloquium, held in July 2012, it was generally agreed by 24 virologists that life on earth would not exist if there were no viruses.

Because its lineage is very old, and could have emerged prior to cellular organisms, Mimivirus has added to the debate over the origins of life. Some genes unique to Mimivirus, including those coding for the capsid, have been conserved in a variety of other viruses which infect organisms from all domains. This has been used to suggest that Mimivirus is related to a type of DNA virus that emerged before cellular organisms, and it played a key role in the development of all life on earth. Furthermore, we, and all living organisms, are all partly virus, both in structure and in our body chemistry.

THE PATHOGENIC OR DISEASE PRODUCING VIRUSES

Name	Where Found	Tissues Affected	Lesions
THE POX VIRUSES *(Poxviridae)*	Pox viruses are not found freely in the environment but only in the creatures they infect. They are unusual in replicating in the cytoplasm of the host cell and not in the nucleus like most other viruses.	The different species of pox viruses all invade the skin cells of the animal species to which they have adapted.	The blisters which the pox viruses cause burst and result in open ulcers leaving the skin open to attack by secondary invading bacteria.

SMALLPOX VIRUS *(Variola)* from the examination of the mummy of the Pharaoh Ramses V, it has been shown this Pharaoh died of Smallpox in 1145 BC. W.H.O. reported the virus was globally eliminated in 1979.	An important human disease believed to have evolved most likely from a rodent (mouse or rat) virus between 68,000 and 16,000 years ago. In ancient agricultural communities rats and mice would have thrived where grain and other food was stored.	Smallpox only infects humans, so there is no animal reservoir of the infection. The virus is transmitted by inhalation of airborne droplets sneezed from an infected person, and by direct contact with contaminated surfaces it is not transmitted by insects.	Causes small blisters on the skin filled with thick fluid. These result in secondary bacterially infected ulcers. Smallpox is often fatal in children.
COWPOX *(vaccinia: from cows)*	First recognised by Dr Jenner in 1796 in cattle and transmitted to milk maids by contact with an infected cow.	Carried by rodents particularly field voles, mice, rats and also by domestic cats. Has infected Zoo kept cheetah kittens kept in an enclosure with long grass where the field voles thrive. Also infected an anteater due to this animal putting its nose down a vole burrow. The virus has the potential to infect most grazing animals.	Causes small blisters on both cow & human skin. Used by Dr Edward Jenner in 1796 to make the first Smallpox vaccine.
MONKEYPOX *Related to Smallpox virus*	Mainly occurs in central & Western	Can infect humans and non-human primates. Often transmitted by some types of rodents	Causes similar lesions in humans

	Africa (particularly in Democratic Republic of Congo) in a variety of different species of monkeys. Has been seen in USA in Pet prairie dogs (a type of ground squirrel.)	e.g. Gambian pouched rats, also rabbits. If virus becomes established generally in rats and mice, could become serious human pathogen.	and animals and *can be fatal.*
PARAPOX VIRUS ORF virus	Only occurs in infected carrier animals, not found freely in the environment. The virus is carried by grey squirrels which are unaffected by the virus.	Can cause infected lesions in cows, sheep, goats, and red squirrels worldwide. Most importantly, causes a contagious pustular dermatitis in humans.	All these pox viruses attack the cells of the skin, mouth and throat.

The different pox viruses not only infect many, if not all, vertebrates but also invertebrates, or as some people like to call them, the ‘creepy crawlies’, for example the insects.

Pox viruses are very large complex double stranded DNA viruses, able to carry out the whole of their replication in the cytoplasm (that is, the main body of the cell) of their host. When doing this, they produce easily recognisable intra-cellular inclusions (so called Bollinger bodies) which, when highlighted with special stains, can be seen with an ordinary light microscope.

The large size of the pox virus is the result of them carrying in their genome numerous nucleotide molecules forming the enzymes necessary to complete self-replication. Canarypox for example, has a genome which is just under twenty times larger that of the common circoviruses, which can also infect many birds. This implies that because they have a large and complex genome, the pox viruses have taken much longer to evolve than other viruses with a smaller genome and with a much less complex structure.

Pox viruses are said to be unable to penetrate intact skin directly, or the inner body covering of mucus membranes of the gut, the air tubes of the respiratory system, or the reproductive and excretory organs. The pox viruses require a break in the covering surface, such as a wound due to a fight or accident, or the bite of an insect. However, it is also suggested that avipox infection of birds may take place via food, water or by inhalation from the air.

Pox infection in the ancient world.

As indicated above, the smallpox virus was certainly around in the time of the Egyptian Pharaoh Ramses V, and probably before that time. Furthermore, it is possible that the human smallpox virus may have evolved from a rodent, such as a rat or mouse, at least 68,000 years ago.

Rats and mice also act as the vectors for some other infectious diseases such a Leptospirosis, Typhoid and *Yersinia pestis* (the cause of the Black Death in 1346 – 53 and the Great Plague of London in 1665-6).

Perhaps the Ancient Greeks noticed the presence of the rodents was associated with an increased incidence of illness and so encouraged the Aesculapian snake (*Zamenis longissimus*) to crawl on the floor of their temples of healing to keep the rodents in check. These healing temples (asclepieion) were where the sick were laid on beds to be treated and one such temple was located on the island of Kos in the Greek archipelago, where Hippocrates (the father of modern medicine) lived. Asklēpios, the Greek god of medicine and healing, is shown as having an Aesculapian snake coiled round his staff, which is now recognised as the universal symbol of medicine and healing.

These snakes are about two meters long and are not venomous but suffocate their prey by constriction. They are still found over large parts of Europe, sometimes called by other names.

POX VIRUSES IN BIRDS

Name	Where Found	Tissues Affected	Lesions
AVIPOXVIRUS viruses of birds. There are at least 36 specific types of Avipoxvirus. Smits et. al. noted considerable variation in the genetic make-up of the different Avipoxviruses. When working in the Canary Isles, researchers surveyed 893 birds of five different species. Some species showed signs of pox infection but others showed none at all.	The genus Avipoxvirus diverged from the common ancestor of all pox viruses about 249 ± 69 thousand years ago. That is before the human pox virus evolved.	Described in at least 230 species of birds and are said to be mostly host specific, being adapted to different families of birds, but the relationship between the different Avipoxviruses is complex.	Cause blisters or ulcers on the skin

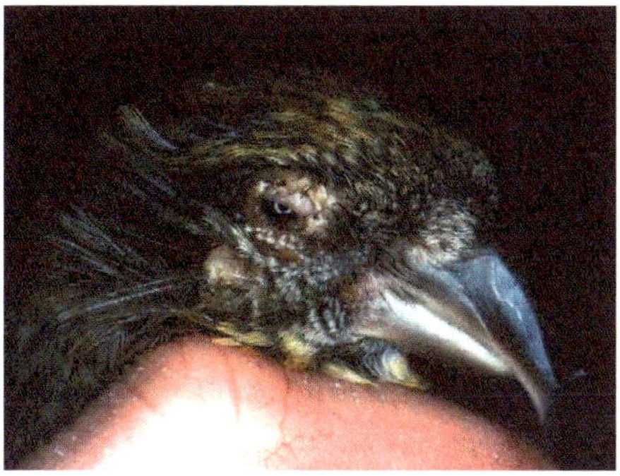

Fig. No. 12 Female Common Crossbill (Loxia curvirostra) showing signs of Avian Pox

However, the tentative diagnosis in the above illustrated case, was not confirmed by laboratory tests, and may in fact be signs of a Papilloma or wart virus infection. The Common Crossbill is found across much of Europe but not as far south as the Canary Isles.

Ostrowski (29) found that canarypox vaccine protected Houbara bustards (*Chlamydotis undulata*), from the Houbara bustard pox virus infection. Moreover, canaries could be infected with H.B. pox virus but this virus was not so pathogenic to canaries as was the specific canarypox virus. Gerlach (30) has also shown a number of avian pox interconnections between domestic chicken pox, falcon pox, pigeon pox, and waterfowl pox.

Plate No.13 Pigeon with pigeon pox

In most of the above cases avipoxvirus overall was not all that pathogenic, except in canaries. Also, pigeon pox virus is more pathogenic in chickens than is the specific chicken pox virus.

The most in depth study of the genetic relationships between all of the avipoxviruses, using an analysis of the genomes of the different bird pox viruses, has been carried out by Susan Jarmin and her colleagues (31). Their work has identified three main groups, labelled A, B and C.

Group A
Within this group is fowlpox, (domestic chicken pox), turkey pox, falcon pox, osprey pox and albatross pox, as well as some pox showing some crossover from pigeon and sparrow isolates.

Group B
This group includes only canarypox.

Group C
This group includes all the viruses isolated from the different parrot species.

The latter viruses form a much more distinct group than those Avipoxviruses included within the groups A and B.

Of course, none of these viruses infect humans or any other animals besides birds.

THE INFLUENZA VIRUSES

This is an important, complex group of viruses with three main types A, B and C, each with a number of subtypes.

<u>Influenza Type A</u> group of viruses. There are *many subgroups* within this group some more serious than others.		This group principally infects *humans, pigs, birds, and some other mammals*. The sub type H3N8 causes serious problems in horses & other equid species.	Type **A** together with type **B** causes yearly winter human flu and usually lasts about 2 days.
<u>Influenza Type B</u> group of viruses.		Only known to infect *humans and seals.*	Also causes a type of *winter flu* usually causing raised temperature, sore throat and headache.

<u>Influenza Type C</u> group of viruses.		Some of these Type C viruses infect both *humans and pigs* but <u>not</u> birds.	Rare but can occasionally cause serious illness in humans.

<u>Bird 'Flu</u>

Also called Avian flu or fowl plague, bird flu refers to all those viruses infecting birds which also cause flu like symptoms in humans. This is usually one of the sub types of Influenza A.

Bird flu is not a new disease and existed well before the well documented 1918 flu pandemic. Historically, it is only by looking at the severity of recorded illnesses, their signs and their rapidity of spread that we can make a guess as to whether that particular epidemic was caused by a human flu virus (B or C), or by the avian influenza A virus. In fact, at the time of the 1918 flu pandemic, it was not known that it was caused by a virus at all. At that time, it was thought to have been due to the bacterium heamophilus influenzea, which can cause a number of bacterial flu-like diseases but is not the primary cause of flu.

Historically, epidemics of fl*u like* illnesses have been recorded since at least 1485 at the time of the battle of Bosworth Field, when Henry Tudor defeated Richard III, the last of the Plantagenet kings. At that time an unknown illness which could have been a flu virus, struck the victorious army and the survivors of this battle carried the disease to London where it 'caused' so many deaths that the coronation of Henry Tudor had to be postponed for 2 months.

An alternative explanation has however, been put forward by other epidemiologists. A mysterious *"sweating sickness"* with similar clinical signs to flu, swept through the country in 1485 just before the Battle of Bosworth Field. This could have been due to a comparatively recently discovered, (identified in 1976,) hantavirus, carried by rodents, which causes pulmonary symptoms in humans.

Since the time of the Tudors, flu-like epidemics have been recorded in 1507, in 1528 (which spread to Germany, causing the so-called 'English pestilence') and in 1551. European pandemics occurred in 1557 and also in 1580, where 8,000 people died in Rome and Spanish cities were devastated.

Nothing was heard for over a century, then there was a European pandemic in 1729, followed by further outbreaks in 1732, 1781, and 1782 (the last two beginning in China). In this last major outbreak, three quarters of the British population became ill and the disease spread to America.

The next major pandemic in 1889-92 was much more serious and is better documented. This epidemic was called 'Russian flu' as it started in St. Petersburg during December 1889 and by March 1890 had spread over most of the world. In those days, transport for human travellers by sea or the early railways was comparatively slow compared with air transport today. Therefore, because of the global extent and rapid spread of some of these epidemics, could they have been avian 'flu, spread by migrating birds?

Lastly, the best known of the previously recorded epidemics was the 1918 pandemic known at the time as "Spanish flu". It is debatable whether this in fact started in Spain or not, as the epidemic seems to have cropped up simultaneously in a number of locations throughout the world.

The first wave of this epidemic is recorded in American army camps in both the USA and France.

The second wave simultaneously started in Freetown, Sierra Leone on the West African coast, in the town of Brest in France and in Boston, USA. At that time, my own father was serving on a warship, the light cruiser Astraea, carrying out convoy duty off the east coast of Africa (based in Sierra Leone), and round South Africa to Durban. He caught the infection and was hospitalized in Cape Town. In a letter to his brother he said that the railway network, as well as everywhere else, was shut down. The 'natives' seemed to catch the complaint quickly and hundreds had died, as well as many white people. There were 10 deaths on his ship, including the captain.

In 1918 there was no long-distance air travel, and travel by sea took a comparatively long time, so was the fact that the infection cropped up simultaneously in widespread parts of the world caused by migratory birds?

At the time, the cause of the pandemic was a mystery, because influenza was not identified as being caused by a virus until the 1930s. However, in 1997 a retired Swedish pathologist received permission to excavate the graves of an Inuit (Eskimo) colony in Alaska that was almost wiped out by the 1918 epidemic, when 85% of the population died. Their bodies had been preserved in the permafrost, so Johan Hultin was able to extract the entire genome of the 1918 virus.

Since that time, the virus has also been recovered from other museum pathology specimens at places such as the Royal London Hospital and the US Army Medical Museum, (which holds over 3 million pathology specimens). All these reports confirm that the same avian 'flu virus caused this widespread pandemic. It is now generally agreed, that certainly during the last 100 years, global 'flu pandemics have **all** been caused by the type A group of avian 'flu viruses. Even though group B and C viruses mostly occur in humans, and they may cause epidemics, they **never** cause pandemics.

The species of birds which have become infected with the avian 'flu viruses include mainly water and shore birds such as ducks, (particularly the Mallard duck, Anus platyryhynchos, which seems to act as a reservoir for the viruses), geese, swans, gulls, terns, herons, flamingos and egrets. Also some birds of prey, such as the Common Buzzard, the Goshawk, the Peregrine Falcon and the

European Eagle owl, have become infected by feeding on ailing birds. Fortunately, few small garden and other small passerine birds have been recorded as becoming infected. Few if any parrot like birds have become infected.

It should be noted that in 2005 in Qinghai province in China, 1500 dead birds were found comprising Bar-headed geese (Anser indicus), Brown-headed gulls (Chroicocephalus brunnicephalus), and Black headed gulls (Larus ridibundis), all of which in that location are migratory.

In the same year, in Huvegel province Mongolia, 89 dead birds were found, a group which contained wild ducks, wild geese and Whooper Swans (Cygnus cygnus).

Any person who casually finds such dead birds, or anyone who is a bird watcher or finds an area littered with a large number of dead birds of whatever species, would be most unwise to touch any of these birds without notifying the authorities. Such birds may have died of Bird 'flu or other causes such as algal poisoning or even botulism.

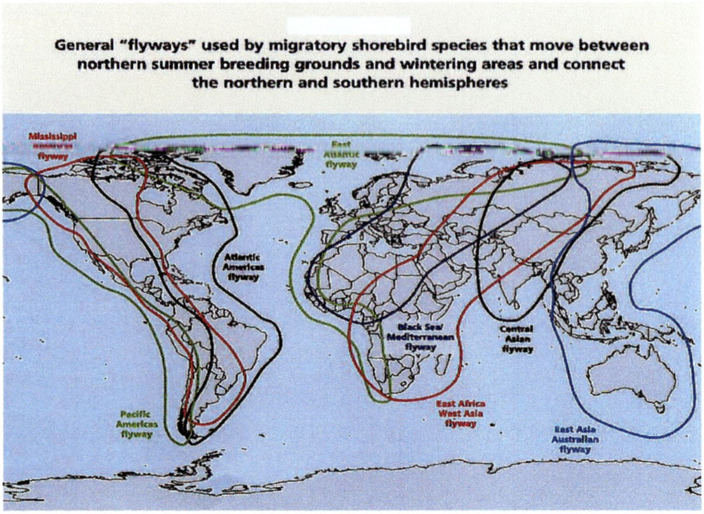

Plate No.14 Major flyways of western migratory birds indicating how they could carry the Avian flu virus.
Credit: Wetlands International and the United Nations Food and Agricultural organisation

Apart from migratory birds, other species which have become infected with Avian flu viruses are pigs, horses, dogs, palm civets, mink, ferrets, stone martins, marine mammals, zoo lions and tigers, as well as domestic cats. Much more detailed information on Avian influenza can be found on the OIE/WHO website www.offlu.net/avian

In 2009, during the course of the recent world pandemic of the H5N1 flu virus, a survey in Java revealed 20% of 500 stray trapped cats were found to be carrying antibodies to the virus. In the neighbouring Indonesian island of Bali, infection has not only been found in cats but also in dogs, where outbreaks of the H5N1 Avian flu virus had occurred. Also in Bali, there were reports of unusually large numbers of dead cats being found around local outbreaks of the disease in poultry. Furthermore, in a survey of 500 pigs in Indonesia, 7.4% were found to be infected with the H5N1 bird flu virus.

The influenza viruses are spread by body fluids (sneezing, coughing, saliva) or by faeces. One gram of animal faeces can contain up to 100 million infective virions (the individual viral particles.)

With the ever-expanding increase in air travel, and the tendency of airlines to reduce the air circulation within aircraft cabins, which helps to save on fuel consumption, there will inevitably be a resulting increase in the spread of human influenza viruses amongst passengers. Apparently healthy, but infected, passengers incubating the virus, will occasionally have attacks of sneezing whilst in the aircraft. The resulting spread of the virus throughout worldwide populations is easy to imagine.

The flu virus can remain viable in soil for many days, and up to 200 days (over 6 months) in contaminated water. In freezing conditions the virus remains viable for very much longer.

The strain of flu which started early in 2009, the sub type known as H5N1, resulted in around 200 human deaths, but there were many more deaths in all types of birds. These occurred particularly in poultry and water birds, and also some types of mammals as mentioned above.

In 2013 the virus mutated again, producing another variant of flu virus, H7N9.This emerged in one of China's live poultry markets. A woman bought a 'healthy' chicken alive, killed it, then cooked it and the family ate it. She died, having been infected by contact with the live bird, but no one else in the family did, as cooking the carcass had killed the virus.

The H7N9 variant of the virus causes no overt signs of illness in chickens, but is carried by them and through which it spreads rapidly. However, it can also be passed from human to human. Earlier in 2013 the same strain of the virus infected 134 people, of which 45 died. Obviously, it has the potential to cause a global pandemic. Again, in November 2014 the H7N9 strain of the flu virus flared up again, and more than 100 cases were reported in China, probably again spread by the live poultry trade.

All three types of A,B & C flu virus can gradually mutate to change their characteristics so as to become more or less virulent disease. Mutation of the virus is particularly liable to happen if two strains, or sub types, of Influenza virus should simultaneously infect pigs. If pigs become infected with more than one strain of the Influenza virus it has been shown that the pig can act as a 'mixing bowl' for the different strains of flu virus. Mutation of the virus then takes place by a process called "re-assortment", Castrucci et al.[100]. In this process, segments (i.e. lengths) of viral RNA forming a group of genes, can swap position in the genome to another position in a neighbouring viral genome. The whole process is rather like the 'cut and paste' procedure used in word processing on the computer. Re-assortment may alter the virulence of the particular virus so that it may become more, or less, harmful. However, re-assortment has been shown to be a complex process and all the factors involved have not yet been explained. Moreover, it is not only pigs, but some poultry species have now also been shown to be able to carry out the process of re-assortment, Keith Hamilton (99)

Constant mutation of the Avian flu virus is hardly surprising, since it is a single stranded RNA virus, and the RNA viruses, in contrast to the DNA viruses, can more easily mutate.

Historically, Avian flu virus was probably in harmony with its 'original' water fowl host, until man started to farm ducks. Almost all domestic ducks are descended from the ancestor of today's Mallard duck (Anas platyrhynchos), which has been spread globally and now hybridises with a number of other species of duck. Original domestication possibly started about 10,000 BC on small farm holdings in Southern China.

About the same time, smallholdings in neighbouring Vietnam started domesticating the Red Jungle fowl (a type of Pheasant), to form flocks of domestic chickens [see Plate No.3 in chapter 1], at about the same time as the domestication of pigs from their wild forebears. This meant that the stage was set for the virus to be released from the stressed ducks, which were incubating the virus, in Southern China. These were then traded to Northern Vietnam to infect more susceptible species of animals, particularly pigs but also domestic chickens. Both of these possibly acted as 'mixing bowls' for several strains of the flu virus so as to produce more virulent strains, which were then able to infect humans.

Even with the extensive use of vaccines, cultured to act against the precisc strains, all of which take time to produce in quantity, some strains of Avian flu will always be with us.

THE PARAMYXOVIRUSES

These viruses form a large family, (at present over 40 have been identified), of single-stranded RNA viruses which cause a number of human and animal diseases. New viruses within this group are constantly being discovered.

The main viruses are tabulated on the following page.

Virus Name	Susceptibility	Occurrence	Symptoms
Newcastle Disease/ Fowl pest in birds	In wild birds susceptibility to the virus is variable and in some waterfowl it can be carried as a latent infection. Overall, ducks and geese, don't seem to be very susceptible to Newcastle disease.	The virus occurs in domestic chickens and it may have originated in water fowl. Over time water fowl may have built up some sort of innate genetic resistance to the virus.	Causes breathing problems, diarrhoea, inflamed eyes and nervous signs. *Humans are slightly susceptible, causing a mild conjunctivitis or 'pink eye'. Also causes slight flu-like symptoms sometimes including mild laryngitis of the throat.*
In 1980 a Fowl-pest pigeon mutant evolved in the Middle East	The pigeon mutant only shows clinical signs in pigeons but a mutant strain is also *carried* by other species such as house sparrows and blackbirds without any signs or apparent harm.		In birds the virus exhibits itself as nervous signs such as a dropped wing or twisting of the neck. Signs which may occasionally be seen in feral town pigeons.

Researchers looking into Newcastle disease virus, have indicated that because this virus replicates more quickly in human cancer cells, it can more readily kill human cancer cells rather than normal healthy human cells. Consequently, the virus is being studied as a treatment for cancer. Nettlebeck et al (25)

A genus (or sub-family) of the Paramyxoviruses is the Morbilliviruses, which is included in the family of viruses the *Paramyxoviridae.* This implies that all these viruses came from a common ancestor. One of the Morbilliviruses is the Measles virus of humans, so the Measles virus is related to Newcastle disease in birds.

THE MORBILLIVIRUSES

Virus Name	Susceptibility	Occurrence	Symptoms
Human Measles virus	Only found in humans		Symptoms include fever, cough, runny nose, red eyes with the body covered in a rash of large red spots, Diarrhoea, sometimes a fatal pneumonia, encephalitis, blindness and deafness. *Altogether a very nasty disease*
Canine Distemper	Mainly seen in domestic dogs	Can infect a range of Carnivores e.g some members of the cat family (*Felidae*) eg Lions but not domestic cats, seals, the weasel family, including stoats, martens, otters &	Purulent ocular and nasal discharge, pneumonia, diarrhoea and vomiting. Later nervous signs such as

		badgers.	fits and *chorea* (a nervous twitching of the legs). Thickening of foot pads ("Hard pad")
Rinderpest (also called ***cattle plague)*** Eliminated worldwide in 2011	Domesticated buffalo European plagues occurred in 17th and 18th centuries and in Africa	All even-toed hoofed animals, wild buffalo, large antelopes and deer, giraffes, wildebeest and also warthogs	Fever, diarrhoea, ulceration of the mouth. High mortality
Hendra virus (HeV) is an emerging paramyxo **zoonotic** virus found in the eastern part of Australia	Old world fruit bats of the family *Pteropodidae* (flying foxes) are the natural hosts of Hendra virus. The virus is transmitted to horses	Can be transmitted to humans by close contact with horses which pick up the virus from fruit bats. Transmitted by saliva and excreta of the bats	The virus causes respiratory and neurological disease and **death in people** as well as horses.

Was the Measles virus originally passed to humans from ducks at a time when these birds were domesticated in China?

Until very recently the Chinese used trained cormorants for fishing, and historically the Chinese people have had a reverence for the Cranes feeding in the rice fields, and these birds are frequently illustrated in Chinese graphic designs. Indeed, some Chinese hill farmers still encourage swallows to nest inside their houses. All these birds could have been carrying the ancestral Fowl Pest virus.

Canine Distemper, Measles and Rinderpest (Cattle plague) are all related morbilliviruses and all probably have the same common ancestor.

According to Crawford (26), by using molecular clock techniques, divergence of Rinderpest and Measles can be pinpointed to around 5,000 years ago, during the development of the early human farming cultures in northern Mesopotamia (i.e. the fertile crescent). Before this episode of human evolution, during the nomadic period of human existence, humans had first domesticated sheep and goats about 11,000 years ago, and then later horses and cattle.

Although dogs had probably been domesticated from the grey wolf, first by hunter gathers some 30,000 years ago, wolves do not associate in large herds or groups, but rather in relatively small packs, and so a pathogenic virus originating in one individual in the pack would soon die out, having eliminated most of the pack before the virus had much chance of being passed to another pack. Consequently, this mobillivirus stood little chance of becoming endemic in wolves, although it may well have been circulating in other small wild carnivores and their prey species at a much lower level of pathogenicity. It is suggested that whilst Rinderpest, or cattle plague, passed to humans (causing Measles) about 5,000 years ago, or somewhat earlier, at about the same time the same virus passed to domesticated dogs kept by humans, resulting in the Distemper virus.

An illustration of a mobillivirus swapping hosts is shown by the following. In 1996 this virus killed over 1000 lions as well as affecting other carnivores including leopards, hyenas, jackals and both silver backed and bat-eared foxes in the Serengeti-Mara reserves in Africa. This was a Distemper virus eventually traced to the Masai tribal dogs which had passed it to hyenas, then passed it on to foxes and thence to jackals, and finally to the lions, all feeding on the same carrion carcasses. Roelke-Parker (27).

Had the virus been circulating for a long time? It was certainly identified in a few lions in 1962, but later, did one or other of these species become stressed because of a gradual reduction of its habitat by an increase in farming, tourism, or drought, fire or a combination of all these factors? When animals are stressed their resistance to a latent viral infection changes.

A similar case of viral transfer between distantly related species occurred in 1994. A number of deaths in Australian racehorses were eventually traced to a Hendra virus. The virus is so named because it was first seen in Hendra, a suburb of Brisbane. This was a latent mobillivirus found to be present in several species of fruit bats (flying foxes) and was discovered in 1994. This virus is still circulating and causing concern in Australia. The virus can also infect and kill humans attending horses.

Since that time, many similar viruses have been found to be carried by different species of fruit bats in S.E. Asia and the Indian subcontinent. An example of this is the Nipah virus, which was identified in April 1999 in Malaysia, and which resulted in 105 human deaths, and disease in a number of pigs, with the result being the culling of over one million pigs.

In all of these cases and the discovery of these viruses, the spread can be explained as the result of the invasion of the bats' normal habitat through destruction of their food sources by the growth of modern agriculture.

The family *Paramyxoviridae* is composed of a diverse group of viruses. There are at present over 40 virus species classified within this viral family. They affect all types of animals whether terrestrial, aquatic or aerial, and undoubtedly more will be discovered.

At one time Rabies was thought to be the only viral disease carried by bats and transmissible to humans. Recent research has shown a number of other viruses are also carried by bats. Moreover, it has now been shown that *bats possibly carry more viruses than rodents*. Also, because they are flying animals which migrate, they have a greater capacity for spreading viral infections. In addition, they also roost together in closely packed colonies so there is easy transmission between individuals.

RABIES VIRUS
(latin: "rabere", Sanskrit: "rabhas", "to do violence")

This is an important virus both from the public health and evolutionary aspect since it is nearly always fatal in humans if not diagnosed early enough. In the Western world, a bite is sometimes not recognized or the potential danger not taken seriously enough.

The problem in diagnosis is that the virus travels **slowly** though the infected person's body, gradually infecting one nerve cell before it travels to the next, before eventually reaching the brain, which may be weeks after the initial infection, when the infection becomes fatal.

Although not common globally, it is widespread with only a few countries entirely free of the disease. The virus does not infect birds or any of the lower vertebrates but it does infect *all* mammals, principally canines and bats. Also, in the USA the virus infects racoons and foxes.

Persons travelling abroad for their holiday are not always vaccinated against Rabies. However, they should be mindful of the risk of befriending any stray dog or cat, when a bite, scratch or *even a lick* from the tongue can transmit the virus. This RNA virus is thought to have evolved within the last 1500 years.

The author has personal experience of this virus as he lost a fellow

National Service colleague from Rabies after he had been licked by an infected dog which he had befriended. This occurred in 1946 whilst serving in the British armed forces in Austria just after the end of the Second World War.

The virus kills about 55,000 people each year worldwide. In December 2013 in the USA, a woman was bitten and infected with rabies virus by a wild bobcat in New York State. Most human mortalities occur in Africa, despite the fact that Louis Pasteur developed an effective vaccine in 1885. Anyone travelling abroad, particularly to a third world country, would be well advised to get themselves vaccinated.

Maryn McKenna (130) reports that there would appear to be several strains of the Rabies virus, with some strains not so virulent as to cause death in the infected person. This is illustrated by the fact that a number of people in a remote part of the Peruvian Amazon have been bitten by vampire bats and have recovered.

A vaccine mixed in bait (for example, chicken heads), has been dropped from the air to vaccinate wildlife and so reduce the risk of persons being infected from wildlife bites such as from foxes or bobcats. This method of reducing the incidence of the virus in wildlife has been used in parts of Europe and North America.

There are other viruses belonging to the same genus as the Rabies virus, such as the *Lyssaviruses (Anc.greek;"lyssa" - frenzy of madness),* which are carried by bats. These are rare, but can infect humans and produce similar symptoms. They have been isolated from parts of Europe, Asia and Australia.

In the UK vaccination is given free of charge to anyone working with bats, such as naturalists.

EBOLA VIRUS is another virus carried by bats.

This virus is so named after the Ebola river in Zaire in Central Africa where it was first identified in 1976. However, it is related to another *filovirus* called Marburg virus which was first noticed in the German city of Marburg in the 1960s.

Both the above viruses are **Filo viruses,** and they diverged several thousand years ago. By using electron microscopy these viruses are seen to be filamentous and worm-like in appearance with a 'shepherd's crook' form at one end.

The Filo viruses cause extremely severe and often fatal haemorrhagic fevers in humans and in non-human primates, with massive internal bleeding. They are carried by bats as well as some small rodents and shrews. It is thought that old world fruit bats, although themselves unaffected by the viruses, act as reservoirs, and the virus may then be transferred from the bats to humans by blood sucking arthropods such as common house flies or ticks.

In the case of the Marburg city virus it is thought that the workers in an experimental laboratory were infected whilst examining the tissues of Grivets, a species of old world monkey.

The most recent and severe outbreak of Ebola virus disease started in July 2012, in which month there were 62 cases and 34 people died. However, by January 2015, nearly 9,000 people had died in this outbreak in East Africa (and this was possibly a gross underestimate). Before being brought under control, the disease was increasing exponentially, being spread across the globe by air travellers, with cases being recorded in Great Britain, USA and Spain. Dr Margaret Chan of the W.H.O. said it was the greatest global challenge since the Second World War.

However, the rate of genetic change in the Ebola viruses are approximately one hundred times slower than that for the influenza A virus. There are at least six types of the Ebola virus originating from various regions in Africa, and being isolated to those regions. The Reston virus found in Virginia USA is also isolated to that area, due to originating from the non-native crab-eating macaque monkeys imported from the Philippines.

Using techniques of paleovirology, the genome of the Filo viruses (including Ebola) has been found to be an endosymbiotic virus (see glossary) of several small mammals such as rodents, shrews, tenrecs, tarsiers, and marsupials, indicating these viruses are at least tens of millions of years old.

It should be noted that the megabats or flying foxes, the colugos (flying lemurs), and the insect eating microbats form a "clade", that is, a group of organisms that consists of a common ancestor and all its lineal descendants, [Tudge page 450]. Probably the flying lemurs crept up trees and then leapt off onto neighbouring trees and so gradually developed folds of skin between their bodies and forelimbs so as to become bats. During this evolution, these creatures carried with them the Ebola viruses, to which they had adapted over many years, whilst they were still ground-dwelling rodents.

Although these viruses are not known to be infectious for birds, it does illustrate that viruses can, and often do, infect many animal species, such as dogs and pigs, but may not in fact be spread by these animals. ***Quite often one type of virus is not confined to just one species of bat.***

Other human viruses carried by bats are SARS (severe acute respiratory syndrome), first identified in 2002/3, and MERS (Middle East respiratory syndrome), a coronavirus found in 2012.

Why don't birds carry or become infected with any of these viruses, including Ebola? The answer is probably that because the avian genomes have become so altered, through mutation, over time from the original ancestral vertebrate genome, they don't sufficiently match these particular viral genomes, and so these viruses cannot be integrated into the avian genome.

And so, from the large to the small viruses…

THE CIRCO VIRUSES.
These are the smallest viruses to affect not only birds, but other animals.

Familiar to most vets dealing with birds is a condition called Beak and Feather Disease seen in parrots. The signs of the disease were first recorded in Australia by Edwin Ashby in 1888, although at that time he did not know it was an infectious disease. Much later the virus was isolated by Pass and Perry (9) in 1984.

This virus has now been spread by the captive pet bird trade to most of the world's parrot species. However, signs of the disease vary between different species of parrots. Budgerigars and African lovebirds, when noticeably affected and diagnosis is subsequently confirmed in the laboratory, often seem to make a full recovery.

Plate No.15. Peach-faced lovebird (Agapornis roseicolis) left: symptomatic, right: healthy specimen

The Peach-faced lovebird inhabits south west Africa. In an unaffected bird the plumage across its back is solid green and not mottled brown as in the bird illustrated.

It is thought that this circovirus has been endemic in Australia for some considerable time, where it affects some wild Sulphur Crested cockatoos which today are sometimes seen in people's gardens.

Plate No.16: Badly affected Lesser Sulphur Crested Cockatoo (Cacatua sulphurea)

Plate No.17: Head of normal, healthy Lesser Sulphur Crested Cockatoo (Cacatua sulphurea)

Whilst some members of a wild flock of Sulphur Crested Cockatoos may be noticeably affected with plumage defects, they are not rejected by the other members of the flock. It would seem that some adult birds are able to carry a latent viral infection which will not flare up unless the bird's immune system breaks down due to stress, such as drought, lack of food, capture or something similar.

This is an immunosuppressive virus, similar to the AIDS virus, and both of these have a predilection for rapidly dividing & replicating body cells. This is achieved in a similar manner to the human immune cell called CD4 Helper T Lymphocyte (a type of white blood cell.)

In the affected birds, it is the rapidly growing skin cells producing new feathers which are affected. Often, infected birds die of a secondary bacterial infection because the bird's defensive immune system is impaired. It is significant that many infected birds seen by veterinary surgeons are newly purchased birds, undergoing the stress of capture and then being passed through a series of dealers before being settled with their final owner. However, unlike the human HIV/AIDS virus, the circovirus is *not* a retrovirus which inserts itself into the chain of DNA of its host's chromosomes. Also, whereas HIV is spread by sexual contact, the circovirus is distributed in the feather dust of the dead feathers.

Several other similar circoviruses have been identified in birds other than parrots. These are:

1. Pigeon circovirus
2. Dove circovirus
3. Black spot in canaries
4. Finch circovirus
5. Black-casqued wattled hornbill circovirus
6. Also identified in southern black-backed gulls, Australian ravens and now recently suspected in a cassowary in Queensland, Australia
7. The echo parakeet (*Psittacula eques echo*), found only on the southern Indian Ocean island of Mauritius

This latter bird virus first emerged in 2004 and it is of concern to the biologists working on Mauritius that the echo parakeet could become extinct if the spread of the virus is not brought under control, *Scott Wilson (64).* The echo parakeet is the last of about 8 species of parrots originally inhabiting the Mascarene group of islands and which have now become extinct.

The virus spreads by direct contact, inhalation or ingestion of dried particles of dust from faeces or feathers. Infectious dust particles can remain viable in the environment for several months. After intensive study, there is some evidence that in a few cases some of these birds may naturally recover. However, it is also possible that some of the apparently recovered birds may be acting as latent carriers of the virus. Moreover, supplementary feeding by the biologists to boost the birds' health status may actually be contributing to the problem, by bringing the birds into closer association at the food containers. This species is, in any case, a social species congregating in flocks.

It is possible that the virus may have been introduced to the isolated pacific island of Mauritius not by the pet trade but by another allied species, the Ring-Necked Parakeet (*Psittacula krameri)?*

This latter species is much more widely spread geographically, ranging from parts of Africa, to India and parts of southeast Asia as well as many of the islands of the Indian Ocean.

The Ring-necked parrot seems to be much more resistant to the virus, indicating that it may have been in contact with this virus for some time.

Whilst in practice during the 1980's, the author saw several black vasa parrots (species *Coracopsis*) purchased by clients through the pet trade. These birds normally inhabit Madagascar. In some of these birds the normal black plumage covering the whole bird, gradually started to turn white and all these infected birds died within a period of 12 months.

Plate No.18: Two normal black vasa parrots.
The larger bird is the greater vasa parrot (Coracopsis vasa);
the smaller bird is the lesser vasa parrot (Coracopsis nigra.)

Specimens were sent to Professor John Cooper working at that time at the Hunterian museum of the Royal College of Surgeons in London. He managed to get electron microscope photographs of a circovirus. Nowadays of course, there are much more rapid and less expensive laboratory tests available for diagnosis.

Some of the lesser black vasa parrots *(Coracopsis nigra)* were at one time kept at Chester Zoo. Then, during December of 1994 the zoo had acquired from a private breeder some healthy looking black cheeked love birds *(Agapornis nigrigenis.)* These birds were placed in the same aviary. Very soon after, the black vasa parrots began to show traces of white feathers in their plumage and were subsequently found to have the incurable circovirus. They had to be put to sleep as there was no cure and they would have suffered a prolonged and painful demise. Moreover, there was a risk that the virus would have infected other species of parrots in the zoo's collection.

Another group of black vasa parrots, the greater vasa parrot (*Coracopsis vasa*), were at the same time kept well away in another aviary and were not affected. This latter species was still part of the Zoo's collection until 2009.

The author suspects that many more circoviruses will be found in the future.

Plate No.19: Two blackbirds (Turdus merula) with abnormal plumage possibly caused by a circovirus. Both birds were seen in the author's garden.

These two birds do not look like normal birds in moult, changing from juvenile to adult plumage. The author has also occasionally seen a few wild birds around his garden with bilaterally symmetrical feather abnormalities which the author suspects may be caused by circovirus infection.

Besides birds, different species of circoviruses may infect mammals. There are two types which infect pigs, causing a post weaning wasting disease. There is a suspected circovirus reported as a cattle-respiratory disease in Canada. Also, a circovirus has now been reported in dogs by Rolando Wer in 2013.

In humans, a transfusion transmitted virus *(Torque Teno Virus, TTV),* first reported in Japan by T. Nishizawa in 1997, was subsequently found to be a human circovirus detailed by Bendinelli et al (34). This human infection is 'subclinical' or latent. TTV, since it was first reported, is found to be extremely common even in healthy individuals and is also worldwide. Possibly in some countries one hundred percent of the population may be infected, whilst in the UK and USA it is probably only ten percent of blood donors who are infected. It is probable that in the past the virus has been overlooked, Handa 2000 (48).

Circoviruses can be seen in body tissues with a light microscope, staining dark blue with a basophilic stain. They are shaped like a cluster of grapes and can be identified in all body cells, but their main target is the immune cells in the lymphoid tissues, which themselves also often show signs of obvious damage.

All circoviruses are potentially immuno-suppressive and these viruses may be more common than hitherto realised. The so called *"emergence"* of circoviruses may be an indication of an increased awareness and refinement of diagnostic laboratory tools, rather than the actual evolution of new viruses.

THE ARBOVIRUSES (those transmitted by Arthropods (insects and ticks)

Some of these viruses are called *Flaviviruses (the yellow fever like viruses including Hepatitis C),* whilst others are labelled *Toga viruses*. Altogether, there are 504 recognised Arboviruses, Karabatsos 1985 (32). Of these, 77 have been isolated from birds. Only a few are mentioned here to illustrate their general characteristics.

THE FAMILY OF TAGO OR ALPHA VIRUSES (IN TOTAL 30 VIRUSES)

The Equine Encephalitis viruses	**Where Found**	**Animals affected**	**Signs and type of disease**
Eastern type *(EEE or Triple E)* commonly called sleeping sickness, first recognised 1831	Eastern United States such as Massachusetts, in wet marshy coastal areas where there are breeding mosquitoes	Horses & humans (30/40% mortality) Also infects many species of birds, reptiles & Amphibia. Transmitted by Culex mosquitoes (*gnats and midges*)	Horses: raised body temperature → fever → infected animals become excessively nervous and sensitive to sound, then sleepy → paralysed → death 90% mortality in horses. In humans: signs include high fever, muscle pain, headache,

			avoiding light, seizures, occurring 3 - 10 days after the bite of an infected mosquito. The number of cases occurring in humans is fortunately quite small.
Western type	Western United States, west of the Mississippi River, and in some parts of Central and South America	Same as above	It is much less common and a less serious human disease except in children and the elderly.
Venezuelan type	Occurs in South America with many local varieties of the virus	Infects many domestic and wild animals *and* birds	As above
Sindbis Virus	A similar type of	Birds and	Causes rash

	Arbovirus occurring in the Middle and Far East & Australia.	humans	and arthritis in humans

Further notes on Eastern and Western Equine Encephalitis Viruses (Tago viruses)

With all the above viruses, although birds may become infected, most show no signs of illness but can act as a circulating reservoir of the infection with increasing amounts of circulating virus both in the infected birds and in the mosquitoes building up during the summer months, when both the birds and the mosquitoes are breeding and contact between individuals is increased.

Signs of disease in infected birds are variable. In some cases, the clinical signs seen are similar to those shown in horses, and have been noticed in a variety of birds including ring-necked pheasants, partridges, pigeons, turkeys and quail. It is to be noted that these are all birds feeding on the ground, and they have probably been picking over the droppings of infected horses. Other types of birds have been shown to be infected with the virus but have shown no clinical signs of disease.

Because of the incubation period of the infection (3-10 days), visitors to the USA from overseas may become infected and may not show signs until they return home. This was the case for a visitor from Scotland, who, in 2007, went on a fishing trip to New Hampshire and fell ill one day after flying home.

THE FAMILY OF FLAVIVIRUSES (IN TOTAL 67 VIRUSES)

(a)West Nile Virus	First isolated in 1937 in a sick woman living in the West Nile region of Uganda. Later found in both tropical & temperate global regions including parts of Europe including the Mediterranean particularly the Camargue of Southern France. Now found over most of North America and parts of Latin America. Endemic to Africa, Asia and the Mediterranean	Mainly infects birds, but also humans, horses, dogs, cats, bats, squirrels, and domestic rabbits. Transmitted by the bite of a Culex mosquito Many humans may be bitten but often show no signs	Infected humans initially show a fever, together with swollen lymph nodes, (swellings under the jaw, under the arm pits etc.) This is later followed with drowsiness, lack of movement, or rhythmic involuntary movements of the limbs. Mortality in Humans about 1%
(b) Japanese Encephalitis viruses	Japan	As above	As above

Further notes on West Nile Virus

Studies of genetic lineages indicate the virus may be at least 1000 years old. Historically, the virus may have contributed to the death of Alexander the Great, as it was said that there were deaths amongst a flock of ravens just after the birds had been exhibiting abnormal nervous behaviour, at the same time that Alexander entered the gates of Babylon, where he subsequently died in 323 B.C shortly after entering the city, Marr JS, Calisher CH (65).

The virus was first identified in the laboratory in the USA in 1999 and is thought to have been transported to North America via an infected migratory bird blown by the jet stream off its normal migratory flight path, **or** in an infected mosquito, which could have been carried in an aircraft to the USA from overseas. In fact, several species of terns, which are migratory, have been suggested as carriers of West Nile virus.

This is not entirely theoretical since the author had an American common nighthawk *(Chordeiles minor)* brought to him in January 2008, which had been blown off course during its annual migration from North to South America. The bird was found in a garden in West Kirby in Merseyside, UK and was brought in by a country park ranger for veterinary examination, to check for injury or sickness. These birds are normally found as far north as Canada and migrate annually to the South American continent as far south as Argentina. They feed on insects hovering over marshy areas. The birds could easily become bitten by mosquitoes and become infected by both the Equine Encephalitis and West Nile viruses. Moreover, nighthawks are sometimes reported to fly at high altitudes (up to 12,000 feet), so this bird could have been picked up by a fast-moving jet stream weather pattern and blown across the Atlantic.
The bird brought to the author was kept alive by being fed on wax moth larvae, kindly supplied by a research worker at Manchester University. It was then flown back to central America courtesy of the Royal Air Force, on their weekly VIP passenger trip, and handed over to the British Consul there, himself a keen birdwatcher, and

eventually reunited with the bird's fellow travellers on their annual migration to South America.

Plate No.20: Hand held Common North American Nighthawk (Chordeiles minor)

Other flaviviruses include ***yellow fever virus,*** so named because it causes jaundice (yellowing of the skin) in humans, and is restricted to the tropical and subtropical parts of South America and Africa.

A yellow fever virus is now, in early 2017, reported to be having devastating effects on South American Howler monkeys. How did it come to infect the monkeys? (Reported in the New Scientist, January 2017).

Also, there is ***dengue fever,*** (so called "break bone fever" because it causes severe pain in joints and muscles), which occurs in many parts of the world including the USA, South America, parts of Africa, India and South East Asia, and Australia. Before 1960 it was present in 9 countries; today it occurs in 60 countries throughout the world.

Another flavivirus is the debilitating ***chikungunya*** virus, which causes a rash, fever and severe joint pain.

Lastly included amongst the flaviviruses, is the recently emerged ***Zika*** virus. Although Zika virus probably first infected monkeys in Africa, it spread to some Pacific islands before causing serious problems in some South American countries.

All these viruses have probably more recently been spread by increased human air travel, and many of the above-mentioned viruses are transmitted by one of the 700 species of the genus of *Aedes* mosquitoes.

Altogether there are about 3,500 different species of mosquitoes but they don't all transmit infectious diseases.

Aedes mosquitoes are small mosquitoes which carry and transmit a variety of viruses causing different types of human disease but do not *usually* attack other animals or birds. They can breed and thrive in small collections of water around human habitation such as ornamental plant pots, rainwater butts, discarded plastic containers and garden ponds.

Apart from infecting humans with various types of viruses, some species of *Aedes* mosquitoes carry *plasmodium gallinaceum,* the organism that causes bird malaria in poultry in Asia and Africa. Whilst infection results in a low mortality rate in the indigenous gallinaceous birds, such as the wild red jungle fowl (*Gallus gallus),* mortality may be as high as 80-90% in domesticated birds.

Also, those mosquitoes belonging to the genus *Culex* may also be important in the maintenance and transmission of some of these diseases.

Additionally, among the flaviviruses is Louping ill virus, which causes infectious encephalomyelitis in sheep.

Louping ill	**Where found**	**Species affected**	**Signs of illness**
An acute viral disease of sheep	Mainly in Scotland	Sheep, birds and humans. The virus is transmitted by the sheep tick Ixodes-ricinus and not by a mosquito	Fever, Trembling, swaying on the legs, collapse, coma → death

The name 'Louping-ill' comes from an old Scottish word describing the effect of the disease in sheep whereby they '*Loup*' or spring into the air.

Until about 1800 much of Scotland was covered in the ancient Caledonian Forest. After the 'Highland clearances' which largely took place between the 1770's and the 1850's, the forests were cleared to create large areas for sheep farming and to create grouse moors for shooting, both activities being more profitable for the landlords than the traditional croft farming. The net result is that the red grouse *(lagopus lagopus scoticus),* and the related ptarmigan both now inhabit this cleared forested area.

CHAPTER 5

The Bacteria

Bacteria were the first recognisable microscopical living organisms to evolve from the primordial slime about 4 million years ago. They mutated into many different species, each with different characteristics including different shapes.

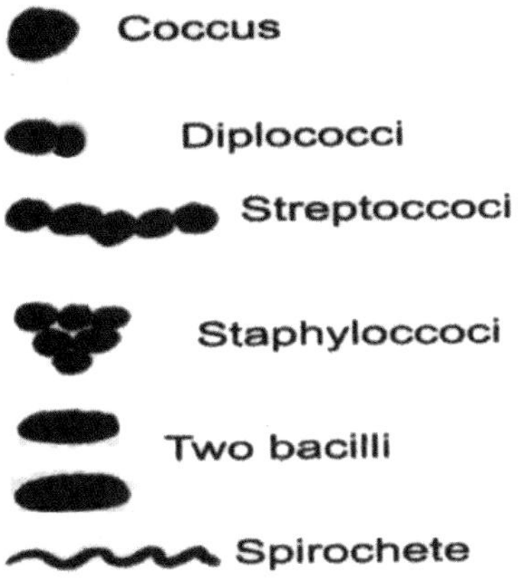

Fig. 1 Different shapes of bacteria.

Despite their different shapes, all the different types of bacteria illustrated in Fig No.1 above, are basically similar in both their design and function, as is illustrated in the following diagram.

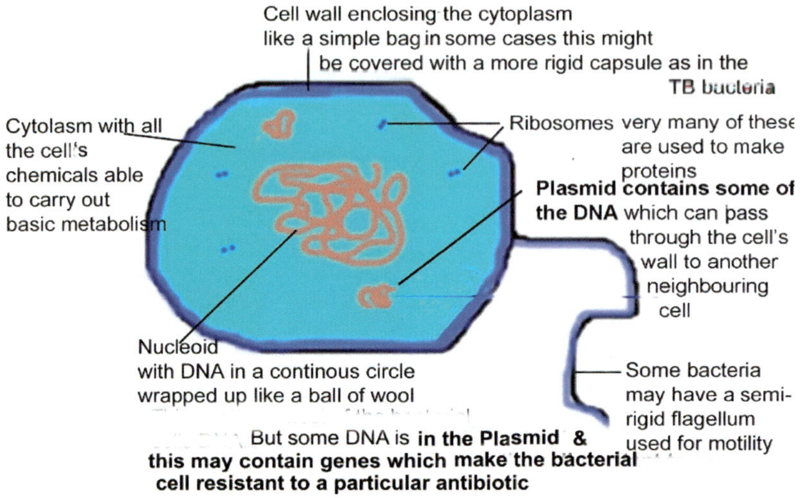
Cell wall enclosing the cytoplasm
like a simple bag in some cases this might
be covered with a more rigid capsule as in the
TB bacteria
Cytolasm with all
the cell's
chemicals able
to carry out
basic metabolism
Ribosomes very many of these
are used to make
proteins
Plasmid contains some of
the DNA which can pass
through the cell's
wall to another
neighbouring
cell
Nucleoid
with DNA in a continous circle
wrapped up like a ball of wool
Some bacteria
may have a semi-
rigid flagellum
used for motility
But some DNA is in the Plasmid &
this may contain genes which make the bacterial
cell resistant to a particular antibiotic

Fig No 6: The structure and organization of a typical bacterium

These most primitive of living organisms are called the prokaryotes [from Greek karuon "kernel"] because their chromosomes, unlike other living organisms, are not enclosed in a membrane separating them from the jelly like mass (cytoplasm) of the cell.

Relatively few bacteria are important causes of infectious disease, but all are a very important part of the web of life, and contribute to the food chain of the more complex life forms.

From the time when life on earth was believed to have started, about 4,000,000,000 years ago, bacteria were thought to be the most advanced and dominant form of life, until at least about two billion years later. During this very long period of time, bacteria, the Prokaryotes, were gradually developing their intracellular complex chemical routines, until the time when the more advanced living organisms, the Eukaryotes, began to evolve.

Bacteria were originally thought to have evolved from the plants. However, the plants, the animals and the fungi are all now known to be quite separate life forms, originally believed to have evolved from LUCA, the last universal common ancestor.

During the late 1970s, another cousin of today's bacteria was discovered, and it is now thought that this parallel type of primitive life form, called the Archaea (Archaebacteria), are in fact the true originators of all the other forms of life, being quite separate from traditional bacteria. There is no doubt that the Archaea are in many ways more closely related to all the animals, fungi and plants than are the true bacteria. The general opinion today amongst most evolutionary biologists is that both traditional bacteria and the Archaea evolved at the same time, as two separate branches from the last universal common ancestor (LUCA). Very soon after the initial evolution of life on earth (LUCA), these two branches took separate paths to evolve (1) into the traditional bacteria and (2) into the Archaea, from which all the other forms of life have evolved.

Altogether, it is estimated that there may be well over 1,000,000 species of traditional bacteria, of which only about 4,000 have so far been classified. However, amazing as it may seem, this identified number is increasing exponentially. Altogether, in total volume, bacteria form the major part of the earth's biomass, which is a greater biomass than all the animals, plants and fungi put together. To quote Dr. Martin Blaser, "We live in a microbial planet which is totally dominated by forms too small to be seen by the naked eye .... millions can fit into the eye of a needle" (144).

Anaerobic bacteria

All members of this group grow and survive in conditions where there is little or no oxygen. Carl Woese speculated that the anaerobic bacteria were probably the first types of bacteria to evolve from the primitive slime when the earth's atmosphere and the oceans had a lower level of oxygen than they have today. This fact is highlighted by Colin Tudge (7), and the observation is also confirmed by the more recent research of Turgeon and Creaser (8). Oxygenation of the earth's atmosphere only began when the early evolved single celled plants in the ocean (phytoplankton), began to manufacture oxygen using photosynthesis as described below. Before this time, when the earth's atmosphere was composed mainly of nitrogen and carbon dioxide, the anaerobic bacteria were getting their energy by splitting apart the molecules of hydrogen and sulphur compounds, which had been formed in the bed rock when the planet was first formed.

Today, most of the anaerobic bacteria are found in the soil and in the ocean's depths. Those which sometimes cause disease, often inhabit the inside of the body cavities of animals, where there is also no oxygen. The internal organs of birds and other animals, including humans, provide suitable places such as the internal surfaces of the gut and bladder, or buried in deep penetrating wounds, away from any oxygen in the air. Listed and tabulated below are a few genera of these anaerobic bacteria, some of which cause disease in humans, in birds and in other animals.

Generic name	**Where found**	**Which animals are affected**	**Disease caused**
Bacillus anthracis causing:- ANTHRAX	Found as long living spores in the soil. These can survive up to 100 years. Can contaminate water supplies.	Most mammal species particularly ruminants but also humans, chimpanzees and gorillas in the rain forest. *However, carrion feeders such as vultures, crows,*	The bacterial toxins of Anthrax cause multiple internal haemorrhages, resulting in sudden death. Recently, during 2014 in

		foxes and wolves may be resistant.	parts of Italy an outbreak was possibly spread by horseflies feeding on infected animals and leading to a slower death.
CLOSTRIDIUM **Clostridium botulinum**	Found in rotting carcasses and in decaying vegetation. Maggots from the eggs of carrion flies, may act as mechanical vectors. The active agent at a *much-reduced dose is a constituent of the cosmetic* **Botox.** This is also used for some medical treatments.	Affects all living creatures including humans. Also, particularly sea gulls & birds of prey *but vultures seem to be resistant.* Can affect other creatures which eat carrion, such as dogs and foxes.	Produces a nerve poison which causes paralysis. In birds this results in *limber* neck or '*Western duck sickness.*' Botulinum toxin is probably the most potent poison known to man.
Clostridium perfringens *(C. septicum, C. novyi,)*	Occurs in decaying vegetation, also **normally found in the gut of many humans**	Affects all living creatures including birds. *One common cause of food poisoning in some humans* who	When the organism gets into affected tissues (e.g muscles) of all animals it

This organism was formerly known as **C.welchii**	who in the past may have had a subclinical infection and so they developed antibodies and so can hold the bacterium in check. Also, occurs in other vertebrates, in insects, and in the soil.	have not developed a natural immunity or are overwhelmed by a large dose of infection. Another cause of food poisoning is improperly cooked or stored food.	produces a poison which kills the tissues & simultaneously produces a gas (composed of hydrogen, carbon dioxide and nitrogen) finally resulting in so called gas gangrene.
Clostridium difficile	Sometimes found as a normal inhabitant of the human gut but held in check by other normal gut inhabitants - *the so called "good bugs"*	Not so far identified in animals, only found in humans but there is no reason why it should not occasionally occur in other species.	*C. difficile* is the most serious cause of antibiotic-resistant diarrhoea in aged humans, where the over use of antibiotics has wiped out *"good bugs",* or in those persons with HIV or people on immuno-suppressive drugs.

Clostridium tetani	Found in the soil, or implanted into deep puncture wounds where there is little or no oxygen.	Occurs in all animals, including dogs & horses. Has been isolated from dead chimpanzees in West Africa. Also in humans globally but particularly in Africa, N.W India & Far East. **Not usually mentioned as found in birds.**	Stiffness and rigidity of the muscles. Helga Gerlach (66)says it is mentioned in older literature as occurring in birds but this is not confirmed by modern laboratory methods.

Gerlach (66) suggests that birds may be highly resistant to tetanus. Bumblefoot, (a penetrating foot abscess), is a condition which is common in all birds, and is a complaint which, at first glance, should favour infection with clostridium tetani, and yet it is not mentioned as being found in birds. Certainly, over evolutionary time, birds would have had the opportunity to develop an innate genetic resistance to tetanus, but there may be other reasons for avian resistance, such as the fact that there is a high oxygen perfusion in the subcutaneous tissues of birds which are well supplied with blood vessels.

After the evolution of the anaerobic bacteria, the earth's atmosphere became more oxygenated due the influence of cyanobacteria also known as blue-green bacteria (or the blue-green algae.)

Cyanobacteria and Chloroplasts

About 2.5 million years ago, after the evolution of the first living organisms, an early evolved bacterial organism, the Cyanobacteria, changed its internal chemistry. Using the energy of sunlight, rather than the chemical energy of deep sea anaerobic chemical reaction, the cyanobacteria began to produce oxygen by splitting a water molecule to release oxygen. At the same time as releasing oxygen, the bacteria was taking in carbon dioxide from the atmosphere to make, or "synthethise," sugars and carbohydrates. Hence this chemical reaction was named photosynthesis.

The Cyanobacteria, also called the blue green algae, either invaded, or were engulfed by, the cells of the common ancestor of all of today's plant species, one of the protophyta. Within the plants the permanently engulphed cyanobacteria became known as the plant's chloroplasts and were acting like solar panels.

The net result of millions of primitive plants acting in this way, was the earth's great oxygenation event. Because of photosynthesis, the amount of carbon dioxide in the earth's atmosphere was reduced from about 20% to about 0.04%.

Subsequently, there evolved a whole range of bacteria either partially or totally dependent on oxygen. Many of these today thrive in aquatic environments.

Apart from green plants, other living organisms such as jellyfish, flatworms, bivalve shell fish and some salamanders make use of the blue green algae to carry out photosynthesis.

In contrast to the benefits of some of the blue green algae contributing to the formation of chloroplasts, other similar, but genetically different, blue green algae, can also flourish in lakes or ponds rich in nutrients to form extensive algal blooms. In some cases, such algal blooms can produce cyanotoxins, or poisons, causing serious disease and even death in humans and other animals which drink the water. In the UK, during the summer months of 2013, this was a particular problem resulting from a prolonged spell of hot weather.

The Proteobacteria

(named after Proteus, a Greek god of the sea)

These are primarily aquatic bacteria and include many pathogens, such as the genera of escherichia, salmonellae and vibrio. Other bacteria in this group are not free-living but include the nitrogen fixing bacteria, found in the root nodules of leguminous vegetable plants of the pea and bean family.

In contrast, in Lake Nakuru, and the other Rift Valley lakes of East Africa, the lesser flamingo gather in large flocks of over a million birds to feed on the blue green algae which are probably, in turn, fertilised by the birds' droppings. However, these particular blue green algae do not apparently produce cyanotoxins. The birds do however need to go to the freshwater streams running into the lake to drink.

Some prominent members of this group of Proteobacteria include the genus Pseudomonas, of which there are at present 191 recognised species.

Generic name	**Where found**	**Which animals are affected**	**Disease caused**
Vibrio cholerae	Found as a tenacious film on the lining of the human bowel	Not known to occur in birds in spite of the fact that the aquatic	Causes the disease *Cholera* in humans. Produces a

		environment of flamingos and other aquatic birds would seem an idcal situation for it to thrive in birds.	potent and often lethal toxin resulting in diarrhoea and vomiting.
Other species of Vibrio	Many other species of Vibrio are found living *symbiotically* in marine creatures such as jelly fish and squid or as a primary or opportunistic pathogens of Lobsters, prawns & some white fish.		

As already described, during the evolution of the early bacteria many bacteria formed interconnected mats or biofilms on various substrates. This characteristic is continued in the adhesive biofilms of vibrio and pseudomonas found attached to the inner lining of a host's gut, urinary tract or airways.

The biofilms or bacterial mats

In some cases, different species of bacteria are arranged one on top of another, like floors in an apartment block. The layers of bacteria are held quite tightly together, and onto their base, by a type of gelatinous glue, which, incidentally, protects the bacteria from penetration by antibiotics and so helps make these particular bacteria more antibiotic resistant. The bacteria making up each biofilm are moreover able to communicate with each other through a system of 'quorum sensing' using chemical messengers (special molecules), which pass through the surface membranes of neighbouring bacteria. The bacteria are then able to compete with other neighbouring bacterial species, Nadell C.D. (6).

They can also, via this system, anticipate how the host, man, bird or other animal or even plant, is going to react to their presence, Atkinson S. and Williams P. (71, 117). This mechanism may, by producing specific chemicals, disrupt the host's white blood cells, which form part of the host's defences (in more advanced animals such as mammals and birds.) This is not a conscious decision made by the bacteria, but it is one which has evolved over time and that benefits the survival of that bacteria.

The biochemical 'cross talk' between microorganisms and their host is being studied by several scientists, amongst whom is Eugene Chang at the University of Chicago (72). This research may result in the manufacture of chemicals which can be used to either disrupt or block this mechanism and be used as an alternative to antibiotics, which in many cases are becoming less effective because certain bacteria are building up resistance to them.

Generic name	**Where found**	**Which animals are affected**	**Disease caused**
Escherichia coli (often shortened to E. coli) There are very many species but only a few are pathogenic. Many strains are specific to different animals.	The pathogenic species can invade any devitalised tissues of the animal body. The harmless non -pathogenic strains of E. coli are often used in the biochemical industry.	Both the pathogenic and non-pathogenic strains of E coli are **found in all species** of animals and birds.	All strains are constantly changing by mutation. In humans, strain No.0157:H7 causes serious disease and many such cases are recorded. See reference (142) In May 2011 another strain

			0104:H4 also caused serious human illness including two deaths.
Salmonella over 4400 serotypes only relatively few of which are pathogenic.	Occur in all animals including poultry & other birds Can become & often are mixed with the non-pathogenic serotypes	Salmonella *enterica serovar Typhimurium* Causes mouse typhoid and has occasionally caused disease in humans.	S.enterica subspecies *enterica* causes Typhoid fever in humans. caused the death of Queen Victoria's husband Prince Albert & also Wilbur Wright of aircraft fame.

Infection and mixed infection with all these bacteria can often be quite complicated as illustrated by the following examples.

Some years ago, samples of bird droppings collected from garden bird tables were found to contain a type of Salmonella. This was found to be the same serovar, (serotype) as that cultured from the faeces of young children with enteritis in a local hospital, indicating the young children may have become infected from a garden bird table. Mice carrying Salmonella typhimurium (mouse typhoid), are often attracted to the seed on which the birds are feeding, and so in turn infect the birds.

In a survey carried out at a zoo during 1969-1992, Salmonella typhimurium was isolated from clinical cases of all the different animals, in total some 80 times. In 57 of these cases the bacteria was isolated from birds. In the mammals, Salmonella typhimurium was also isolated on a number of occasions, but in addition 11 other different serovars were also isolated. Of the reptiles, none were carrying Salmonella typhimurium but these animals were shown to be infected with other types of salmonella on 22 occasions. In none of these cases were they Salmonella typhimurium, but there were 14 other different serovars not carried by either the birds or the mammals.

Generic name	Where found	Which animals are affected	Disease caused
Campylobacter jejuni A motile corkscrew like organism. Similar species infect cattle and sheep causing spontaneous abortion in these animals.	An important human aquatic pathogen inhabiting the human intestine. Wild birds pecking at milk bottle tops can contaminate the milk in the bottle.	Although it does not cause disease in birds they do act as carriers. Often, they may be contaminated with the organism.	In humans Campylobacter can cause painful and bloody diarrhoea. Has been shown that about 75% of all supermarket chickens sold as 'oven ready' are contained in packaging contaminated with Campylobacter .
Treponema pallidum. The cause of the human venereal disease Syphilis.	Spread by sexual intercourse. It later spreads to other body organs including the nervous system.	Treponema is only found in humans in which it causes Syphilis and Yaws.	Also called the **Great pox** (smallpox is a generalised viral infection.)

Well known historical figures believed to have been infected with Syphilis include Adolf Hitler, Tolstoy, Lenin, Al Capone, Franz Schubert, Mozart and Beethoven.

Borrelia A genus of *Spirochaete* with at least three distinct species.	All carried & transmitted by ticks which infect a number of animals including birds.	Causes **Lyme disease** in humans.	In humans results in flu like symptoms sometimes involving the nervous system. *See Louping ill virus*

A group of bacteria having a thick water repellent waxy cell wall are the **Mycobacteria**. In humans and some other animals, this bacteria cause tuberculosis. In the eighteenth century, the disease was known as consumption because it seemed to "consume affected persons from the inside" and was romanticised, as the disease from which Violetta dies, in Verdi's opera, La Traviata.

The author has a personal interest in this disease because as a newly qualified Vet, he spent the first three months in general practice doing nothing else but testing cattle for bovine TB. At the same time, a close relative had the disease for at least ten or twelve years without being properly diagnosed, because a thorough clinical examination had not been carried out by a succession of GPs.

A characteristic of the Mycobacteria is that they do not readily produce quick-acting acute toxins to poison the host's tissues, so the disease just slowly progresses. Because of the bacterium's waxy cell wall, the host's immune defence simply surrounds the bacterium with macrophages and other inflammatory body cells. These tend to isolate or "wall off" the bacteria, rather than directly killing it off. The net result is the formation of small granulomas or tubercles. This tends to result in a latent infection which only flares up into a fullblown infection if the host is weakened in any way and the immune system as a whole is impaired.

Generic name	Where found	Which animals are affected	Disease caused
<u>Mycobacteria</u> A complex group with many related species All are much_ slower growing than other bacteria by about 100 times this allows the formation of a latent infection.	Found in the soil and water, but <u>do need</u> oxygen to survive. Very resistant to many antibiotics and disinfectants.		
<u>Mycobacterium Tuberculosis - TB</u>		The major cause of TB in humans.	Causes multiple nodules or tubercles in the main body organs particularly the lungs.
<u>Mycobacterium Bovis</u> related to M. tuberculosis	Mainly infects all body organs of cattle and can sometimes infect humans.	Can infect many other species of animals besides cattle including deer, badgers, dogs, cats, foxes, pigs, horses, and in New Zealand the possum.	Causes disease similar to that in humans.
<u>Mycobacterium microti</u>	Causes tuberculosis in voles, mice and cats.	Can also infect rats, stoats, ferrets, foxes, and deer.	
Many other related species of mycobacteria in the same		Infects seals, goats and humans in Africa (serious).	Similar to the above.

complex			
Myco-bacterium marinum	Infects all species of fish.		Causes opportunistic infections in humans and sometimes causes a rare disease called aquarium granuloma, typically affecting people who work with fish or keep home aquariums.
Mycobacteria Avium complex		Infects many species of birds particularly water birds and cavity nesters such a starlings & sparrows. Avian TB also infects ostriches.	Causes multiple tubercles similar to those in humans Often infects people debilitated by the AIDS virus.
Paratuberculosis Related to the above		Principally attacks the small intestine of cattle and sheep.	Causes Johne's disease resulting in persistent diarrhoea.
Mycobacterium Leprae (Hanson's disease) Also, recently discovered in 2008,	Causes **leprosy** in humans. A disease much feared in biblical times and recorded in 1400 BC (Book of Leviticus 14:57)	Only other animal regularly infected is the American **nine-banded Armadillo** which is infected because of its low body temperature.	Much slower growing than other Mycobacteria. Incubation may take as long as 30 years or may

Mycobacterium lepromatosis. This organism occurs in Mexico and the Caribbean and causes an extensive form of Leprosy, It seems to have evolved by reductive evolution having lost some of its genes	Infected persons were seen as unclean and were quarantined. The areas of dead flesh become secondarily infected causing the patient to smell so they were regarded as unclean.	The bug was brought to America by infected immigrants. Probably doesn't infect birds because their body temperature is too high, and the organism is very slow growing and so the lifespan of most birds is too short.	be as short as 5 years. Some infected persons are unaware they are infected. About 80 people a year in USA are infected from Armadillos which in Louisiana and Texas are hunted and eaten. Immune system attempts to wall off bacteria results in clumps of dead white blood cells and dead tissue.

There is also a type of leprosy, Mycobacterium lepraemurium which occurs in rats and which can infect cats.

Yersinia pseudotuberculosis (Yersinia pseudoTB)

This bacterium is interesting because on post mortem it looks rather like tuberculosis. The bacterium is carried by rats, mice and other small rodents as well as wild birds. It is common in those wild birds which flock up in winter and in birds which visit sewage farms.

The author has diagnosed this disease on many occasions in aviary kept birds where the mice enter the bird's enclosure looking for dropped seed. It also occurs in zoo animals, again from infection by rats and mice.

The author and others have also noticed that zoo-kept tropical birds such as toucans and barbets seem more susceptible to Yersinia pseudo TB than other birds. Toucans and barbets are both in the family Piciformes, and are both frugivores and omnivores. Both are also widely distributed in South American tropical forests. Consequently, under natural conditions, these types of birds probably spend most of their time in the forest canopy and they don't have much contact with animals on the ground such as rodents or their ectoparasites, the fleas. As a result, there is not much chance of these birds coming into contact with rodents or where these creatures have been on the ground and so becoming infected with Yersinia pseudo TB. Therefore, these types of birds will not have had the chance to build up an innate genetic immunity through frequent contact with this organism. Yersinia pseudo TB can infect humans and cause Far East scarlet-like fever.

It is to be noted that the closely related bacteria Yesinia pestis, which is the cause of Bubonic Plague (the Black Death), has been shown to have evolved from Yersinia Pseudo TB, Achtman, Mark et al (128).

A third organism, Yersinia enterocolitica which is closely related to both Yersinia pestis and Yersinia pseudo TB, does infect birds as well as many farm animals and humans. In fact, investigations are being carried out to develop an attenuated strain of Yersinia pseudo TB to be used as an inexpensive oral vaccine for humans against Yersinia pestis. Taking into account that two of the many species within the Genus Yersinia both infect fish, (Yersinia frederiksenii and Yersinia intermedia), the originator of the genus Yersinia, like many other bacterial organisms, possibly evolved in the ocean. From the fish, it could have been passed on to those birds feeding on the fish, and at the same time, been picked up by scavenging rats.

Why shouldn't the principal vector of Yesinia pestis, the rat flea (xenopsylla cheopis), attack birds? Fleas generally are not particular onto which animal they will jump and both dog or cat fleas will jump onto humans. However, they do have their preferred hosts, and there is a related species Ceratophyllus gallinae which attacks poultry. Fleas are attracted to humans and other animals by the amount of carbon dioxide they breath out, so perhaps the amount of carbon dioxide exhaled by birds is too high? Birds certainly have a different respiratory system to humans.

Bubonic plague, and Yersinia pestis, is still with us. One entry in Wikipedia states that "every year, thousands of cases of plague are still reported to the World Health Organization although with proper treatment, the prognosis for victims is now much better. A five to six-fold increase in cases occurred in Asia during the time of the Vietnam War, possibly due to the disruption of ecosystems and closer proximity between people and animals. The plague also infects many species of mammals and has been detrimental to some of these animals, such as in the United States of America, animals such as the black-tailed prairie dog. Colonies of these animals can extend over quite large areas of several square miles and contain large numbers of individual prairie dogs, a small rodent. Also the endangered black-footed ferret which preys on the prairie dog is under threat from the disease". In addition, David Eads of Colorado State University says that reduction in the numbers of the black-tailed prairie dogs is affecting the connection between the grasslands of the prairie and the whole ecosystem.

Yersinia pestis and the plague, is thought to have originated in Asia where it is harboured in the guts of several species of small rodents such as marmots and gerbils. However, the disease is first mentioned as the plague of the Philistines of Ashdod, (recorded in the First Book of Samuel, chapter 5, in the Old Testament of the Christian Bible), and dated to approximately the second half of the 11th century BC. There is no scientific evidence that this was the well-known bubonic plague, as any serious epidemic disease would at that time have been considered a plague by the ancients. Nevertheless, those persons affected were said to have been troubled by the swelling of their 'emerods' (which could mean haemorrhoids or tumours) in their private parts.

The Philistines were a tribe of the 'sea peoples' and Ashdod was a coastal city just north of present day Gaza. Like many tribes recorded in the Bible, these people were great consumers of alcohol. Also recorded in the Old Testament, the Philistines were said to have had the reputation of being producers of strong beverages and distillers of fine wines. They were recorded to have indulged in week long alcoholic wedding celebrations. Excessive consumption of alcohol may well have had an adverse effect on their gut flora. Moreover, the Philistines were said to have been afflicted with a plague of 'mice' (which was more likely to have been rats), which would have helped to spread the disease. The foregoing is of course pure speculation on the part of the author.

Later known recorded outbreaks of the disease were firstly, the Plague of the Roman Emperor Justinian (AD 541–542), a pandemic that afflicted the Eastern Roman Empire (Byzantine Empire).There were similar local outbreaks around various ports in the Mediterranean in the 4th, 5th and 6th centuries, but these gradually became less virulent.

Recent research, using ice cores, together with the archives of the British Antarctic Survey and several other international institutions, have indicated that there were two massive volcanic eruptions in northern America in 535 and 536 which had a profound effect on the global climate. There was a marked drop in temperature, due to a huge and intense dust cloud. This resulted in a prolonged winter with no spring, followed by drought. Crops and fruit failed to grow or ripen, resulting in famine. All this would have reduced peoples' resistance to infectious disease.

Second came the Black Death, or the great bubonic plague of the European Middle Ages, which was a pandemic from ~1340 to ~1400. This spread from central Asia to the Mediterranean and Europe, possibly brought into Europe via the Silk Road, the ancient network of trade routes.

Other, more localised, epidemics periodically cropped up in Milan, Seville, Vienna, the Baltic, Marseille, and even in Australia as recently as 1925.

The last plague pandemic occurred from 1866 to the 1960s, spreading from China to various places around the world probably by ship born rats. It reached India and the west coast of the United States.

Research published in the Lancet Infectious Diseases (141), indicates that, using DNA sequencing from two skeletons buried in a cemetery in Bavaria, and the DNA extracted from a skeleton in the London cemetery of the same time, that the plague which struck Europe in the 1340's did not have the same genotype as the plague of Justinian in AD 541. This would indicate that the Yersinia bacteria had 'jumped' at least twice from its rodent host to humans, and it could do so again.

Bacteria, having invaded the body, unlike the viruses, do not usually invade the body's cells but stay in the tissues *between* the individual body cells.

However, a few bacteria, once classed as viruses, such as the Rickettsia bacteria, *have* invaded the tissue cells of more advanced creatures and have developed into intracellular, obligate parasites because, rather like viruses, they depend on the host cell for their replication. They have become some of today's most serious pathogens causing typhus and other infections such as Q-fever and Rocky Mountain spotted fever (so named because of the characteristic skin rash it produces in humans). There are quite a number of other spotted fevers including Japanese spotted fever and Mediterranean spotted fever, or Boutonneuse fever, occurring in France, Italy and Denmark. In fact, the various forms of typhus can sometimes produce a spotted rash which could be confused with that of measles, which is a virus.

In 2006, a newly discovered organism called Rickettsia helvetica was isolated from a patient in Sweden exhibiting meningitis K.Nilsson (120). All Rickettsia are transmitted by ticks, fleas and lice, all of which are transported by animals, including birds. All these different species of Rickettsia bacterial spotted fevers are so named because they not only cause a fever but typically produce a rash of spots on the skin.

In areas where rats are not common, typhus may also be transmitted through cat and opossum fleas.

Most of the above infect a range of animals, including birds. A similar organism, although not strictly a Rickettsia, is

Chlamydophila which causes psittacosis, or parrot fever, in humans. This organism can infect a variety of birds other than parrots, when the disease is then called ornithosis. It has also been found to infect some other mammals besides humans such as cattle, pigs, sheep, horses and even tortoises. However, unlike the Rickettsias, this organism is not transmitted by ticks, fleas or lice, but by contact and inhalation of dust. Susceptible species of birds include sparrows, ducks, chickens, gulls but more particularly, pigeons. Many of the wild pigeons seen in our town and city streets will be infected with Chlamydophila.

Because this organism is carried by all pigeons, any person encouraging a wild pigeon to take food such as bread, held between their lips, as the author has observed in some public parks such as London's Green Park, are running the risk of catching the disease. People may not appreciate this, but the habit carries risk, and can be regarded as rather foolish.

Rickettsia bacteria are able to make metabolites, necessary for their own growth and most, but not Chlamydophila, have an ATP transport system, so starving the host of all energy resources.

Interestingly the Rickettsias are genetically related to the mitochondria, which were once independently living bacteria and which have become an essential part of most eukaryotic cells. Mitochondria are to be discussed in Chapter 6 on the more advanced unicellular organisms.

Before we leave these early evolved forms of life, as has been already indicated, the different species of bacteria are continually evolving by mutation into slightly different forms and so eventually will go on to produce different species, some of which may, or may not, be resistant to antibiotics.

The *Good* Bugs

Besides those bacteria which cause infectious disease, there are very many other non - pathogenic species of bacteria, which do not cause disease in other living creatures. There are also other non - pathogenic microorganisms, including yeasts, which normally inhabit the gut and aid in the digestion of food. This not only occurs in the digestive tract of birds and other animals, but also in the human bowel. These microorganisms adhere to, proliferate and colonise the lining of the gut.

These so-called good bugs also influence the immune response of the cells lining the bowel, and they also synthesise some B-vitamins. It is estimated that the average human normally carries in their gut at least one kilogram of microbes and up to a quarter of a kilogram in or on other parts of their body.

Humans cannot digest cellulose, a main constituent of most plants, but cattle and other ruminants are able to carry out this digestion because they have a special stomach called the rumen. The rumen contains special bacteria and other simple unicellular organisms which have the necessary enzymes to break down cellulose. This can then be digested normally after being further passed along the gut and mixed with the digestive juices produced by the cow.

Animals such as deer, buffalo and sheep are also ruminants. When these animals are ruminating, or are said to be "chewing the cud" they are regurgitating the contents of the rumen and mixing this with saliva in their mouth to complete digestion, after which it is then swallowed and by-passes the rumen to travel further along their gut.

A similar process occurs in the ostrich, an early evolved type of bird known to exist from about 2,500 million years ago, and which feeds on seeds, shrubs, grass, fruit and flowers. However, in the ostrich, unlike other birds, there is no crop at the base of the oesophagus. The food is collected in the mouth to form a bolus, which is then swallowed, and can be seen to travel directly down the neck and then into the bird's stomach (the gizzard). Here it is mixed with previously swallowed small stones and ground up by the strong gizzard muscles, after which the processed food passes further down the alimentary canal to be absorbed.

Bacterial fermentation starts in the Ostrich's fore stomach, but these birds do not actually ruminate by passing the food back into the mouth.

The capercaillie or wood grouse *(tetrao urogallus)* a large member of the grouse family which can weigh up to 16lbs, is primarily a vegetarian, feeding on blueberries and fresh shoots of sedges and grasses in the summer. This changes to a diet of mostly conifer pine needles and cones in the winter. It has two long appendices (humans have only one appendix) as part of its gut. These appendices are filled with symbiotic (friendly) bacteria and they enlarge during the winter, to aid in the digestion of the capercaillie's rather course vegetable diet. The winter diet consists mainly of coniferous pine needles containing various oils and resins, some of which would be poisonous to other animals.

Plate No. 22 The male capercaillie

During the summer the young, growing fledglings and adults feed on invertebrates (breeding insects and their larvae), which provide plenty of protein needed by the young birds for growth, and on more succulent, growing vegetation.

Plate No.23 The bearded reedling (panurus biarmicus)

Again, the bearded reedling undergoes a change in the structure and function of *its* gut according to seasonal changes in the environment and the bird's seasonal nutritional requirements. These birds may be feeding themselves and their offspring on a high protein diet of insects and larvae in the spring when rearing their hatchlings. After the breeding season, when the birds go back onto a diet of seeds, the stomach then develops hard internal plates on each side and, at the same time, the bird takes in small stones to help grind up the seed like a flour mill. In line with this, the bacterial population of the bird's gut also changes.

The same changes will occur with the bacteria in our own human intestines, which have bacteria adapted to our own individual diet. That of the vegetarian or vegan will differ from that of the person who eats meat, for example. Lawrence. A, et al, writing in Nature (131), and citing many other references, has indicated that the microbiome of humans changes quite rapidly when a person's diet is switched from one containing mostly animal based protein, to one composed mostly of plant material. Moreover, there will be a difference between the bacteria required to digest cooked, (thus killing off food borne microorganisms), and uncooked food.

Paolo Lionetti and colleagues, at the University of Florence (67), compared the gut bacteria of children in a rural African village in Burkina Faso with those of children in Europe. He found that breastfed infants in both countries had similar bacterial profiles, but in older children the gut microbiota was different. The children living in Africa ate more, and could digest more easily, fruit and vegetables than the children living in the so called more advanced nations. In addition, it was interesting to note that the children living in Europe had a much higher rate of allergies.

Many more lowly creatures make use of bacteria, such as the various species of termites, which feed on wood and are aided in their digestion by bacteria in their gut.

A group of bacteria known as wolbachia inhabit the gut of some insects, such as the mosquitos, and some worms. Without these symbiotic bacteria, some of the host creatures cannot reproduce or even survive. Wolbachia make their host resistant to some viruses, so that by killing off the wolbachia with antibiotics, it is possible to kill off some mosquitos, and also to weaken the larvae of the nematode worm *(onchocerca volvulus)*, which causes river blindness in humans.

Bacteria are all around us, in and on the surface of the soil and in our houses, even deep below the earth's surface in the rocks and in the ice of the glaciers. They have invaded the more evolutionary advanced life forms such as all the different animals and birds. Their hosts have, for the most part, accepted them as useful helpers or symbionts: whilst providing these bacteria with food and shelter, the bacteria in turn aid in the digestion of their host's food. Some bacteria and the more advanced living creatures have become interdependent for each other's existence. We humans and all the animals could not live without them. Moreover, many of the contained bacteria, the so called 'good bugs', help to shield us, by competing with their more pathogenic cousins via the system of quorum sensing, already mentioned.

Many biologists consider the alimentary canal, or gut, as functioning *together* with its microbiota, and all should be considered as one of the body's major defence organs.

You may recall that Sir Alexander Fleming discovered the antibiotic properties of the common soil fungus Penicillium, when he noticed the staphylococci bacteria (a disease producing pathogen) on one of his culture plates, were inhibited from growing when they were near a mould of the ubiquitous fungus, penicillium notatum. The spores of the fungus had accidentally contaminated the culture plate and were exuding a substance, subsequently called penicillin, by a process somewhat similar to the quorum sensing substances exuded by bacteria as mentioned above.

In addition, in helping shield us and all animals from their pathogenic cousins, the "good bugs" have a constant interaction between these bacteria and other biota (including fungi and amoeboid like organisms) in the host's gut and the host's immune system. The inside mucosal surface of the gut is the animal body's largest immune surface, interacting with the world 'outside' the body. The lumen, or hollow cavity, of the gut is technically outside the body's tissues. Persistent stimulation by the gut biota of the host's immune system helps to keep the latter in trim. Humans, together with all the animals, including the birds, have their own internal eco-system which, if disrupted, leads to trouble.

A major problem today is that, because of the over extensive and often inappropriate use of antibiotics, many of the so called 'good bugs' have been reduced, or even killed off entirely, as well as the pathogens, so that the whole balance of the normal gut biota has been disturbed. This fact is highlighted by Martin Blaser in his book 'Missing Microbes'. He believes that many of our modern-day plagues such as type 1 diabetes (juvenile diabetes), coeliac disease, irritable bowel disease (IBS), ulcerative colitis and Crohn's disease are all due to this disturbance.

Also, although not considered to be a problem of the bowel, the recent increase in the incidence of asthma, hay fever and other allergies, including those to peanuts, and also some types of autism, may be due to disruption of the human microbiome. The author knows from personal experience, having witnessed the problems experienced by his severely autistic grandson, that there is undoubtedly a connection between the diet and autism. The range of autism spectrum disorders was hardly recognised by the medical profession 20 years ago, but is undoubtedly becoming increasingly prevalent today.

In addition to the foregoing, bacteria can reproduce themselves rapidly, some even doubling their number four times a day, and each time reproduction takes place, there is a chance happening of a mutation in their genome. One such mutation may be a resistance to a particular type of antibiotic. In addition, bacteria are able to pass on such mutations stored in their genomes to other neighbouring bacteria which may not necessarily be of their own kind. They are able to carry this out because some of their chromosomes, unlike those in the more advanced multicellular creatures, are stored in the bacterial cell in small circular packets called plasmids. These can pass through the outer cellular membranes, and so become inserted into neighbouring bacteria, a process called lateral or horizontal gene transfer. This mechanism is now being exploited by some scientists to develop DNA vaccines.

The hypothesis regarding the balance between good and bad bacteria in the gut is not new. The idea was originated by the Russian biologist Ilya Ilyich Metchnikoff, who noticed that the rural population of the Russian Steppes and Bulgaria were exceptionally long lived and had a diet largely composed of fermented milk. The milk was fermented by the bacteria lactobacilli, the lactic acid acting to inhibit the growth of more harmful bacteria, such as the clostridia, which produce detrimental toxins to the human body and advanced ageing.

Also, the German professor Alfred Nissle treated shigellosis infection in 1917, with a benign strain of E. coli., shigellosis being a type of food poisoning caused by shigella, a genus of bacteria closely related to both the bacteria E. coli and the bacteria salmonella. Globally, shigellosis occurs in at least 80 million people and results in about 700,000 deaths a year. Most cases occur in the third world but there are about 500,000, usually non-fatal, cases in travellers from industrialized countries.

Research indicates that both humans and other living creatures all host a vast complex of approximately 100 trillion micro-organisms. These, together with their host, form a complex "super-organism". The microbiome is composed mostly of bacteria, but also smaller numbers of protozoa, archaea, fungi, viruses and even the various worms, all together form an essential organ of the living body of the human, and of all other animals, including the birds.

Another aspect of the relationship between the human host and their microorganisms has recently been highlighted by the research of T. Andrew Clayton and his colleagues. They have found that the commonly used painkiller paracetamol (acetaminophen), is influenced by the composition of your gut bacteria (106). At one time, it was thought the metabolism, or break down, of all drugs, and toxins or poisons, was entirely carried out by the liver. However, it now appears that the microbiome of the gut, working in parallel with the liver, plays an important part in this process. Those people who say they can't take this or that drug, are possibly indicating that their microbiome is different from that of the "average" person. It might be that there is something unusual in their diet which influences this. If this occurs in humans, there is absolutely no reason why this mechanism should not occur in birds and other animals.

There is increasing scientific evidence that the rise in the incidence of some allergic conditions and autoimmune disease in humans, may be due to alterations in this balance of the microorganisms in the gut.

There is a valid argument that his could have been initiated by the so-called "hygiene hypothesis," which contends that, because everything in today's human environment is so "super clean", the young child is not exposed to infectious agents and parasites, and therefore the development of a healthy immune system is suppressed, thus leading to an increased susceptibility to allergic diseases. There might be something in that old saying, "a little dirt does you good".

Not many allergic conditions are seen in birds! Some will say that this is due to better diagnosis in humans, but is it? Remember the wading birds seen frequently in the glutinous mud of estuaries, or on sewage farms mentioned at the end of the first chapter in this book.

Alternatively, the balance of the different types of organisms in the gut, and the increase of allergic conditions in Western societies, may be due to a decrease in the amount of fibre in the diet. This is proposed in a paper entitled "Gut microbiota metabolism of dietary fibre influences allergic airway disease and haematopoiesis," published by Benjamin Marsland of the University Hospital of Lausanne in Switzerland, and supported by 43 references (145).

Quite apart from allergic conditions occurring in human patients, there is growing evidence of the importance of how the disruption of the gut biota influences other conditions of the body.

Alex Khoruts, MD a doctor working in the University of Minnesota Medical School, treated an eighty-nine-year-old human patient who was severely ill and near death, suffering with an overwhelming infection caused by clostridium difficile. The doctor's treatment was to use a faecal transplant, which consisted of an infusion of faeces obtained from a near relative, the patient's son. The patient had been previously treated with all the latest and most powerful antibiotics and had not responded. Dramatically, within 24 hours of starting treatment, Dr Khorut's patient showed a sudden improvement in her condition and she was able to return home in a short time. This was not the first successful faecal transplant which was carried out by Dr Khoruts. This doctor, and the Australian gastroenterologist Dr Thomas Borody, have now carried out 1500 of these procedures (94).

Many doctors don't recognise this procedure, which, until very recently, remained on the outside of recognised medical practice. However, it is now slowly being accepted as standard medical practice. In the minds of many doctors, there is little connection between the microbiota of the gut, the immune system, and the rest of the body, and the generally accepted opinion is that it is safer, and more acceptable, to use expensive antibiotics. In 2007 in England

and Wales, according to the Office for National Statistics, there were eight thousand hospital deaths related to clostridium difficile, far more than the number of deaths due to road traffic accidents which was just under three thousand.

Perhaps it might be prudent to ask whether it could have helped to at least try faecal transplants? A great deal of money might have been saved on expensive antibiotics, if only the medics and their patients could have overcome their fear, and perhaps distaste, of faecal transplant therapy. As Dr. Thomas J. Louie, MD, who is a Professor of Medicine, at the Department of Medicine and Microbiology-Infectious Diseases, University of Calgary in Alberta, Canada, and Medical Director for the infection prevention and control programme in the Calgary health region has stated, "There is a fair amount of loathing for things that are regarded as dirty. There is a huge yuck factor."

It has been suggested that if the procedure was referred to as a "microbiota transplant" (as it sometimes is), it might become more acceptable. However, the idea is in fact slowly being taken up by the medical profession. In fact, some unlicensed clinics and online forums are marketing the idea as a cure for all sorts of conditions from irritable bowel syndrome to Alzheimer's disease. There is even a move now to manufacture a pill containing the correct mix of live bacteria to correct the balance of the human microbiome. Unfortunately, unless the procedure is properly controlled, there is a risk that unidentified organisms and unwanted side effects, such as excessive weight gain, may be introduced, and it is essential therefore that the whole process is properly controlled by law.

Another idea, about the relationship between the microorganisms inhabiting the human gut and the rest of the body, has been advanced by Professors John Cryan and Timothy Dinan of the University College of Cork in Ireland. They have found that some signalling molecules used in the brain, such as serotine, dopamine and GABA (gamma-Aminobutyric acid), are manufactured by some gut bacteria. These can influence some behavioural conditions such as depression and obsessive-compulsive disorder (134). It has also been suggested that the increase in autism in young children, (a condition hardly recognised 20 years ago by the average GP), may be partly due to a change in their gut bacteria because of overuse of antibiotics.

Although microbiome transplantation may be offensive to us, from my own observations I have seen captive budgerigars eat their own, and the droppings of other birds in the same cage. Many other species of animals are coprophagic, including ostrich chicks. Also, pandas, koalas, hamsters, hippopotami and elephants, all eat the faeces of their mother to obtain bacteria to enable them to properly digest their food. It is reported that when these animals are born, their intestines are completely sterile. This is logical, because during development, the developing embryo of the vertebrate animal is isolated from the outside world, and coprophagia helps to populate the new intestine with suitable bacteria, not only engaged in the digestion of food, but also to act as a deterrent to colonisation by harmful species of bacteria. It has also been established that children born by caesarean section do not acquire from their mothers a healthy microbiome, which would have been acquired during a normal vaginal delivery.

In some of these cases, for example in rabbits and hamsters, coprophagia is carried out to obtain extra vitamins, after the ingested food has then been passed twice through the gut and been reprocessed by bacteria. In other cases, coprophagia enables the young immature animal to populate their intestine with specific bacteria needed to break down and digest the plant food diet containing cellulose.

The foregoing paragraphs about the co-operating bacteria, refer to the so-called 'good bugs,' and this is the principle behind the use of probiotics, mainly based on varying species of lactobacilli which are believed to be beneficial to humans who consume them. These are distinct from prebiotics, which are nutrients believed to encourage the growth of probiotics. Synbiotics are a combination of both probiotics and appropriate prebiotics, put together so that they work synergistically.

Plate No.24: A young elephant eating the droppings of an adult elephant which has just defecated

CHAPTER 6

A further evolutionary advance in the complexity of living organisms.

After the *relatively* simple structure of the bacterial cell, there evolved from a parallel group of bacterial organisms, the Archaea, a vast number of more complicated single celled microorganisms.

In contrast to the traditional bacteria, these new organisms had their chromosomes with the DNA wrapped up in a 'bag' (the nuclear membrane), away from the other departments of the cell. The chromosomes then formed the separate compartmented "nucleus" of the cell. These organisms are called eukaryotes, the name being derived from Greek, meaning 'true kernel', since their chromosomes were now separated from the rest of the cell.

Both the eukaryotes and the less complicated bacteria, or prokaryotes, were probably evolving in parallel rather than in a direct line of descent, as ancestors and direct descendants. Like the bacteria, the vast majority of eukaryotes are microscopic and cannot be seen by the naked eye without the use of a microscope. Despite this, the eukaryotes include all the larger multi-cellular 'higher' animals (which obviously *can* be seen by the unaided human eye), and the plants.

Some of the early evolving eukaryotes were referred to as the Protozoa, or the very first animal-like organisms. Just like a minority of the bacteria, only *some* of these microorganisms, the first eukaryotes, are the cause of infectious disease in other living creatures.

Apart from the separation of the chromosomes encased in the nuclear membrane, the eukaryotic cell is overall a more advanced form of life than that of the bacterial cell. It is generally larger and has a more rigid structure than a bacterial cell, because it contains within the body of its jelly-like cytoplasm, a cytoskeleton anchored to the surrounding cellular membrane. In addition, during cell replication, as takes place during normal growth, for example when tissue such as the skin expands to enclose the growing creature, the eukaryotic cell divides into two separate daughter cells by the process called **mitosis** (in chapter 2). This complex, staged and highly regulated process, is preceded by the cell's chromosomes splitting longitudinally into two identical halves, so dividing the DNA into two identical halves. The result of replication is the formation of two daughter cells which are each exact replicas of the original mother cell.

In contrast to mitosis, during replication of a bacterial cell, replication takes place by simple binary fission or straightforward splitting into two equal halves. This process is what takes place in all the bacteria, and in a few other simple organisms such as *some* protozoa.

As already indicated, the Archaea, originally called Archaebacteria are believed to be the forerunners of the eukaryotes and were first recognised by Carl Woese and George E Fox in 1977. These organisms have metabolic (i.e. chemical) pathways similar to those of the typical bacterial cell.

The Archaea were originally discovered in the oceans and today are now found to form a large percentage of the plankton. Also, the so-called 'bacteria' found in the rocks and in glacial ice are mostly Archaebacteria. Overall, Archaebacteria form approximately twenty percent of the Earth's biomass and they are an important source of various enzymes, which are utilized in the laboratory to produce medical and agricultural products.

Cellular Energy and Mitochondria

During the same period as the evolution of the Archaebacteria, a type of early bacterium evolved, which was the forerunner of today's intra-cellular (i.e. within eukaryotic cells) mitochondria. These bacteria had 'learned,' or evolved, to use the oxygen which became available in the Earth's atmosphere resulting from early plant photosynthesis.

The Earth's atmosphere, during the initial period of the evolution of life, was without oxygen and therefore anaerobic. However, as time advanced, atmospheric oxygen eventually became available, after the cyanobacteria had entered the early plants to become the plant's chloroplasts. The early mitochondrial bacterium used the same mechanism of endosymbiosis (i.e. they either invaded the other primitive bacteria actively, or were captured by the very early bacteria) as had the cyanobacteria with the early plants (see Chapter 5.)

The mitochondrion organism incorporated itself into the universal ancestor of all of today's living animal cells. This change possibly took place between about 1.7 and 2 billion years ago. Through the course of evolution, mitochondria have become the dedicated "powerhouses" of **all** present-day animal cells. Mitochondria carry this process out by using atmospheric oxygen to 'slow burn' food products used in the cell. The mitochondria now provide a versatile package of chemical procedures which supply the energy for all the metabolic reactions of all living animals.

There are however, a few primitive eukaryotes which do not contain mitochondria. These are Giardia (mentioned below) and its relatives, some primitive fungi (microsporidians), and also the arch-amoebae (see below). These organisms are the most primitive of the unicellular eukaryotes and it would seem likely that they had evolved before the origin of mitochondria.

Nuclear DNA and Mitochondrial DNA

The certainty that mitochondria were once independent living organisms, is indicated by the fact that they have retained their original cellular membrane, so that in their new eukaryotic cellular home they are enclosed within a double cellular membrane (their own, together with that of the host cell.)

Moreover, like other living eukaryotic cells they have their own DNA ("mitochondrial DNA"), organized in several copies, contained within a circular chromosome. This is distinct from the nuclear DNA of their host cell. Consequently, when DNA is recovered from any human, perhaps to investigate a person's ancestral origins when researching family history, it is necessary to distinguish the host cell's nuclear DNA, obtained from the original host cell, from the separate cellular mitochondrial DNA, derived from the once independent mitochondrial living cell.

Host cell nuclear DNA is formed by a combination of half from the male parent side (sperm derived DNA), combined with half from the female side (egg derived DNA), both sperm and ovum having combined, to form a single celled zygote. The single celled zygote then repeatedly divides into many body cells, and subsequently develops into the adult animal. Mitochondrial DNA in the final adult originates **only** from the female side. This is because the ovum (the unfertilised egg), goes to form the bulk of a fertilised egg (the zygote), compared with the much smaller bulk of the male gamete (i.e. the sperm), which has no mitochondrial DNA. Unfortunately, there is a downside to some mitochondrial DNA. About 1 in 5,000 children born in the UK, and possibly worldwide, carry a defective mitochondrial DNA mutant which can cause problems such as blindness, seizures, dementia or mental impairment.

Once inside their parent eukaryotic cell, the mitochondria are able to replicate within the host cell, so that an individual eukaryotic cell may have just a few, or many, of these mitochondrial miniature chemical factories. They vary in number according to the need in each cell, from one, to up to several thousand and can increase in number when greater energy requirements are needed, Also, the mitochondrial genome is very small (in humans 16,500 base pairs, compared with 3 million in the human host genome.) Mitochondria can migrate around the cell and may fuse together to form a web and then split up again.

Apart from mitochondria being the primary energy generators of the eukaryotic cell, recent research has indicated they also have other important and protective functions:

(a) They influence ageing, the combating of stress, and disease.

(b) They influence working memory, migrating into the synaptic junctions of the neurons when required.

(c) They produce the haemprotein used in haemoglobin.

(d) They control the availability of calcium.

(e) They synthesize steroids.

(f) They synthesize humanin, a small protein preventing the formation of amyloid plaques found both in the brains of Alzheimer patients, and in Arteriosclerosis (the thickening, hardening and loss of elasticity of the walls of the arteries.) This protein is produced by the genome of mitochondria.

The mitochondria genome produces thousands of other small non-coding RNAs, which influence how the nuclear genetic code of a genome is expressed, by the process of methylation. This was mentioned above, in Chapter 2 regarding epigenesis and the expression of genes. The incorporation of mitochondria into the Eukaryotic cell may have influenced the evolution of the multicellular organisms. Moreover, because the mitochondrial genome is small and subject to much more rapid mutational change than the nuclear genome of the host cell, it has a more rapid influence on how the host genome is expressed. Additionally, mitochondrial change may proliferate at different rates in different parts of the host's body according to varying need, adapting to the cellular environment. (New Scientist, 20 September 2014, Garry Hamilton.) It has been shown that it is possible to slow the process of aging by taking more exercise, which produces energy requirements and so produces more mitochondria (5 months of endurance exercise of 45 minutes, 3 times a week, resulted in a complete mitochondrial overhaul.)

The Eukaryotic cell also has a number of other intracellular organelles (i.e. minute packeted structures within each cell, carrying out a specific function for that particular cell.) These are (1) the Golgi apparatus, which processes proteins, particularly for secretion, and (2) the ribosomes, molecular "machines" for helping to accurately replicate DNA for the nuclei in the production of new body stem cells. Also, the ribosomes in the reproductive organs help to produce either the female gamete (the egg) or the male gamete (the sperm.)

PROTOZOA

The early animal life forms are generally referred to as the Protozoa, whilst the early forms of plant life form the Protophyta. These include the minute Amoebas, which can only be seen with a microscope. These organisms will be familiar to anyone who has studied biology at school.

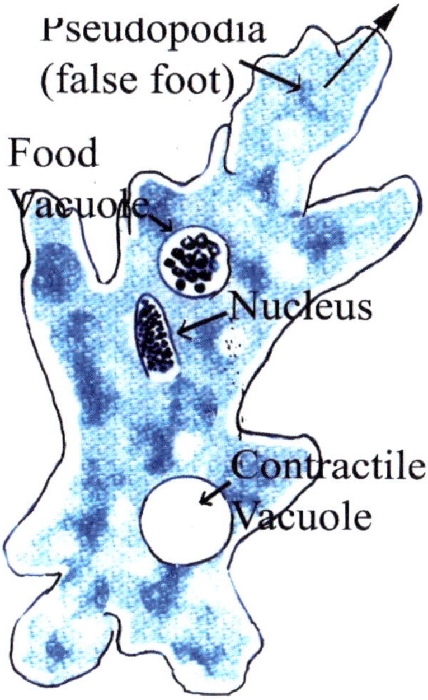

Figure no.6 A diagrammatic representation of the jelly like creature with the arrow indicating how this organism just flows forward in its direction of movement

There are many different types of amoebae within the Phylum Amoebozoa. These are mostly living harmlessly in soil or in water, ingesting nutrients by simply flowing over their prey, which may be a small specimen of algae, bacteria or other minute living organism.

However, a few amoebae do cause disease in the higher animals. All the various types of amoeba have certainly been around for a very long time and are amongst the most primitive and early evolved animals and some authorities classify them as being in their own Phylum. There is indirect fossil evidence that they may have evolved around 715 million years ago. The very early evolved so called archameoba are quite closely related to the slime moulds mentioned above at the end of Chapter 3.

Of the type of amoeba which produce disease there are a number of species in the genus Entamoeba, which live in the gut of many animal hosts. Entamoeba histolytica predominantly infects the primates (humans, apes and monkeys.) Occasionally, it infects some other animals but does not cause significant disease. It has not been recorded in birds as causing disease, although sometimes unidentified symbiotic types may be present amongst the many thousands of species of non-pathogenic microorganisms inhabiting the avian bowel, and for that matter, the bowel of all other animals.

If surrounding conditions become unfavourable, all Amoebae can secrete a fluid which hardens, to wrap the whole organism in an environmentally resistant cyst. The cyst is the principle mode of infection and transmission of the pathogenic species of Amoeba. Infection of animals takes place by means of the cyst entering the mouth of the host. Also, the amoeba may exit its host, wrapped up in a cyst, via the host's anal passage, together with the rest of the host animal’s excreta.

When the pathogenic Entamoeba invades the host, the cyst-like hard outer covering dissolves and the organism resumes its normal physical form. This can then invade and destroy some of the host’s cells lining the gut and the adjacent blood vessels, so resulting in a severe, bloody enteritis. Disruption of the host's gut lining cells enables the amoeba to enter the bloodstream of the host and then be transported around the body. The result is a possible liver amoebic abscess. During its passage around the host's body, the amoeba can replicate, so that when it is finally eliminated from the body of the host, the number of individual amoeba has multiplied. Moreover, Entamoeba histolytica can imbibe into its body, and transport to a new host, some viruses such as HIV.

Serious epidemics of human amoebic dysentery have occurred in recent times in Australia and Norway. Also, it is believed that amoebic dysentery occurred amongst the Crusaders in the twelfth and thirteenth centuries.

Another type of amoeba, *Acanthamoeba,* living commonly in soil and fresh water, can also infect humans and other animals although again, it has not been reported in birds. In humans, the organism may rarely cause eye, brain and gut infections.

It has recently been found that this amoeba can also engulf and ingest the bacterial Staphylococcal organism MRSA (Methicillin-resistant Staphylococcus aureus). This particular bacterium is commonly the cause of resistant antibiotic infections, particularly in hospitals. Within the hospital environment, the bacterium can become trapped within the encysted amoeba but remain alive, and the MRSA bacterium can multiply whilst within the cyst (Sharon A. Huws et al (56)). The dry, persistent cysts may then be an important cause of airborne transmission of the bacterium, which is carried in the dust accumulating in the environment, which is particularly problematic in hospitals where debilitated humans are concentrated.

The reader will remember that Mimivirus, mentioned above in Chapter 4, was first discovered in an *Acanthamoeba.* In fact, a lot of research is being undertaken by a number of scientists, cited by Francoise Bichae and colleagues, who are looking at how many types of bacteria, and other pathogens, have evolved by being protected in the cysts of amoebae and other waterborne microorganisms.

Rather like the environmentally resistant and infectious cysts of the amoebae, there are many parasitic protozoans which produce spores able to persist in the environment and which carry the parasite to a new susceptible host. An important group of these single celled spore producing parasites are collectively known as Coccidians. They inhabit the guts of many species of birds and also cattle. Amongst these are the various species of the genus Eimeria, consisting of at least 1771 species. Infection with these parasites, results in a disease called coccidiosis, familiar to poultry farmers.

Plate No. 25 The crested wood partridge (Rollulus rouloul)

The Crested Wood Partridge *(Rollulus rouloul)* and the Palawan peacock pheasant *(Polyplectron napoleonis)* below, are both members of the pheasant family *(Phasianidae)*, as is the domestic chicken *(Gallus gallus)*, as mentioned in Chapter 2. These types of birds inhabit the same tropical rainforest region of southeast Asia, and all are susceptible to coccidiosis.

Plate No.26 Palawan peacock pheasant (Polyplectron napoleonis)

The infectious Coccidial oocysts, originating from the parasite in the infected bird's bowel, are passed out in the bird's droppings. These lie on the forest floor or poultry pen to be picked up by, and infect, another bird of the same or a similar species.

Besides chickens and their relatives in the pheasant family (Phasianidae), similar species of coccidial organisms occur in many other species of birds, both captive and wild. The result of infestation is a serious inflammation of the lining of the gut, sometimes resulting in a bloody diarrhoea and in loss of bodily condition, ending in death in severe cases. The disease thrives in groups of overcrowded and stressed poultry being kept in insanitary conditions on some poultry farms, such as in closely packed rearing sheds. In contrast, in their natural environment of the rain forest, the susceptible birds are not closely confined so an overwhelming infestation does not usually occur, and an ongoing, periodic, re-infection by a small number of oocysts picked up from the forest floor has enabled the wild birds to live in relative harmony with the parasite. They have been able to build up a gradual, innate resistance without being overcome by an overwhelming infection.

This particular avian coccidian does not infect humans.

There are many other similar genera of parasitic protozoans, and these are Isospora, Dorisiella, Tyzzeria and Wenyonella. These different species of coccidians infect different groups of birds but again, are not reported to have infected humans. Nevertheless, other species of coccidians can infect rabbits, dogs, calves, many wild animals and some reptiles.

However, one of the most serious spore forming parasitic protozoans causing disease not only in birds but also in humans, in cattle, sheep, dogs, cats, mice and even reptiles, are the Cryptosporidiae.

This family of parasites is distantly related to the malarial parasites Plasmodia and to another spore forming parasite, Toxoplasma, both to be discussed below.

Cryptosporidiosis, is one of the most common waterborne diseases and is found worldwide. It can live in the gut of the infected host, sometimes causing severe diarrhoea, particularly in immuno-compromised humans. In infected animals, such as sheep, goats and cattle, the spores produced in the intestine are passed out in the droppings. This results in contamination of the soil or surface water which may be used as a source of drinking water by hill and mountain walkers or campers, who may get their water from lakes, hill streams or even ponds. Humans drinking untreated or un-boiled water in these circumstances are at high risk of infection, and should always take care to wash their hands and boil the water before drinking it.

Like Campylobacter mentioned above in Chapter 5, in the UK particularly, garden birds pecking through the foil bottle tops to get at the milk delivered and left on a customer's doorstep, has resulted in the infected birds contaminating the milk within the bottle with Cryptosporidium. Most animals, including birds, who carry the organism, are merely acting as vectors, as they are not usually pathogenically affected by this organism. Interestingly, Cryptosporidium has been shown to be pathogenic in some reptiles.

Amongst the same group of spore-forming protootozoan parasites is Toxoplasma. The organism is ubiquitous, causing disease in many species of mammals (even elephants), in reptiles, in amphibians, in birds and in fish. In infected animals, the parasite tends to form cysts in the muscles of the host. It can infect all species of birds, generally causing a chronic debilitating anaemia, and has been reported to have caused a fatal disease in a captive parrot collection.

Most importantly, in humans, Toxoplasma can be a serious problem, particularly for pregnant women, as the parasite can infect the developing unborn child, and for immune-compromised people such as those carrying the HIV virus. However, Toxoplasma's 'definitive' host, only in which the parasite is able to complete its life cycle and so produce infective cysts, are members of the cat family. Humans can become infected via direct contamination with cat faeces or from places contaminated by cats, such as the soil of a garden flower border. However, cats generally are meticulous in washing themselves and burying their faeces in soil.

The most important source of infection for humans in general, is eating unwashed vegetables and salad foods, or eating improperly cooked meat (from any animal), which may contain the cysts in its muscle. It is estimated that around thirty percent of humans worldwide carry the parasite. In most people, apart from being problematic for pregnant women, there are usually no signs of disease. Sometimes infection can produce mild fflu like symptoms, but it is very rare that a severe infection results in inflammation of the eye or brain. In pregnant women, because the parasite can cross the placenta to reach the foetus, this can result in serious disease in the unborn child. Also, in 2007 the psychiatrist Fuller Torrey carried out a meta-analysis of 42 separate studies, and found that people who suffer from schizophrenia are three times as likely to be carrying antibodies to this parasite as those people who do not have the condition, Priya Shetty (88). It should be noted that there seems to be an overlap in the genetics of schizophrenia and bipolar disorder, a condition which has come much more into the public eye recently, as reported by Craddock N. and Owen M.J. (105).

Similarly, another related protozoan parasite Neospora, which in the past has often been misidentified as toxoplasma, can only complete its life cycle in the dog and other canines such as foxes. It does not, so far as is known, infect humans or birds. However, it can cause neuromuscular disease in dogs, and it is an important cause of abortion in dairy cattle causing, up to 40% of abortions within a herd in some cases. It does also infect many other animals such as sheep, horses and foxes. It has been demonstrated that some species of birds such as sparrows, magpies and buzzards, can pick up the cysts and act as carriers.

Another genus of parasitic Protozoans, (about 130 species in all are recognised at present), to infect a very wide range of host species from reptiles and birds to mammals, including humans, is Sarcocystis.

This parasite is so named because, like Toxoplasma, the organism can form cysts in muscle or flesh (from Greek sarx, sarkos.) Although infection in some human populations can be as high as twenty one percent, the majority of human cases show no symptoms and infection is usually caused by eating undercooked meat. People who prefer their meat served 'rare' should be aware of the risks they take. In some animals, infection can result in disease of the heart and of other body muscles.

All spore forming protozoans will have evolved from a common ancestor and over millions of years have developed, through mutation, into slightly different genomes, resulting in their individual life histories. The important idea to grasp is that as each species of 'higher animal' has evolved, it has acquired its own species of parasitic protozoan, each adapted to the new host; put another way, the parasite has evolved alongside its host.

It might begin to feel as if the world is full of different kinds of these early evolved and primitive forms of life, all ready to invade humans and other living creatures, and to cause disease. However, it is important to remember that these organisms and their ancestors, were here on this planet long before humans, birds and other more highly evolved animals arrived. We humans, and our fellow creatures, have all developed and 'learned' to grow up with, and live side by side with, these more primitive life forms.

During the unimaginably long period of evolutionary time, all living creatures, including those already mentioned, together with other prospective host creatures such as sponges, worms and crabs, developed effective defence mechanisms against disease producing organisms. All of these biological defence mechanisms depend upon specialised cells within the bodies of the host being able to distinguish other individual cells as being “self” or “non-self,” or, in other words having the ability to 'say', “is it one of us?” and then deal effectively with any foreign invader.

In the higher animals, including humans, these specialised defence cells form part of their immune system. This system is based in special organs which include the spleen, the lymph nodes, some parts of the gut and some blood cells, all of which can sometimes become disrupted by viruses such as HIV, birnaviruses or circoviruses.

The important point to remember is that there are many more protozoans which evolved long before the more complex animals (including humans) evolved. Most of these protozoans still remain to be identified, because at present they are not causing any obvious disease.

Also, there are many protozoans spending part of their life living in the guts of birds and other animals such as dogs, cats and cattle, as well as humans, many of which are harmless symbionts. These, together with benign bacteria already mentioned above at the end of Chapter 5, help to form the so called 'good bugs'.

Like bacteria, the relatively few protozoans which do cause disease do so usually in immuno-compromised animals or people. The resistance of birds to some pathogenic protozoans can also become reduced if they are exposed to stress or to environmental toxins.

A group of protozoans which are flagellated with their long tails, and are therefore motile, are the trichomonas. Different species of these organisms infect not only many species of birds, but also some species infect humans, for example trichomonas vaginalis. It is estimated that 29% of black American women carry this infection whilst 38% of women in Nigeria are infected.

Related species of this group of parasites also infect cattle and probably many other animals.

In those birds infected with trichomonas, the parasites are found in the throat. They often infect birds of prey, in which case falconers then call the disease Frounce, a condition recognised since the thirteenth century. The infection is picked up when the hawk or falcon catches an infected prey species.

Dr. Jamie Samour reported that 63% of captive falcons in Saudi Arabia (97) are infected. Ewan D. S. Wolff and colleagues believe they have evidence that this organism even infected a dinosaur (86), which is not surprising, since the trichomonas will have evolved long before the time of the dinosaurs.

Trichomonas infection is currently a serious problem in garden birds, where they are spread by infected but apparently healthy birds which contaminate bird seed feeders, resulting in other, less resistant, song birds becoming infected. This could be prevented if people using garden bird feeders regularly washed the feeder before refilling with seed. Trichomonas are possibly responsible for a decline in the UK population of the greenfinch *(carduelis chloris).*

Other flagellated motile parasites related to trichomonas, and which probably evolved from the same ancestor, are histomonas and cochlosoma, both of which are well recognised pathogens found in the gut of some species of birds, but not in humans. Histomonas meleagridis is principally found, and causes disease, in turkeys (blackhead disease), but it is also found in other gallinaceous birds, whilst cochlosoma is found in some finches.

Another flagellated and primitive protozoan parasite, but which is not related to trichomonas, are the species of Giardia. of which about forty species have so far been described from different animals, although some of these might not be truly separate species. Unlike most other protozoan creatures, they do not have mitochondria.

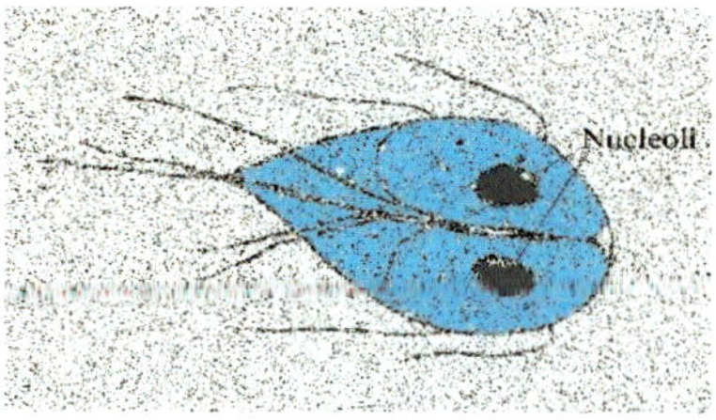

Fig No.7 Giardia

All Giardia are formed of two cells, each with its own nucleus and with four flagella. Unlike many other protozoans, Giardia do not form true spores, but do form resting cysts. Most of the time they are motile microscopic discrete double celled anaerobic parasites, living in dirty water and within the bowels of many animals, including birds. People such as campers often become infected by what looks like sparkling fresh water from natural sources, like a mountain stream. but this unsterilised water is often contaminated with animal faeces from sheep, cattle and deer for example, which carry Giardia as well as cryptosporidium mentioned above.

In humans, infection with the parasite can cause diarrhoea, together with excessive gas production in the intestine, resulting in marked abdominal pain, together with flatus. In the USA, infection with this organism is sometimes called beaver fever.

A further group of early evolving parasitic protozoans living in the blood of the higher animals are the trypanosomes, which, by comparing their DNA, have been found to be related to the free-living euglena. Euglena is a motile protozoan found in ponds and other fresh water environments but it does not cause disease.

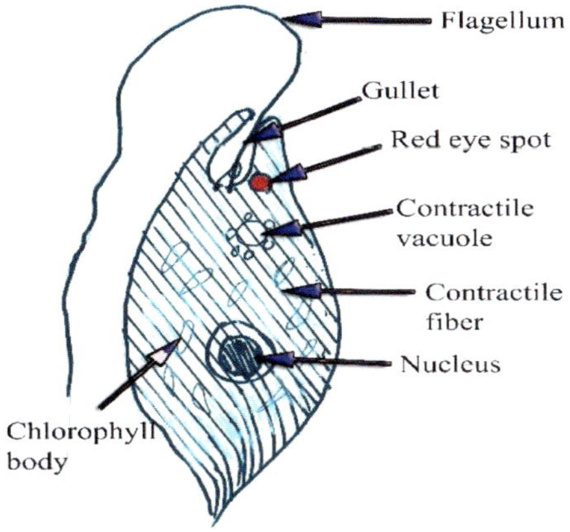

Fig. No. 8 Euglena

This green single celled organism is often so numerous as to form a green scum on the surface of the water. The organism's red eye spot directs the creature towards the light. Euglena moves through water by using both the flagellum at one end and by altering its shape, as if being squeezed, using contractile fibres spaced across the organism's outer cell membrane.

Although a primitive animal species, euglena is often thought of as a plant because of its green colour. Like all plant species, it is able to carry out photosynthesis using energy from the sun's rays. During the course of time, by means of the evolutionary process of endosymbiosis, euglena has taken into its single celled body, free living cyanobacteria to form, like the plants, chloroplasts. These are normally found in all green plants (see Chapter 5), and are what give the plants their typical green colour. In this instance however, they have invaded, or been taken in by, euglena's animal ancestors. As mentioned above, other living animal organisms such as jellyfish, flatworms, bivalve shell fish and some salamanders, make use of blue green algae to carry out photosynthesis.

The Trypanosomes

These are blood parasites of some of the vertebrate animals which inhabit some regions of Sub-Saharan central Africa, south east Asia and South America. In humans, the parasites cause the illness known as 'sleeping sickness.' A similar and often fatal disease, 'nagana' affects horses, and some species of cattle (the zebu or brahman type; that is, those with a fatty hump), in east Africa. However, other species of cattle in west Africa, together with most of the indigenous wild hoofed animals in these regions, are usually resistant. These resistant species, have, over evolutionary time, built up an innate resistance to the disease caused by the parasite.

The trypanosome blood parasites are transmitted between mammals by the tsetse fly. This fly is similar to, and indeed related to, the common housefly although it is somewhat larger. Likewise, the horsefly, which is sometimes mistaken for a housefly, but again is somewhat larger and has a more painful bite. Furthermore, the horsefly belongs to the same generic family, the Tabanidae, as the tsetse fly.

Three species of trypanosomes have been recorded as being found in many species of birds, not just in Africa but worldwide, including common garden birds and pigeons. In birds generally, they do not seem to cause much harm, probably because over aeons of time the birds have developed an innate resistance to the parasites.

In birds, trypanosomes are transmitted between their avian hosts by numerous blood-sucking insect carriers, such as the flat or louse flies, (the hippoboscids - see plate 32), which are often found on sheep. Many, but not all, of these flies have wings. Including the various sub-families, there are over two hundred different species of flat flies. Also, some species of biting flies (the Simuliidae or black flies of North America, Scotland and New Zealand), as well as parasitic mites, suck blood and transmit trypanosomes in birds.

So how did the trypanosomes evolve from their aquatic euglena-like cousins, and come to reside in the blood of many host species causing serious disease in some mammals such as humans, horses and domestic cattle?

The author speculates that possibly, in the distant past, millions of years ago, both euglena and trypanosomes evolved from their common ancestor and lived in water. Here the ancestral trypanosomes were taken up by the ancestral arthropod of the tsetse fly. In fact, all arthropods (the scientifically classified group which includes the insects), are believed to be related to, and possibly to have descended from, their common ancestors, the velvet worms. Today, the velvet worms (onychophora), are often brightly coloured (blue, green or red), look rather like slugs with legs and have mouth parts which are generally always open. They evolved in water where today, the one hundred and twenty or so species, continue to live. The ancestors of these creatures probably did not have to actively feed, their food just flowed into their constantly open mouths. Today's velvet worms do actively investigate their prey with their two front tentacles. After this, they envelope and immobilise the prey in a slime, before it is ingested.

The protozoans (including the ancestral trypanosome), were also simultaneously evolving in water and possibly just swam into the gut of the ancestral velvet worms. Then, not being actively digested by the ancestral velvet worm, the 'trypanosome' just swam into their open fore-gut, rather like today's small fish are passively taken into the open mouth of the basking shark. Not all of these ancient protozoans may have been digested, some of these creatures may just have "taken up residence," feeding on the cells lining the gut of the velvet worm, thus establishing themselves in the lining wall of the fore-gut of their newly found host and so became established for part of their life cycle inside the 'ancestral insect.'

However, there may well have been other routes by which these parasites established themselves as blood parasites of the vertebrate animals, as is indicated by the studies of Hughes and Piontkivska (107), also Simpson and colleagues (108). Both groups of workers have been intensively studying the DNA of these parasites, trying to work out their evolutionary history. All that is certain is that these flagellated parasites were around, together with their biting fly vectors, at least one hundred million years ago, and probably much earlier, because they have been discovered in Burmese and in Dominican amber (see the chapter on dinosaurs).

Of course, the larvae of the tsetse fly are not found in water today, but their ancestor probably did evolve in an aquatic environment. Today, tsetse flies are found in bush or woody vegetation, bordering on the banks of rivers in tropical African climates.

The common ancestor of euglena and the trypanosomes, together with the ancestral arthropod, probably co-evolved as parasite/commensal and host, forming their present relationship. Today, the female tsetse fly does not lay eggs, but directly gives birth to larvae which pupate and then, after falling to the ground, develop directly into the adult flies. Having found its host, be it human or animal, the adult tsetse fly bites the host to obtain a meal of blood and simultaneously injects some of its saliva (which acts as an anticoagulant) containing the parasitic trypanosomes. Inside the human or animal, the parasite travels via the bloodstream, to invade the host's lymph nodes and eventually reaches the brain causing the sleeping sickness.

In the Americas, another trypanosome (T. cruzi), causes Chagas disease in humans. The infection is believed to have arisen in South

America and it is now estimated that as many as eight million people worldwide are infected. In North America, it is possible that 330.000 US citizens carry the disease. These people are mostly very poor American citizens of Hispanic origin.

Overall, Chagas disease probably kills more Americans than does Malaria. However, in contrast to the situation in Africa, this trypanosome is transmitted by Triatominae, the assassin, or kissing bugs, (of which there are many species), which also had a common ancestor in the ancient velvet worms. These bugs hide in cracks in the woodwork of sub-standard housing. The assassin bugs feed not only on the blood of humans but also of domestic and wild mammals which form the natural reservoirs for T.cruzi. Although Triatominae bugs do feed on birds, the birds appear to be immune to infection by T. cruzi and therefore the birds are not infected.

In the United States those animals on which the Triatominae bugs do feed include armadillos, squirrels, opossums, wood rats, and mice. All these animals act as a reservoir for the parasite.

It is believed that Charles Darwin may have become a victim of Chagas disease, transmitted by the bug Triatoma infestans. Darwin describes in his diary being bitten by a large black bug of the pampas which swelled after sucking his blood.

Some zoo vets have exploited the habit of Triatominae bugs to suck blood from animals, and use these bugs to collect blood samples from those zoo animals which are dangerous or difficult to handle. The Triatominae bug is a large insect, about one inch long, which swells markedly when it has sucked blood from its prey. Having sucked the blood, the sample can be extracted by hypodermic needle and syringe from the bloated body of the Triatominae bug, Stephanie Sanderson (81).

Another group of related Protozoans are a number of species in the genera Leishmania, there being at least thirty-five different species of this parasite. Leishmania are transmitted by various species of blood sucking sand flies. The protozoan causing Leishmania have a reservoir in many warm blooded animals such as rodents and other animals such as dogs and foxes, and also, in Africa, in hyraxes. However, all these animals may not be carrying the same species of parasite as that which occurs in humans.

Plate No.14 Rock Hyrax

The *Leishmania* parasite, as seen in blood samples, does not look unlike the Trypanosome protozoan.

The female sand fly carries the Leishmania protozoa from an infected animal after feeding on their blood, and then carries the parasite to another host species be it human, hyrax or another animal, thus transmitting the disease and causing sand fly fever. In contrast to the female, the male sand fly feeds on plant nectar because it doesn't need the animal protein to nourish eggs developing in its body like the female. Female sand flies lay eggs in batches, in cracks and crevices which are dark and rich in organic matter such as dry sand or even in wall cavities.

In the New World, a species of sand fly feeds on bats. There are no records of these flies feeding on birds or transmitting Leishmania parasites to them. Again, the ancestor of the sand fly probably evolved in water in the same way as that of the tsetse fly.

There are a number of types of leishmaniasis in humans, the most common form of which is the cutaneous form which causes severe ulceration of the skin (sometimes described as "flesh eating") and is seen mostly in the Middle and Far East but it can occur in southern France. In humans, occasionally, these parasites can invade the internal organs of the body and cause serious disease.

The parasites can also cause the same type of disease in dogs, but these signs may not be seen for months, or, as in one reported case, up to six years after the dog had returned to the UK from a holiday abroad. All the cases of canine leishmaniasis seen in the UK are diagnosed in dogs which have been abroad. The sand fly vector does not, as yet, occur in the UK. As climate change takes place the Phlebotomine sand fly is expected to invade the more northerly parts of Europe from the warmer climatic regions, particularly from the Mediterranean.

Malaria

Moving on now to malaria, first mentioned in the introduction to this book, and the subject which initially stimulated the author's interest in the evolution of infectious disease.

Malaria, so-named because it was thought to arise from the bad air of swamps and marshes; hence the name derived from mediaeval Italian 'mala-aria.'

At one time this disease was not uncommon in many parts of the Western World. Oliver Cromwell, the Lord High Protector of the Republic of England, Scotland and Ireland (1653—1658), was thought to have suffered with it. Affected persons show a fever with shivering and intense sweating called "the ague" or marsh fever. At present, globally, 300 million people suffer from malaria with over a million deaths in children annually. Most of these cases today occur in Africa and unfortunately, in its early stages, malaria is often difficult to differentiate from viral Ebola fever.

The evolutionary scenario for the malarial parasite is probably similar to that suggested above for trypanosomes. Plasmodium, the malarial blood parasite, originally got into the salivary glands of the mosquito when the ancestors of both the mosquito and the malarial parasite, were jointly evolving in an aquatic environment. The result is that the malarial parasite is now injected into its final and definitive host by the female mosquito when the insect bites its victim to obtain a meal of protein rich blood.

The present-day larvae of the mosquito still breed in water and their ancestors, relatives of the velvet worms, probably took up the ancestor of Plasmodium in a similar way to the ancestors of the Trypanosomes.

Plasmodium has now been found by some research biologists, using molecular taxonomy, to be related to Paramecium, the slipper animalcule again familiar to some of us from our biology lessons.

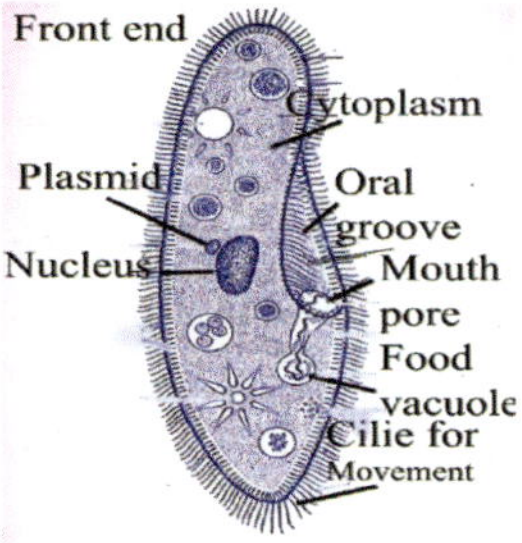

Fig. No. 9 Paramecium

This microscopic protozoan is very common in pond water and easy to culture. As a schoolboy, the author was fortunate enough to have a second hand Leitz microscope. It was easy enough to make an infusion of hay or dried grass, rather like making a pot of tea, then when cooled, to inoculate this with a little pond water. By the following day, the water was teaming with Paramecia which were fascinating to watch as they glided through the water.

The ancestral form of this organism could have been swept into the mouth of the larva of an ancestral mosquito (a velvet worm), and entered into some sort of symbiotic/commensal relationship. Again, there could have been co-evolution between ancestral parasite/symbiont and ancestral host, so that they both arrived at their present-day relationship.

Today, the mosquito, when biting and sucking blood from an infected human, at the same time injects some of its saliva, containing malarial sporozoites. These will have developed and multiplied in the wall of the mosquito's gut. After injection into the human host, the sporozoites travel, via the bloodstream, to invade the liver cells of the victim and multiply many thousands of times before being released back into the human host's bloodstream. After this, they are then taken up again by another biting mosquito to repeat the life cycle. This is the broad outline of the life cycle. There are actually more changes of the parasite in both the mosquito and the host before the life cycle is completed.

Similar species of Plasmodia infect many other species of animals such as reptiles, monkeys, chimpanzees, rodents and birds. In fact, Sir Ronald Ross, a British doctor working in India in 1898, worked out the life cycle of the malarial parasite firstly in birds. He demonstrated that avian malaria was transmitted from bird to bird by a species of mosquito belonging to the genus Culex. However, a year later, Giovanni Batista Grassi and Raimondo Filetti working in

Italy, demonstrated that human malaria was transmitted by another type of mosquito, the Anopheles mosquito. For his work, Sir Ronald Ross received the Nobel Prize in 1902.

Altogether to date, over 200 species of malarial parasite have been identified, of which eleven infect humans.

As mentioned earlier, Plasmodium is also distantly related (by its DNA) to Crytopsporidium, another type of protozoan parasite found in water. In fact, all the protozoans will have had a common ancestor in an aquatic environment, as is also the case with all the bacteria.

In humans, malaria is mainly caused by three principle Plasmodium species; *P. ovale*, *P. vivax* and *P. falciparum*. The last one of these causes the most severe form of the disease and it is postulated by Waters et. al (10) that this type of malaria appears to have occurred relatively recently. Waters believes that the parasite was acquired by man as a result of lateral transfer between bird and human hosts. Using DNA analysis, these workers confirmed that there is a close relationship between *P. falciparum* and one of the avian malarial parasites. Perhaps the same species of mosquito was simultaneously feeding on both human and avian blood. It is suggested that this change possibly took place about 10,000 years ago, at about the time of change from the nomadic to an agricultural village lifestyle in humans. Possibly the birds were attracted to agricultural sites by the grain and other food crops produced by agriculture and so came to be more closely in contact with humans. The Chinese were also cultivating rice in their paddy fields as long ago as 10,000 years and this watery environment would have been an ideal habitat for mosquitoes to breed.

The same human cultural change was occurring simultaneously in the Euphrates and Nile valleys. There are some texts recorded on papyrus by Herodotus dating from 3,000 BC, which mention the 'pest of year' when the population slept under nets at the time of the Nile flood.

Joyce Filer (11) states there is also evidence of malaria in a number of Egyptian mummies when these have been examined by paleo-pathologists. Moreover, recent studies using DNA evidence, indicate the type of malarial parasite is *P. falciparum*.

What happened with the ancestors of the Trypanosomes and Plasmodia exemplifies what has happened throughout the evolution of life on earth. As each new organism has evolved, it has gradually exploited the whole of its environment, including its association with other neighbouring creatures, to eventually become either a symbiont, or, in a few cases, a parasite. Furthermore, as each newly evolved potential host has appeared, it has gradually been invaded by a multitude of different, potentially parasitic, organisms. Of course, as both host and parasite have eventually become recognised to be distinct, individual species, they have each been evolving in tandem from their particular ancestors. In turn, the host's genes have gradually mutated and adjusted to accept the invader, or 'fellow passenger', so that there is a continual ‘arms race’ between the two organisms until eventually a state of equilibrium will be reached. Moreover, although the mosquito has been described as the vector (transmitter) of the malarial parasite, there are about 3,500 species of mosquito and the same species do not all transmit malaria in humans (Anopheles mosquitos) whilst other kinds of mosquito do so in birds (Culex mosquitos).

Why is it that, although Trypanosomes and Plasmodia are found in a large number of avian species, they are not usually so pathogenic in birds as in humans? The possible explanation is that Trypanosomes and Plasmodia have been associated with birds for very much longer in evolutionary time than is the case in humans. During this period, many species of birds will have built up a long established innate genetic resistance to the parasites. There is in fact good evidence that the Dinosaurs (the ancestors of the birds) were infected with the malaria organism Plasmodium. This we will come back to in the chapter dealing with dinosaurs.

Whereas birds started evolving from the dinosaurs 100 million years ago, Homo sapiens was only evolving 160,000 years ago, and even its forerunner Homo habilis was only evolving from its primate ancestors 2 million years ago. However, the Primate ancestors of humans will have built up at least some genetic resistance to the parasites which will have been passed in their genome to their descendants.

However, was this the case? Beatrice Hahn (82) of the University of Alabama, USA, after analysing three thousand samples of ape faeces from across Africa, found evidence of six species of the malaria parasite, all of which were ten times as genetically diverse as those species which infect humans. From this, Hahn concludes that the Apes were probably infected with a species of Plasmodia causing a type of malaria long before the humans. Moreover, humans and the Apes (gorillas and chimpanzees etc.), all evolved from the same common ancestor. In conclusion, it would seem that malaria in humans may have arisen from more than one source.

Quite a lot of study has taken place since the early 1950's, into the genetic resistance of humans to malaria. The best known of these genetic resistances is that of sickle-cell anaemia. Here if a person has one copy of a particular gene and is a heterozygote, that person will have some resistance to malaria. If a person has two copies of the same gene, so that the person is a homozygote, then they develop the fatal disease of sickle cell anaemia. In this disease, the red blood cells become distorted so that they tend to block small capillaries in the body. The disease is eventually fatal.

Looking at the case in birds

Avian malaria can be quite a serious disease in a few species of birds such as some penguins, poultry and pigeons. It may be carried as a latent infection by many Passeriform birds, (that is, over half of all bird species) as exemplified by the common house sparrow and the thrushes. This latent infection serves to constantly stimulate the bird's immune system, to guard against a pathological re-infection. Penguins, in their wild habitat, do not normally become infected with the bird malarial parasites, because they mostly inhabit the Antarctic where the mosquitos which transmit the parasite cannot breed in the very cold salt water. The only penguins which usually become clinically infected, are those captive in zoos or private collections.

The blood parasites of birds, which are (1) Plasmodium, (2) Leucocytozoon and (3) Heamoproteus, are all similar in appearance. Using DNA techniques, they are all thought to have evolved from the same, more primitive, common ancestor Paraheamoproteus.

Heamoproteus is the most primitive form of malarial parasite, and is found in many types of birds, even sea birds such as gulls, but not in most tern species. This is probably because terns nest in places where mosquitoes and gnats do not breed. Biting midges (small mosquitoes) spread the parasite. Also, the blood parasite Heamoproteus is found in amphibians and reptiles, the parasite being spread by these same insects. Both the blood parasite and the midges containing Heamoproteus, have been identified as fossils in both Burmese and Lebanese amber, George and Roberta Poiner (53 & 54). In many cases, with all these avian blood parasites, wild birds may act as latent carriers, indicating that there has been a long association between host (birds) and parasite.

In consequence, although Heamoproteus is common in many species of birds, it does not often cause serious disease. Consistent with this concept, when looking at the blood parasite Leucocytozoon in ducks, Dresser et. al (12) found that in wild ducks, densities of the parasite in the blood were typically low and they were carried as a latent infection. However, mortalities could reach one hundred percent in young ducks kept on farms where new ducks were continually being introduced. Siegmund and Fraser (13), further investigating this scenario, found that the ducks became stressed so that their immune systems were depressed, and in consequence the birds became overwhelmed by infection.

This is a good illustration of the continuing balance between the integrity of the host's immune system and the potential pathogenicity of the invader.

An interesting and comparatively recent illustration of how some species of birds are able to build up resistance to the malaria parasite is that of the Hawaiian honeycreeper or Hawaii Amakihi (Hemignathus virens).

Plate No.15 Hawaiian Amakihi (Hemignathus virens).

These little brown and yellow birds belonging to the family of so-called honeyeaters are about the size of a common sparrow and are also called Hawaiian finches. They live on the Hawaiian Islands in the Pacific Ocean and are well isolated from the infectious diseases of mainland birds. They originally occupied both lowland and highland habitats on the islands. However, with the arrival of man on the islands in approximately 1600 AD, thc lowlands were cleared for agriculture, mosquitoes started breeding in static water and those carrying malaria were inadvertently introduced. These and other changes introduced by humans, severely threatened the Amakihi with extinction. However, within the last decade, Bethany Woodworth and her colleagues (89) have reported recent emergent populations of recovering Amakihi in lowland areas despite the continuing extremely high prevalence of avian malaria. Therefore, this species of bird must have evolved some resistance to the parasite.

CHAPTER 7

The fungi

Another very important group of living organisms are the Fungi. These total an estimated 1,500,000 species and only about 72,000 have so far been classified. The Fungi are familiar to us as mushrooms or toadstools and as the mould growing on stale bread. Most fungi are terrestrial and grow as tubular, elongated, filamentous structures called hyphae connected together to form a web or "mycelium." From this, they secrete liquid enzymes which digest the surrounding organic material on which they are growing, so forming an easily absorbable 'soup.'

Fungi disperse by forming dust like spores and are a very important part of the world's ecology. Together with the bacteria, they are one of the great recyclers of dead organic material. They are ready to invade any devitalised tissue or substrate. Apparently, they will attack and cover hibernating bats in a thick mould, if these animals become too cold and so sluggish that they fail to occasionally stir themselves. Another type of fungi, the yeasts, which do not form hyphae, are important in industrial fermentation such as in brewer's yeast (a type of fungus) for the production of beer, wine and spirits like whisky, brandy or vodka.

Yeasts are separate, single cell organisms, although some yeasts join together to create a chain of single cells, forming a so-called "false hypha" as seen in the mould on bread.

Another type of yeast is used by bakers for bread making, and other yeasts are used in the making of some cheeses such as Camembert, Brie, Gorgonzola and Stilton.

Interestingly, all the different above-mentioned fungi are close relatives of the fungus Penicillium notatum, used to produce the antibiotic penicillin. Yeasts are essential for the manufacture of other antibiotics besides penicillin, are also used in the manufacture of hormones and again in many other processes of today's biotechnology, including antidotes for many toxins. A number of other fungi also have medical uses, some as anti-cancer drugs.

Historically, it is known that the ancient Chinese, the ancient Egyptians and even today's indigenous Amazonian peoples use moulds or fungi to treat wounds.

There are many cases of symbiotic mutualism between fungi and other organisms, where two different life forms associate to their mutual advantage.

The many different groups of lichens which are shown as the green colouring on stone work and some types of tree bark, are a good example of mutualism, in which the fungus is associated with green unicellular algae. It is said that eighty-five percent of all plants have a mycorrhizal (that is, a filamentous mould-like growth) around their roots, in many cases required in order for the plant to thrive. However, modern farming methods which make use of fungicides tend to reduce these useful fungi. The great trees of both temperate and tropical forests depend on a mycorrhiza on their roots to absorb basic nutrients from the soil. In each case, the plant in its turn, provides the fungus with the manufactured nutrients produced by the plant's photosynthesis, Tudge (14). *Armillaria solidipes,* known as the honey fungus, is found in the conifer and hardwood forests on the western side of the Rocky Mountains in the USA. One particular single specimen is thought be about 2,400 years old and to cover an area of 3.4 square miles (8.4 km^2). It is said to be the largest living organism.

This relationship with the trees and other plants, is probably how the fungi first evolved in a terrestrial habitat. The animals, the plants and the fungi probably all came from the same common ancestor (an Archaebacterium) when life on earth first started, approximately 3.5 billion years ago. These different life forms gradually diverged from each other and are now classed as being in three separate Phyla; the Animals, the Plants and the Fungi.

Until relatively recently, fungi had been traditionally classified with plants, but DNA research now indicates that fungi's relationship is in fact probably much closer to the animals. In other words, the plants formed a completely separate branch of living organisms long before the fungi, and the animals split into two separate branches, or Phyla, of living organisms.

The cells of fungi are encased in chitin (a fibrous substance), like that found in the arthropods and nematode worms, and are not enclosed in cellulose, like the cells of plants. Chemically, chitin is a strong flexible polymer consisting of polysaccharide cellulose, and ways are being developed to use it industrially.

The Pathogenic Fungi

The readiness of fungi to attack devitalised tissue, makes them important pathogens of birds, humans and other animals which may be less than one hundred percent fit, or just not able to keep the invasion of their tissues in check.

Aspergillus

Aspergillus is a genus of fungi, of which there are over two hundred species. Not all species cause disease. Some are saprophytic, living on dead or decomposing tissue. However, some Aspergillus species do cause disease.

Aspergillosis is a serious fungal infection of both birds and humans. Commonly confused in humans with an allergic bronchopneumonia, it is sometimes called "bird fancier's lung," it may also be mistaken for asthma, which is caused by an a hypersensitivity to bird proteins, contained in feather dust and in bird droppings. Most humans inhale some Aspergillus spores every day, particularly if working in dusty environments. Such places are where there is mouldy hay, straw or wood chips, or in damp, old buildings. Also, people who breed birds of prey in close boarded aviaries where there is little air movement, and where the floors are not cleared out and cleaned regularly, are at risk.

In a healthy person, the inhaled spores are quickly dealt with by the immune system. People most at risk are those who are immuno-compromised, perhaps because of infection, such as with AIDS, during treatment for cancer, or from immuno-suppressive drugs dispensed to them after having had transplant surgery.

The most common pathogenic fungus is Aspergillus fumigatus. In birds, this infection is commonly seen in cage birds such as parrots, in bird rehabilitation centres, where injured water fowl are housed whilst they recover from injury, or again, possibly in captive overfed and under-exercised falcons. It could be that in all of these cases, the birds are not getting sufficient exercise to thoroughly flush the air which is carrying the spores though their lungs before it has had time to settle and develop a mycelium. Once this happens, the fungus can establish itself in the lungs.

In a few avian clinical cases, some veterinary surgeons may make injudicious use of antibiotics to deal with supposed infections of pathogenic bacteria, which then act to kill off the 'good bugs' as well as any pathogenic bugs. Alternatively, they may use corticosteroids, which temporarily shut down the bird's immune system. Use of either of these treatments acts to hclp the fungus establish an infection in the bird.

However, massive die-off's can occur naturally in wild birds. Such an occurrence of Aspergillosis was responsible for two thousand mallard duck deaths in Idaho in the USA, where the birds were feeding on mouldy grain left on the fields. Another similar case was reported, of five hundred mallards in Iowa, USA. In both instances, these massive die-offs could have been mistaken for avian 'flu or even botulism, both causing similar signs of disease, if a thorough investigation had not been carried out.

Aspergillosis is particularly common in captive nectar feeding birds such as lorikeets and honeyeaters, because of the sugary solution on which they are fed which encourages fungal growth.

Candida (Monilia)

This is another fungus belonging to the yeast group. There are nearly fifty recognised species of Candida of which Candida albicans is the most common, and which causes disease in humans. In the mouth, candidiasis is commonly called "thrush" but can also affect the throat and other parts of the gut, the vagina and urinary tract. It is an opportunist pathogen taking advantage of a debilitated individual. It also infects other animals including birds.

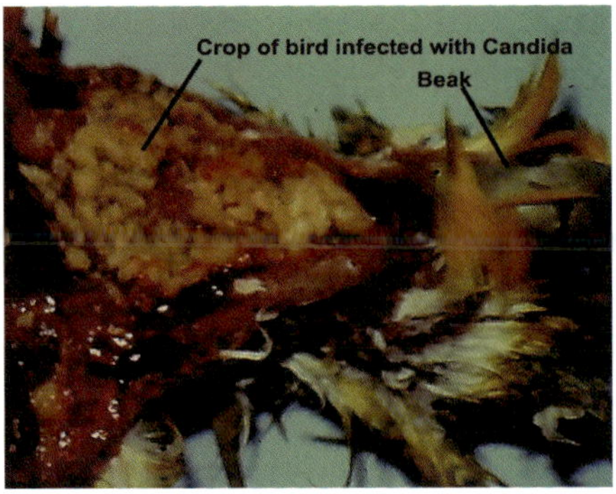

Plate No.16 The head of a parrot showing the opened crop (part of the food tract) situated in the bird's neck grossly infected with Candida.

Cryptococcus (Also known in North America as blastomycosis.)

This is a yeast type of organism, living on dead plant material and rotting wood. It infects all species of birds and other animals and is a serious hazard for humans keeping birds in insanitary poultry houses and dusty aviaries which are not frequently and thoroughly cleaned. It may also be carried as a normal non-disease producing inhabitant in the gut of some pigeons.

In those individual animals which have become infected because their immune system is suppressed, the fungus primarily causes a type of pneumonia and can spread via the bloodstream to the rest of the body.

Histoplasma

A similar type of disease-producing fungus which can exist either as a yeast or a mycelium. Histoplasma species reside in soil and on any surface contaminated with bird or bat droppings, hence histoplasmosis is called *cave disease* in some parts of the world.

Trychophyton genus

A further group of fungi which cause one type of ringworm infection in humans, observed on human skin as obvious raised red circular areas often about 1-1.5cms in diameter. A similar fungus can cause athletes foot and similar diseases of the nail, beard or foot.

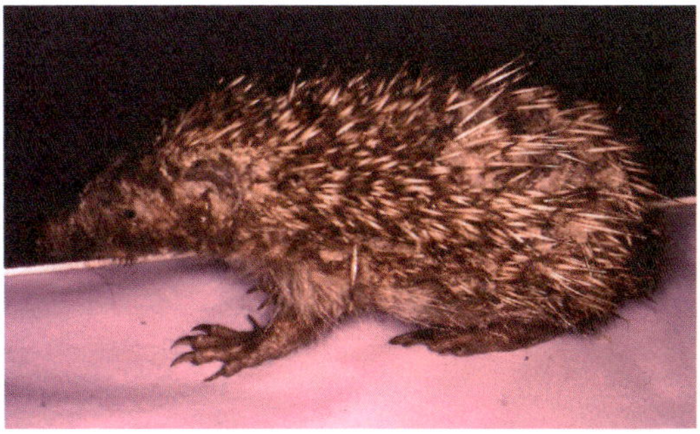

Plate No.17 Western European Hedgehog (Erinaceous europaeus) badly infected with ringworm type fungi.

This type of fungus can infect quite a wide range of animals, from which it can be transferred to humans.

Infection is not uncommon in some cattle, often forming obvious grey crusty plaques on the neck, the animals possibly being infected, and transferring the infection between each other, by rubbing the itching skin on wooden gate posts and the like. As well as having been infected himself, the author has seen this infection many times in children who grow up on farms. The organism also infects birds, but humans rarely become infected from this source.

Coccidioides immitis

This fungus causes coccidioidomycosis, known as valley fever in humans in the USA. Whilst this is usually a mild disease with flu like symptoms, accompanied with mild muscular pain and a skin rash, sometimes the infection can develop into a serious systemic disease in immune-compromised individuals.

Coccidioides immitis is an opportunistic pathogen mostly affecting the skin or the gut. It is normally a soil inhabitant which, although very occasionally is seen in other parts of the world, mainly resides in the western hemisphere, being endemic in California, Utah, Nevada and other parts of Southern USA and South America. The fungus is dormant in the dry season but when the rains come and the soil is disturbed during farming or during building work, the fungus develops a mould from which can break off airborne infectious spores, which are inhaled and then cause infection.

This fungus infects a wide range of domestic and wild mammals but, strangely enough, has not been reported in birds. It is possible that the birds generally have developed an immunity to this pathogen.

Chytridiomycota (Chytrids)

These are primitive, aquatic, single-celled organisms, which Colin Tudge (101) suggests may be the closest to the ancestral fungal form. Moreover, they are the only fungi to have a flagellum, and so are motile. They are mostly found in fresh water or in moist conditions.

These fungi are able to break down keratin, which is a principle component of the skin of the higher animals. There are over one thousand species of chydrids, a few of which are saprophytic fungi living on dead or decomposing material, whilst others reside in the guts of herbivorous animals. Apparently, different species of chytrids live in the hind gut of ruminants from those that inhabit the rumen, (one of the four stomachs of cattle and other similar ruminant animals.)

Since 1993, one species of chydrid has been identified as being at least one cause of a serious and fatal disease in the world's amphibians (frogs, salamanders and newts), leading to a dramatic global decline in this group of animals.

Although this particular species of fungus has existed for many millions of years, it has either recently undergone a genetic change so that it has become a more virulent pathogen, or alternatively, some environmental factor has possibly induced an epigenetic (see glossary) change, so that the balance between the host and parasite has altered. It seems unlikely that the host resistance of many different species of amphibians has simultaneously changed. It is more likely that the virulence of the parasite has been enhanced, possibly by a change in the aquatic environment, which may, in turn, be linked to global warming.

Chytrids only appear to be pathogenetic in amphibians, that is, frogs, newts and salamanders. They are not pathogenetic in birds, reptiles or mammals, (as noted above, some species are in fact symbionts in cattle, living as beneficial "bugs" in their gut). This is possibly because, unlike other animals, the skin of amphibians is different, being porous and well supplied with blood vessels, so that amphibians are able to take in oxygen, expel carbon dioxide and absorb water through their skin.

Amphibians are unable to drink though the mouth. Consequently, amphibians must live in an aquatic, or at least a moist environment. James Voyles (39) has suggested that the amphibians' ability to regulate the balance of the electrolytes sodium and potassium in their blood via the amphibian skin, is impaired by the presence of chytrid fungi. The presence of the fungi causes a drop in the sodium level by 20%, together with a drop in the potassium level of 50%. Those who have studied the workings and control of the heart in higher animals including humans, will know that an imbalance of sodium and potassium blood levels results in heart failure. The heart just stops beating.

As an aside, it is worth mentioning that whilst still at school studying biology in the late 1940's, the author learned that frogs can breathe through their skin and thought that it should be possible to anaesthetise frogs for a short time by immersing them in fresh water which had been shaken up with ether. When ether is mixed with water and then shaken up, the two fluids are not completely miscible and don't mix completely but form a so-called partition co-efficient (or distribution ratio). This just happens to result in the amount of ether retained in the water being the right strength for administering ether as an anaesthetic to frogs. Inhaled ether was one of the earlier anaesthetics used on human patients (by Joseph Glover in 1877), and it has been used on other animals. The author, Coles B.H. (62) has used this anaesthetic on birds, even as large as a mute swan (*Cygnus olor.*)

Having anaesthetised the frog by immersing it in this mixture of ether and water, it was then possible to place the frog on its back and position the web of one of its feet under the microscope and watch the blood circulating through the almost transparent skin. The frog could then be placed back into fresh water, in which it made a full recovery. Nowadays of course, it is likely that a Home Office license would be needed for this procedure, and school children are not encouraged to use either live or dead animals when learning about biology.

Coming back to the spread of the chytrid fungi, it has been suggested by Reid Harris (75), that this may have originated in sub-Saharan Africa and has been spread by the use of the African clawed frog (*Xenopus laevis*), in widespread biological research, including human pregnancy testing. Apparently, this species of frog is not itself affected by the chytrid fungus.

It has also been found that the normal balance between bacteria and fungi, or naturally occurring ecosystem, of frog skin, may have been altered so that the fungus has not been held in check. Bathing the frogs in water containing a particular bacterium (*Janthinobacterium lividum*), which naturally produces an antifungal compound that kills the fungus, results in the frogs surviving chytrid infection. It is possible that chytrid fungal infection could be another problem brought about by human influence on environmental change, such as pollution of the environment with substances such as PCBs or even glyphosate, an organophosphorus compound which is the active ingredient in the weed killer "Roundup" produced by the company Monsanto. It has to be said however, that the rise in the observation of the chytrid problem seems to have occurred before glyphosate started to widely contaminate the environment.

Barbara Bowman et al (15) have indicated most of the fungal pathogens have close relatives amongst the non-pathogenetic species of fungi, just as is often the case with the bacteria. Consequently, Bowman considers that pathogenicity amongst the fungi has arisen independently on several occasions. The original non-pathogenic fungi have been quick to exploit any 'gap' in their environment.

It is therefore quite possible that other pathogenic fungi will be found in the future, as has avian gastric yeast (*Macrorhabdus ornithogaster*). This is a pathogen of budgerigars, canaries and other birds, which has only comparatively recently been identified as an opportunistic yeast, rather than, as it was originally thought to be, a bacterium and was thus named Megabacteria.

Microsporidia

The Microsporidia were once thought to be separate group of protists without a cell wall, but are now known to be true fungi. They are spore-forming, single-celled parasites, classified with the fungi and considered to be a related group of the fungi, which only form spores and not a mycelium. There are now approximately 1,500 named species and probably more than one million species exist. They parasitize only animal hosts but not plants, and all major groups of animals can act as hosts to microsporidia. Mostly they infect insects such as bees and mosquitos, but they can also infect all species of animals including some fish and crustacea, and humans.

'Helpful' pathogenic fungi

Some fungi, such as Beauveria, attack insects and can be used as a method of controlling insect pests instead of using potentially environmentally harmful chemicals. However, great care has to be taken whenever humans "make use" of naturally occurring organisms for their own benefit, as this fungus has also been reported to kill alligators.

CHAPTER 8

From the single cell organisms to the origin of some multicellular organisms

Approximately 542 million years ago, at the beginning of the Cambrian geological period, a so called 'explosion' of living creatures took place. Prior to this period, most forms of animal and plant life had been just single celled, soft bodied creatures. These delicate forms of life sometimes left their imprints in sediments such as sand or volcanic ash, after being glued together and onto their substrate. Secretions from the microorganisms formed slimy substances which held them together, forming what are known as microbial mats. Evidence of such imprints are found most prominently displayed in the Ediacara Hills of Southern Australia, approximately 650 kilometres north of Adelaide. The Ediacaran geological period immediately preceded the Cambrian.

During the Cambrian period, the single celled organisms were *gradually* evolving to become creatures composed of many cells, often arranged in layers of more than one cell. Some of these creatures left their remnants as fossils, buried in the sands and mud of that time. Most fossils are composed of the hard parts of animals and plants which, unlike the softer tissues, have not been degraded by bacteria and the environment, Dawkins (35). It was during the Cambrian period that many organisms were increasingly able to make use of the changes in seawater chemistry, by incorporating minerals into their bodies (biomineralization) to form a supporting skeleton.

Biomineralisation resulted from the increased availability of calcium ions, bicarbonate ions, phosphate ions and silicon dioxide. Also, some evolving organisms were then able to make use of silica (radiolarians and diatoms), and calcium phosphate (trilobites), to strengthen their 'skeletons' and these mineral substances subsequently contributed to their fossil remains.

It is estimated that about 30 billion species of microscopic life forms, such as the bacteria and amoebae, are thought to have lived ***before*** the Cambrian period, when the multi-cellular organisms first started to appear on earth. During the Cambrian period a vast array of living organisms, now classified into some 30 Phyla, started to *gradually* become more complex in the way their bodies were built. However, at the present time, of these multi-cellular organisms, **99.9%** have become extinct, a fact which is often not appreciated by many conservationists, who want to keep the planet as we see it today, since *biological evolution is an ongoing process.*

During the Cambrian period, the ancestors of all those animals with hard body parts which exist today, such as those with back bones (the vertebrates), and the arthropods with their hard, external skeletons, became much more evident to us today by leaving behind their fossilised remains.

The fossils of the earlier evolved multicellular creatures such as the sponges, the corals and the sea anemones, although all part of the evolutionary process, do not really concern us here, because they do not contribute to causing disease in other animals. *Nevertheless,* all of these creatures were gradually evolving in an aquatic environment.

Some of the early evolved animals may not even have looked like their modern descendants. They may have been much smaller, or much larger.

It should not be assumed that the evolution of life progressed in the form of a straightforward hierarchical ladder, from the lowest proteo-bacterium or Archaea to the 'highest' multicellular creatures, the vertebrates. The latter of course, eventually gave rise to the birds and to the Primates, and ultimately led to the evolution of humans. The evolution of all life forms is more like a branching bush, with numerous lineages forming offshoots to coexist simultaneously. When one branch is unable to compete with a "neighbouring" life form, it withers away, and becomes extinct.

During the Cambrian period, the invertebrates, or those animals without backbones, flourished, so that today they comprise 97% of all living multicellular creatures. Such were the various types of worms, insects, starfish, shrimps, krill, shellfish, octopuses, molluscs, slugs and many other wondrous marine creatures. Only those causing disease in the higher animals will be considered here.

The Worms

Quite how the worms evolved as a distinct group from the simpler one celled organisms, is still a bit of a mystery. It is known that these were amongst the first multicellular animals to evolve, and from the point of view of causing disease as parasites in other animals, they are an important group to be included here.

The **nematodes or roundworms** are much less complex worms than the familiar segmented garden earthworm, which is a more advanced but non-disease producing creature. Overall, 28,000 species of nematode worms have so far been identified. Roundworms are ubiquitous and can be found in garden soil, in ponds, in the deep-sea ocean trenches, as well as on trees and other vegetation. They are also found throughout the bodies of the more advanced animals ranging from whales to birds and humans. However, not *all* nematode worms cause disease. Of the total number of species so far identified, only about 16,000 are parasitic.

Again, it is important to stress that as each new type of creature has evolved from its ancestor, it has slowly changed in order to exploit its environment. Included in this environment will be other living organisms, both animal and plant, and so it has to be remembered that both parasite and host were evolving at the same time from their own individual ancestors, on parallel courses.

It has been said that every living species on this planet has its own personalized species of nematode, Colin Tudge (28). There is even a nematode worm which attacks garden slugs, and the larvae of these worms can be purchased with the specific purpose of controlling slugs.

The nematode worm lives in the gut of its host, producing eggs which are passed out mixed in the faeces of the infected host animal. In the case of the non-parasitic nematode worms, the eggs are just freely cast into the environment. The eggs then hatch to form juvenile forms which subsequently grow into adult worms.

However, if the particular nematode species is one of the parasitic types, the eggs are picked up by an uninfected animal, often of the same species as that in which the worms have developed. Once swallowed, the eggs hatch inside the new host to form larvae (immature replica worms). These then proceed to invade and burrow through the body organs (viscera) of the body of the new host; a process called *visceral larva migrans.*

Many species of nematodes are not strictly limited to one particular host species. Humans can pick up the eggs of the canine parasitic roundworm, *Toxocara canis* (which is also parasitic in foxes and other canids), or alternatively those nematodes found in cats (Toxocara cati). It is during the migration of the parasitic larvae throughout the body of humans that serious disease is sometimes caused. This could be the invasion of the heart muscle (resulting in a myocarditis), or of the brain (resulting in an encephalitis, causing fits), or of the eye (causing a type of tumour and blindness). Rarely, if ever, do all of these pathological changes occur simultaneously in the same individual human host.

Infection occurs by ingestion of the infective eggs of the parasite directly from the soil or from soil contaminated surfaces, and children can become infected in this way. It is important therefore for children to always wash their hands after playing outside. Very young children who put their fingers in their mouths are at greatest risk. In the USA about 100,000 clinical cases are seen by medical authorities annually, and of these, about 700 involve tumours of the eyes, resulting in blindness in the affected eye. The incidence of the condition is highest in US citizens living in the poorest inner-city areas of the Southern States, where sanitation and hygiene standards may sometimes be compromised.

On a global scale, 340 million people are estimated to suffer serious side effects from these worms. All of this can easily be prevented by (1) regular worming of dogs, (2) hygienically picking up and disposing of dog faeces and not leaving it exposed to flies, which can act as airborne carriers for the worm eggs, and (3) by making sure children wash their hands regularly. It should also be remembered that in addition to domesticated pet dogs, foxes also help to spread the worm eggs around the environment.

Grazing animals such as sheep, cattle or rabbits may occasionally pick up the eggs of the parasite, and these, during their larval migration, may become encysted in the muscles of these animals so that their uncooked meat can, very occasionally, be a source of human infection. The worm eggs are very hardy and can resist drying, frost and extreme temperatures, as well as quite powerful disinfectants. They can remain viable in the environment for at least a year.

Ascariasis, (infection by Ascaris nematode worms), is also familiar to some people who keep birds, particularly parrots, and to bird veterinarians. However, the Ascaris nematodes found in birds are not the same species as those found in dogs. The intermediate hosts for the Ascaris worms in birds are crickets, beetles and earwigs, all of which had evolved by the time of the dinosaurs, the ancestors of the birds. Badly infected birds are seen to lose weight or even die because of a simple mechanical blockage of the gut, due to a heavy worm infection.

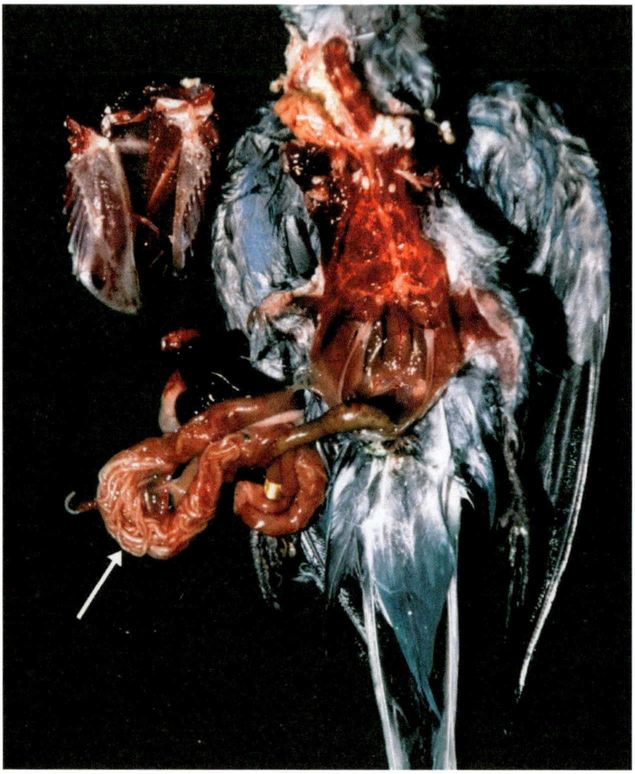

Plate No. 18: The post mortem picture of a Bourke's parrot (Neopsephotus bourkii.) The bird's gut is impacted with Ascaris worms, as indicated by the arrow.

Bourke's Parrot is a small bird, a little larger than a budgerigar, which like the budgerigar, inhabits central Australia. Of course, in its natural home environment, this species of bird is unlikely to become badly infected by this particular worm. The bird shown above probably became infected in a bird keeper's aviary, where it may have picked up a beetle or similar flying insect. Fortunately, there are no recorded cases of humans ever having picked up this species of Ascaris roundworm from birds.

Another roundworm which can cause problems in birds is Syngamus trachea. This is well recognised in poultry, resulting in a condition called 'the gapes', because the parasite irritates and partially obstructs the trachea or windpipe of the bird in which it lives. This partial obstruction causes the bird to gape for air.

Whilst a student in the 1950's, the author was once told by one of his professors, that he didn't think wild birds became infected with this parasite, "it only occurred in poultry." From the author's own subsequent observations, and what he learned from many others, it is now clearly found to be common in many species of wild birds. This is particularly the case with song birds, and those feeding on the ground, such as rooks. The eggs of the parasite are passed out in the droppings of the bird and are taken up by a transport host. The transport host can typically be an earthworm or a snail or beetle. The eggs hatch in the transport host to form larvae, which are then taken in by the bird when the bird eats the earthworm, snail or beetle.

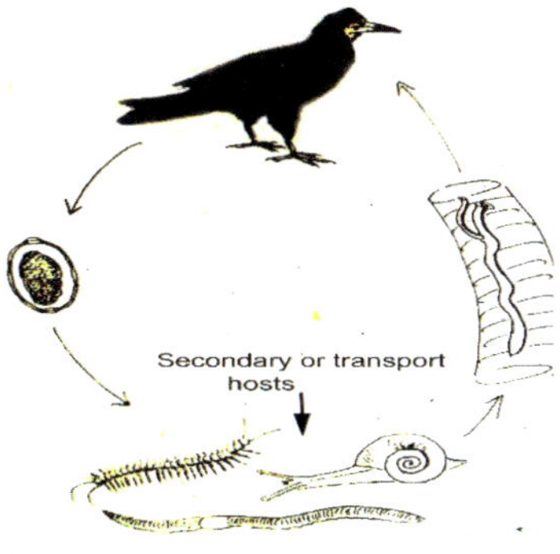

Fig No.10: Life cycle of Syngamus trachea in the rook.

In the bird's gut, the larvae penetrate the body, passing into the bloodstream, and are thence carried around the bird's body eventually reaching the bird's wind pipe or trachea, where they fully develop into adult worms and cause irritation. Why don't they kill wild birds? They certainly will do, if the bird is badly infected, but most wild birds tolerate them if the number of parasites is not too great.

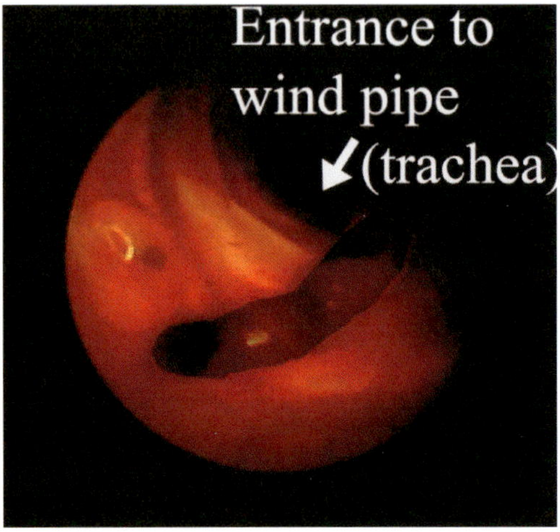

Plate No.19: A view of the gape worm Syngamous trachea as seen looking down an endoscope passed into the bird's mouth to view the opening into the 'windpipe' in a rook.

Interestingly, in rooks, the incidence of infection in young birds was found to be of the order of 99%, whilst older birds become progressively more resistant. By the age of one year, the birds were showing an incidence of 40% and in the more adult birds, infection was only 8.6%. This indicates that this species of bird at least, gradually builds up an immune resistance to the parasite.

Mammomonogamus is a genus of parasitic nematode related to the Syngamous parasite seen in birds. These worms are found in the windpipe or trachea of sheep, goats, deer, cats and have been reported as infecting orangutans, and even elephants. This worm can also occasionally infect humans, another mammalian host.

The infection in humans is very rare, with only a few cases being diagnosed from the Caribbean, China, Korea, Thailand, and the Philippines. The mammomonagamus worm parasite usually inhabits the upper airways and can cause chronic coughing and asthma-like breathlessness. In some human patients, they might think they have just been smoking too much.

To the reader, it may seem horrible that we are surrounded by a variety of worms just waiting to invade and parasitize us. However, this is all part of the normal natural environment in which we live and the world has not suddenly become a more dangerous place because of them. With good basic hygiene such as washing one's hands regularly and being careful what you eat, particularly in a tropical country, there is very little chance of picking up these parasites.

Other nematode parasites related to Syngamous trachea affecting birds, are the species of the genus Cyathastoma bronchialis. These parasites can infect a variety of birds, such as birds of prey, gulls, wading birds, crows, herons and water birds including ducks, geese and swans. In the host bird, the parasite resides around the eye and nasal cavities of the head causing a localized inflammation. A very unusual massive infection was once diagnosed in a 4-year-old horse in France. The author has never heard of these infecting humans.

The reader may well ask, how did Syngamus and its relatives evolve to become established as a parasite of the trachea and upper airways of many types of animals? The author's hypothesis is as follows. During the evolution of the vertebrate breathing system, several stages occurred. As the ancestral primitive fish, the Chordates, (those which had evolved around a cartilaginous back bone), gradually hauled themselves out of their watery environment onto the land, they simultaneously, and gradually, dispensed with their gills because they slowly became air breathing animals.

Their gills had enabled them to absorb oxygen from the water and to get rid of the carbon dioxide produced in their bodies. This gaseous exchange took place as the water, with dissolved oxygen and carbon dioxide, passed through the membranes of the gill slits.

The early Chordates, being bilaterally symmetrical, elongated creatures with a dorsal spine, then gradually evolved a different type of respiratory system suitable for the interchange of oxygen and carbon dioxide with the surrounding air in which they now lived, instead of being surrounded by water. The trachea or windpipe, and later the lungs, were gradually being formed during evolution from a pouch on the floor of the primitive fore gut. Over time, the pouch slowly closed over to form a tube, and from this tube, there slowly developed the trachea and lungs now seen in the land living and air breathing animals.

During the course of evolution, the aquatic ancestor of Syngamus possibly parasitized the foregut of the ancestral fish. Later, the parasite then slowly took up residence in the developing pouch on the floor of the foregut. The ancestral parasite has stayed there ever since, gradually evolving alongside its host. Of course, if we go back far enough in evolutionary time, both birds and mammals will have had a common ancestor. Some of the ancestral parasites, such as Syngamus, will have stayed with the birds, whilst others, such as Mammomonogamus, will have been trapped with the mammals, each having undergone genetic change to adapt to their particular type of vertebrate host.

The above explanation is not entirely hypothetical, being largely based on the theory of recapitulation put forward by Karl Ernst von Baer (1792-1876), and Ernst Heinrich Haeckel (1834-1919). The former had noted that the embryos of developing vertebrates such as fish, birds and humans, were quite alike when they first emerged from the fertilised egg. The different embryos only gradually began to diverge into their different forms as they developed towards their final "adult" stage.

Haeckel further developed this idea and stated that 'ontogeny recapitulates phylogeny', which, in effect, means as each vertebrate animal embryo develops it goes through all those stages of evolution which brought it to its present form, such as the adult bird, reptile or mammal, including humans. However, Haeckel's theory has been somewhat discredited by modern evolutionists, because the drawings in the original publication were not strictly accurate according to Nick Hopwood (143).

The subject of the early evolution of the vertebrates, and the common ancestral origin of both the birds and the reptiles, was briefly mentioned in chapter 2, when discussing the influence of the HOX genes.

Another variety of respiratory system infectious parasite, found not only in humans and birds but also in many other animals, has probably evolved in a similar way.

Various species of Baylisascaris, another related genus of nematode worm, are found in many species of birds, although are not as often reported as they are in mammals. Some of these nematode worms have evolved to pass the first part of their life cycle within another intermediary or transport host. Such intermediary hosts are snails, ants, beetles and earthworms. These are then eaten intentionally, or possibly accidentally, by any species of bird, whether the invertebrate is part of the bird's normal diet or not. If this happens, there is no reason why that bird should not become infested with the parasite, in the same way as it does with the more common bird parasite Syngamus trachea.

An additional nematode commonly known as rat lungworm, Angiostrongylus cantonensis, is primarily found in the pulmonary arteries of several species of rat, but is also found in a variety of mammalian species, including humans. The eggs from the female worm of this species are passed out in the faeces of the rat, later to be taken in by an intermediate host which includes several species of slugs and snails. Within the snail, the eggs hatch to produce larvae which can directly infect the final host when these are eaten by the rat. Alternatively, they may first pass through another subsidiary host, such as freshwater prawns or crabs, before they are finally eaten by the ultimate host. This nematode was first reported in a human patient with eosinophilic meningitis by Nomura and Lim in Taiwan in 1944.

In 2004 this parasitic nematode was reported by an Australian veterinarian, Dr. Deborah Monks and her colleagues (37), in a yellow-tailed black cockatoo (Calyptorhynchus funereus.) Simultaneously, it was also found in two tawny frogmouths (Podargus strigoides); all of these birds were being kept in the same zoo in Australia. Dr. Monks noted that although snails and slugs are part of the normal diet of the free living tawny frogmouth, in the case of the cockatoo, an infected snail or slug was probably amongst the food items unintentionally introduced by the zookeepers into the bird's aviary. Black cockatoos normally feed by digging into the bark of certain trees searching for the wood boring larvae of moths or beetles and they have a beak shaped and adapted for digging out such larvae from the wood of the trees. This instance was the first reported case of the parasite occurring in species other than in a mammalian host.

Dr. Monks also notes that this particular nematode parasite has gradually been extending its geographic range throughout South East Asia and the Pacific Basin since the mid-20th century. This is indicated by most cases of human eosinophilic meningitis being caused by angiostrongyliasis, which is itself caused by this parasite, and also because of the increasing popularity of raw prawns and snails in the human diet, together with the global transportation of food. This gives a good indication of how infectious disease in humans and other animals is slowly evolving globally.

A further species of this genus of worms is Angiostrongylus vasorum, which attacks a variety of canine species including dogs, many types of foxes, the wolf and the European badger. This particular worm has a worldwide distribution and again, its secondary hosts are several species of snails and slugs.

Apart from those already mentioned, there are many other related types of worms. Such are the gizzard worms, commonly found in wild waterfowl, and the hookworms found in both humans and some other animals.

The roundworm Strongylus vulgaris, or blood worm, is a common and serious intestinal parasite of horses. However, because of the intensive use of anti-worming drugs specifically directed at this nematode parasite, the balance of intestinal parasites has been altered. This larger nematode, Strongylus, has been replaced as the most common intestinal parasite of horses by a smaller type of nematode worm, Cylicocyclus nassatus which is not so sensitive to the same anti-worming drug. This echoes the effect seen in the increase of antibiotic resistance developed by some bacteria.

The Flatworms (The Flukes and Tapeworms)

Somewhat later in evolutionary time, after the nematodes or the roundworms had emerged, came the flatworms. This is another important group of intestinal parasites infesting all the vertebrate animals, including birds and humans. Altogether there are 25,000 known species of flatworms, most of which are free living and only relatively few of which are parasitic.

Included in the phylum flatworms, are at least 9,000 species of parasitic flukes. Flukes are mostly flat, leaf-like, soft bodied, small creatures which have no body cavity. There is a tube-like gut that is sometimes branched, which increases surface area for the absorption of food material. The gut branches throughout the soft multicellular body mass, there being no body cavity unlike the higher animals, like mammals and birds. Sometimes there is an anus, or back passage, for waste food material to be discharged, and most flukes are hermaphrodites, that is, individuals have both male and female reproductive organs.

The first flukes to evolve, known as the Monogenea, are simple parasites which cling to the outside of their host, usually fish. Gradually during evolution, from clinging to the skin of their host they crept into the external orifices, such as the mouth or the gills and then gradually further inside their host's body. They cling to the lining of their host's gut with suckers.

The parasitic flukes slowly evolved and developed more intricate life cycles, and becoming dependant on more than one type of host. Their principal, or primary, host is a vertebrate and the subsidiary, or secondary, host is a snail. Because the Flukes depend on snails as the secondary host, they are mostly associated with a watery or moist environment. Sometimes more than one intermediate host (that is, more than one type of snail) is involved. Many people, particularly farmers, who deal with sheep, will know about the common liver fluke which can parasitize sheep, goats and cattle, and occasionally, even humans.

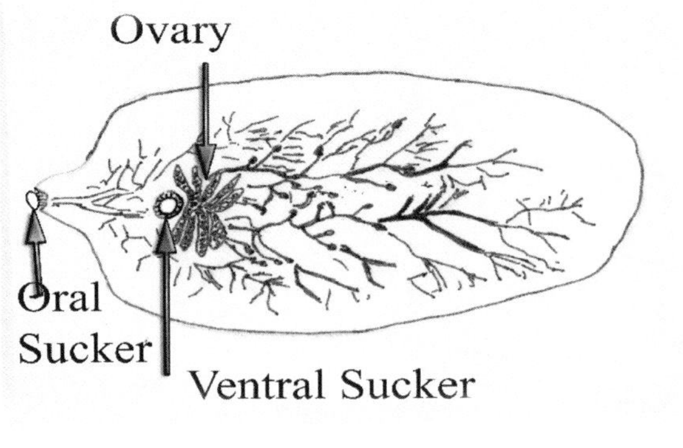

Fig. No. 11 The Common Liver Fluke of sheep (Fasciola hepatica.)

In life about 3 centimetres in length.

A survey carried out at Liverpool University in 2006/2007 found that 72% of dairy herds in England and 84% of herds in Wales were exposed to this parasite. The survey also indicated that those parts of the country which had experienced warmer and wetter weather due to climate change, had seen an increased incidence of these flukes. The climatic conditions favoured an increase in the numbers of snails which transmitted the parasite.

There are many different species of liver flukes which have evolved to parasitize a variety of different species of animals.

The adult flukes can inhabit the bile ducts, the gall bladder, and the substance of the liver itself, where they feed on the blood of the host. Since the flukes are hermaphrodites, cross fertilisation can occur between two flukes inhabiting the same part of the host's gut. Once the adult fluke has produced fertilised eggs, these are then passed into the intestine of the host and then outward, in the host animal's faeces, to be taken up by the secondary host and so on to repeat the life cycle.

Another fluke species which typifies the life cycle of flukes in birds, is Leucochloridium paradoxum. In this case the main hosts are various woodland birds, while the intermediate hosts are various species of snail. As with the common liver fluke, the adult parasite lives in the bird's gut where it produces eggs. These eventually end up on the ground in the bird's droppings, often on moist soil. When the eggs hatch in warm, moist conditions, they release a type of actively mobile larvae called a miracidium. The miracidium possesses a flagellum or mobile tail, so enabling the parasite to move around in the moist woodland environment. The miracidium subsequently burrows into an intermediate host, a small snail living in the moist surroundings. Once in the snail, the miracidia change into another type of mobile larvae called a cercaria.

The cercaria then proceed to invade a second type of intermediate host, which is possibly another species of snail, a small fish, or even an insect. In the second type of intermediary host, the cercaria become encysted forming a small cyst. When the secondary host has been eaten by a bird, the cysts develop inside the bird's gut, and become adult flukes.

Overall there are about 20,000 species of flukes and several hundred of these species attack birds.

Although the flukes usually require a particular species of snail as the subsidiary host, these parasites are not so particular about the spectrum of final hosts, Horák P., Kolářová L. Adema C.M. (102). Infection of the bird with the parasite is sometimes much more dependent upon the type of environment in which the bird finds itself, such as being captive in a zoo or a garden aviary with a small pond. In the zoo, they may be associating with a species of bird brought in from the other side of the world, or have access to drinking water contaminated with unfamiliar insect larvae or an unfamiliar snail.

Recently, the unusual fluke Paratanaisia bragai was identified in the kidneys of a red bird-of-paradise (Paradisaea rubra) at Chester Zoo.

Plate No.20 Red Bird of Paradise (Paradisaea rubra),a native of New Guinea.

The mollusc by which this fluke was transmitted has been provisionally identified as one of two species of evolutionarily related small snails, either A. clavulinum or S. octona, both of which been frequently found in the aviaries at Chester Zoo. These could possibly have been introduced into the aviaries when replanting with suitable foliage took place. These small species of snail are cone shaped, measure about 20mm x10mm and are commonly found globally in tropical greenhouses. Although the red bird-of-paradise is normally frugivorous (eats fruit), it is known to consume a small number of invertebrates and may have been looking for small snails. After researching the subject, it was found that this particular parasite has been reported in the following birds; the Ring-necked pheasant (Phasianus colchicus),the domestic pigeon (Columba livia domestica), the blue-and-gold macaw (Ara ararauna), a white-eared parakeet (Pyrrhura leucotis), toucans (Ramphastos), domestic chickens (Gallus gallus domesticus), turkeys (Meleagris gallopava), the helmeted guineafowl (Numida meleagris) and the laughing dove (Spilopelia senegalensis), all of which will take small snails. Since the finding in the zoo at Chester, the parasite has also been found in some other birds in the zoo, all of which had occupied the same two aviaries, Steve Unwin et al (57).

The questions which this case posed were;

1. Since this particular species of fluke can affect a number of species of birds, is this parasite more common than previously recognised? Have cases not been reported because in-depth investigations, (such as histopathology, or microscopic examination of the kidneys, or other laboratory methods such as PCR screening), have not been carried out consistently?

2. Is it possible that this particularly small snail has been inadvertently imported by the gardening staff with the snail attached to some 'exotic' vegetation? This may have been

placed in the bird's aviary to make the aviary as near to the bird's natural rainforest environment as possible.

Adult parasitic flukes of whatever species may remain permanently in their final host, be that bird or mammal, throughout the host's life. Often the parasites are well tolerated and do not cause significant disease. In this case of the red bird-of-paradise however, the bird was showing progressive kidney failure, and was lame on the right leg due to pressure from an enlarged kidney on the right sciatic nerve.

A few species of flukes can cause epizootics (animal epidemics), particularly if large numbers of flukes are picked up at the same time. This can result in the mortality of thousands of waterfowl. Such an occurrence was recorded by Rosemary Drisdelle (38) in the Great Lakes region of North America.

A dramatic outbreak of parasitic disease like this, resulting in multiple deaths, is often caused by large numbers of migratory birds landing on the water together, combined with an increased density of first and second intermediate hosts, namely, the snails. The snails may increase beyond normal levels because of an increase or change of local vegetation influenced by local climate change. Also, the age and nutritional state of the birds may influence the scenario. Referring back to Desser S. (12), already mentioned, in relation to the increased mortality caused by blood parasites in ducks (see Chapter 6). In that instance, there was increased stress and possibly a low immune response due to a decreased state of nutrition.

Now we return to the swifts circling in the sky, with a description of which this book began. During the period 2006 to 2008, Marko Legler and his colleagues at the University of Hanover in Germany carried out a number of post mortem examinations on casualty wild swifts which had been brought into his veterinary clinic. During the examinations, he found that, of the adult swifts, 15% were carrying trematode flukes in their intestine. In contrast, 38.3% of the juvenile birds were found to be carrying the same parasites. All the swifts mentioned in this study were brought to the clinic as injured wild casualties and they were all in good bodily condition but had died, not because of fluke infection, but as a result of collision injuries.

The reader might ask, if the birds were otherwise healthy and in good condition, why did they become causalities? The Author knows from personal experience, that some birds such as swifts *do* make mistakes when flying and become casualties. When the author lived in a five-storey house during the 1940s, the swifts, nesting in the eaves just above the upper bedroom window, would sometimes misjudge their approach, crashing into the casement window and slip down between the two glass window panes, when coming in to approach their nests. They then had to be carefully extracted by hand. These birds were thankfully not injured, only dazed.

The fact that the birds in Hanover were in good bodily condition indicated that the parasitic flukes in the intestine were living in relative harmony with their avian host and were not having any significant adverse effect on the swifts' health. Also, as the birds got older, their immune system was building up a resistance to the parasites, as was indicated by the differential infestation between adult and immature birds. Using geolocators, a type of satellite tracking device weighing just a fiftieth of an ounce, attached to the individual birds, scientists from the British Trust for Ornithology in 2010/2011, worked out that these small migratory birds covered over 3,000 miles in just 5 days during their outward migration to the Democratic Republic of the Congo in Central Africa. Some of the birds flew as far as South Africa, Angola and Mozambique. One bird covered a total distance of 17,000 miles. The birds were able to maintain an average speed of about 25 miles per hour during their outward and return journeys. All of which would tend to indicate that the parasites could not have had any significant adverse effect on the physical fitness of these birds.

Swifts spend the whole of their life airborne, only coming down to roost when nesting. They even sleep and mate whilst in the air. However, they do come down to skim along the surface of water when drinking. They feed aloft while trawling with their mouths wide open, producing a wide gape, catching aerial plankton containing small insects. It is in these insects that the encysted cercaria of the trematode flukes are found and which infect the swifts in flight. When the infected swift comes down to skim on the water to drink it *probably* defecates, passing its droppings, containing the fluke eggs, into the water and so completing the flukes' life cycle.

Some flukes which infect humans, use quite a large variety of secondary hosts, particularly several species of small snails, to transmit their larvae. This point emphasizes the importance of thoroughly washing all salad vegetables before eating them. Those purchased in supermarkets may have been flown in from overseas, where the conditions surrounding their cultivation may be variable.

The author is aware of the story of a retired couple, holidaying in Spain, who had a salad meal in a village eating house. To them the salad was excellent, but soon after the couple returned to the UK the husband developed what their local GP thought was cancer of the liver. Further investigations revealed it to be a liver fluke infection.

The author's own grandfather, a market gardener in the 1930s, had watercress beds growing along the banks of the river Cray in Kent which would undoubtedly have contained snails, some of which may have been infected with the liver fluke from sheep grazing in the nearby meadows.

An important group of flukes are the blood flukes, the ***Schistosomes.*** These flukes are elongated and live in the blood vessels of the intestine or urinary organs of birds and mammals. The flukes which infect human blood vessels are mostly found in tropical countries, often affecting people planting rice seedlings and spending a lot of time standing in water. The parasite causes a chronic disease known as bilharzia.

In this case, the adult female fluke lays her eggs in the small blood vessels lining the intestine of the host. The blood vessels rupture and the eggs pass into the interior of the host's gut, to be passed out with the host's faeces. Eventually, because human faecal matter is used in many third world countries to fertilize the soil, the eggs often get into neighbouring water courses. There they hatch, to produce flagellated mobile miracidia, which next penetrate a specific kind of water snail. In the snail, the miracidia become sporocysts, which in turn produces cercariae. These resemble miniature adult flukes. The cercariae make their way into the watery environment until they come into contact with the skin of a human standing in the water. The human host's skin is penetrated by the mobile cercariae. The life cycle is completed when the cercariae make their way into the human host and eventually into the blood vessels lining the intestine or the tubes leading to and from the host's kidney. When the infected human urinates or defecates, the parasite returns to the water to repeat the process, by forming a sporocyst which in turn produces cercariae. The cercariae then make their way into the next human host.

Fig No.12 The life cycle of Schistosoma japonicum or blood fluke which causes the disease bilharzia

Included within the scientific family of the **Schistosomatidae** is the genus ***Trichobilharzia,*** which infect birds. This is the largest group within the Schistosomatidae and includes about 40 species of bird parasites. They attack mostly water birds and are not too particular which species of birds they parasitize. However, the different species of miracidia (from the various species of Trichobilharzia) are generally much more particular about the species of *snail* they invade. This may indicate that during evolution their association with the aquatic snails has been much longer over time, and that the immune defences of the snails have had longer to mature, as indicated by Horák mentioned above.

The Trichobilharzia parasites of water birds are distributed quite widely globally and are found in many freshwater habitats, so that it is not uncommon for the free-swimming cercariae to attack the skin of any human swimmer worldwide. This is at first just noticed as a "swimmers itch." However, a second attack by the cercariae often results in a more severe allergic cercarial dermatitis. The fluke however, does not *usually* complete its life cycle in the human host, although very occasionally the parasites may migrate through human tissue and even into the nervous system.

Another type of bird fluke with a similar life cycle is that illustrated in figure 13 below, Echinostoma revolutum. It is of interest because, although primarily a bird parasite, it occurs in many parts of the world and it can occasionally parasitize humans. It is endemic in China and some countries of S.E. Asia, and has been reported as affecting US travellers returning from parts of Africa.

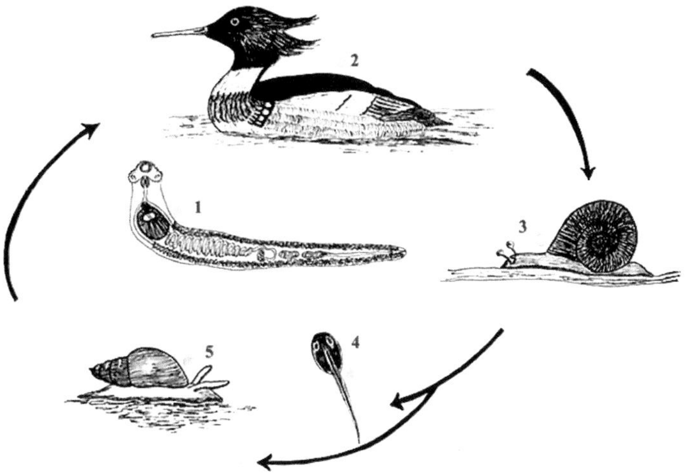

Fig. No. 13 Life cycle of Echinostoma revolutum.

1. The fluke Echinostoma revolutum which resides in the rectum and caecum of the infected bird *(and occasionally humans.)*

2. The fluke infests **many** species of duck, although the one illustrated is a red-breasted merganser. Also, it attacks partridges, poultry and any bird which may eat the snails.

3. A water snail of thc genus *Helisoma.*

4. Another intermediate host, a frog tadpole, which may be eaten by a bird which would become infected.

5. A second species of snail a pouch snail of the genus *Physa.*

In all the secondary host species infected by the fluke it is generally fairly benign.

<u>Tapeworms</u>

These are another type of flatworm with life histories in many ways similar to those of the flukes. The many species of tapeworms mostly live by attaching their head onto the inner lining (the mucosal surface) of the host's intestine, by means of suckers which are sometimes combined with hooks. Tapeworm hosts include all species of vertebrates including humans and, again, the parasites are dependent upon a mobile secondary host for their distribution amongst their primary hosts.

The tapeworm is a flat ribbon-like creature, divided into segments, called proglottids. The segments are budded off gradually from the head of the worm. As each new segment is formed, the one behind it progresses towards the tail of the tapeworm. During this progression towards the tail, the individual segment gradually matures, forming eggs. Each of these eggs, when fertilised, will eventually develop into an adult tapeworm. Each proglottid has no mouth or intestine, so the 'soup' formed from the host's digesting food in the host's gut where the tapeworm lives, just soaks through the worm's outer covering. The individual proglottid has both male and female reproductive organs, each with separate ducts leading to a genital pore. The creature is, again, an hermaphrodite. Either self-fertilisation, or cross-fertilisation between the proglottids of neighbouring tapeworms, can occur when sperm are produced to fertilise the eggs. When the eggs have matured, the proglottid breaks off at the terminal end of its parent tapeworm, to be passed out with the host's droppings or faeces. When the discarded proglottid becomes dry, it, in effect, becomes a packet of fertile eggs.

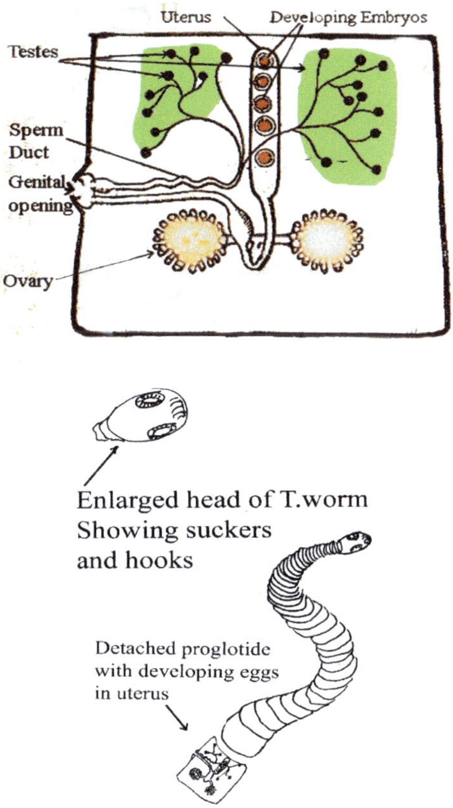

Fig. No.14 (Top) An enlarged and detached proglottid of a typical tapeworm

(below) The complete tapeworm

Coming back to the story of the swifts circling in the summer sky, the researchers in Hanover also found evidence of tapeworms in the swifts. Infection of the swifts by tapeworms probably occurred in a similar way to infection by the flukes. Moreover, the life cycle of these tapeworms was possibly completed in a similar manner to that of the flukes. Packets of mature eggs from the tapeworm and the fertile fluke eggs would both have been taken up by the larvae of the flying insects which were developing in the water, before the larva matured into an adult fly. The adult parasitized fly, carrying the larvae, was eventually eaten by the swifts during their trawl through the sky for aerial plankton.

There are very many species of tapeworms which infect different birds, including sea birds, such as terns. Nonetheless, because all tapeworms require an intermediate host to complete their life cycle, these parasites are less often found in seed or fruit-eating birds. The main exception to this rule is the case of young nestlings which may be fed insects or insect larvae by the adult bird. Many so-called songbirds such as thrushes and titmice, which many people might think of as only seed eaters, eat quite a lot of invertebrates such as insects, spiders, slugs and snails when feeding nestlings. None of the flukes and tapeworms found in the swifts and other birds are infectious to humans.

However, in the case of the 'beef tapeworm' (Taenia saginata), humans are the definitive final host of this parasite and cattle are the intermediate host. Fertile eggs produced by this tapeworm are taken in by a cow eating grass contaminated by human faeces. In the case of the pork tapeworm (Taenia solium) again, the human being is the final host and the pig is the intermediate host which becomes infected by feeding on food contaminated by human faeces. It is found mostly in third world countries where hygiene may not be so good. It is rare in the Muslim world, because the eating of pig meat is forbidden. In both cases of the beef and the pork tapeworm the proglottids containing the fertile eggs may have dried and been blown by the wind to contaminate the food source.

In the intermediate host (which in the above cases is a cow or pig), the fertile tapeworm eggs hatch in the host's gut producing a six-hooked embryo. The tapeworm embryo then bores its way through the hosts' intestinal wall and into the cow's or pig's blood vessels. Then it is carried by the circulating blood to eventually reach and form a sac or 'bladder' in the cow's or pig's muscles. If uncooked meat is eaten by a human, the bladders in the muscle of beef or pork can, after the meat has been digested by the human host, develop into adult tape worms which in the case of Taenia saginata may be up to five metres long. The parasite is not uncommon in Africa, Eastern Europe and Latin America. Consequently, any visitor to these countries, who prefers their beef slightly under cooked or rare (pink), is taking a risk.

Tapeworms live in a variety of animals. The broad fish tapeworm *(Diphyllobothrium latum)* lives in fish and can reach up to sixty feet long. Again, consumption of raw or undercooked fish by humans poses a risk of infection.

Another small tapeworm *(Echinococcus granulosus)* lives in the intestine of dogs, and humans can occasionally become infected by allowing an infected dog to lick their face and hands. It is however, easy to eliminate this parasite from the dog by routine and regular worming with suitable anti-worming drugs. The intermediate hosts of *Echinococcus granulosus* are the sheep or cow, where the parasite eventually ends up in the sheep's muscle to form a type of cyst called a hydatid cyst. Hydatid cysts form little subsidiary cysts within their own globular cavity. Occasionally, infected humans can develop hydatid cysts in the brain (resulting in epilepsy), in the liver or in the eye. This was, at one time, a not uncommon diagnosis in Liverpool hospitals where patients were brought in from the sheep rearing areas of neighbouring North Wales.

Like the other organisms inhabiting the gut of humans or other animals, such as the bacteria, the viruses and protozoa, the various worms and flukes all interact with and may stimulate the host's immune system. This was first demonstrated by John Turton (79) working at the UK's Medical Research Council Laboratories in Surrey in 1976. He intentionally infected himself with hookworms. Hookworms are not a tapeworm, but a small type of roundworm. He was attempting to combat his allergy to pollen and thus his suffering from Hay fever. His experiment worked, but did not continue once he got rid of the worms in his gut, using an anti-worming drug. The worms in the gut would normally only survive for between four and six years. Again, Professor David Pritchard and Alan Brown (111) at Nottingham University, working both in Papua New Guinea in the late 1980s, and later in the University, infected themselves with a small dose of hookworms (Necator americanus). Pritchard also used some volunteer students to find out if this worm infection influenced the human immune system. He wanted to find out if the immune system became less affected by autoimmune disease such as some allergies like Hay fever, asthma, Crohn's disease, ulcerative colitis, multiple sclerosis and possibly rheumatoid arthritis. The hypothesis put forward by Professor Pritchard and Alan Brown is supported by 29 other references attached to their paper and given by their colleagues working in this field.

It is interesting to note that paleontologists studying human excrement, have found an increasing frequency of historic human societies being infected with the various types of worms and flukes. This has been fore-shadowed by man's increasing association with animals from hunter-gatherers to the domestication of poultry, sheep, wild boar and cattle, Kate Ravilious (129). It seems to be more and more apparent that living in a more 'hygienic' society may have produced some autoimmune diseases which could be described as the "diseases of civilisation".

CHAPTER 9

The Arthopods

After the worms, the next most important, and largest, group of animals to evolve which were to have a profound influence on the development of infectious disease in all animals including birds and humans, were the arthropods.

The arthropods have an evolutionary link to the velvet worms already mentioned in Chapter 6. There are about 80 species of velvet worms living today, and some extinct specimens are well represented as fossils in the Burgess Shale Formation. This is a geological formation found in part of the Canadian Rocky Mountains in British Columbia.

The arthropods are creatures with jointed limbs, but with all the soft body parts enclosed within a hard, outer coating of Chitin (a long chain-like molecule derived from glucose) rather like a suit of a mediaeval knight's armour. This contrasts with the vertebrates, where the supporting bony skeleton is surrounded by muscles, whereas in the arthropods the muscles are enclosed within the skeleton. In some cases, the chitin is mineralized, adding extra strength.

Some arthropods are important regarding the causation of infectious disease in animals, where they often act as the carriers of a disease. This group includes the insects, the mites, the ticks, the fleas and the lice.

From an evolutionary aspect, the ticks were probably the first arthropods to act as vectors, transferring infectious disease between individual vertebrate animals. Such diseases include Lyme disease, Rocky Mountain spotted fever and Q fever, all of which infect both humans and birds.

Next to evolve were the blood sucking flying insects like the mosquitos and midges, transferring such diseases as malaria, and the tsetse fly which carries the trypanosomes.

The Insects (biological class: Insecta)

The estimated total number of insect species is 8,750,000, (three quarters of all animal species), whilst the named species are only 1,025,000. They may be small, but from the time they evolved some 350 million years ago, the insects have had a profound influence on the evolution and ecology of all other land dwelling forms of life by their influence on the food chain.

Plant eating insects probably consume more vegetation, both wild and cultivated, than all other herbivorous creatures. Consequently, they are in competition with humans, and their domestic animals, for food resources. Throughout history, plagues of desert locusts (a type of grasshopper), have been documented in both the Bible and the Qur'an aa having stripped large areas (up to 400 square miles at a time) of all vegetation, and caused famines.

Amongst those insects that prey on other animals, the biting and blood sucking types, such as mosquitoes, are responsible for forming a deadly relationship with many microorganisms. These include the blood parasites causing malaria, leishmaniasis, trypanosomiasis, the arboviruses causing yellow fever, West Nile fever and those resulting in types of encephalitis.

Also amongst the insects are the flies, classified as the Diptera, which again, are important mechanical carriers of human disease such as tuberculosis, salmonella and bacillary dysentery. In addition, there are the carrion flies, causing blowfly strike in animals such as sheep, when the insects lay their eggs on the skin of animals so that when the eggs hatch they produce larvae (maggots). These maggots then feed on the flesh of the animal on which the eggs have been laid.

This is most commonly seen in sheep around the moist matted wool of the anus. Blowfly strike causes the Australian sheep industry millions of dollars each year. The author has also seen this happen in birds, which may result from the animal having open wounds caused by injury. It can also occur in humans, particularly in tropical countries causing so called Myiasis.

A. The common housefly

The commonest of the flies, and the one with which everyone is familiar, is the common housefly (*Musca domestica*). This insect, being a flying creature, is responsible for routinely carrying on the surface of its body hairs, vomitus and faeces from sick animals including humans.

It is said that the common housefly is capable of carrying over one hundred pathogens, such as those causing typhoid, cholera, salmonellosis, bacillary dysentery, tuberculosis, anthrax, the viruses of poliomyelitis and enteroviruses and also the eggs of parasitic worms.

This fly is believed to have evolved about 65 million years ago, which is about the time of the extinction of the dinosaurs, so these creatures could not have been troubled by houseflies.

B. Hippoboscides (flat flies or louse flies)

These flies are members of a super-family which includes the Tsetse flies, both of which are dependent on biting and sucking blood from other animals as a food source for their survival, meaning that they are obligatory parasites. Flat flies are common insect parasites found particularly on swifts but also on other wild birds. Anyone who handles swifts, because the birds may be wildlife causalities, or for ringing purposes when used to record migration patterns, will soon find the very active flat flies jumping onto them. Animal nurses hate them because they can easily jump into a person's hair and are difficult to extract.

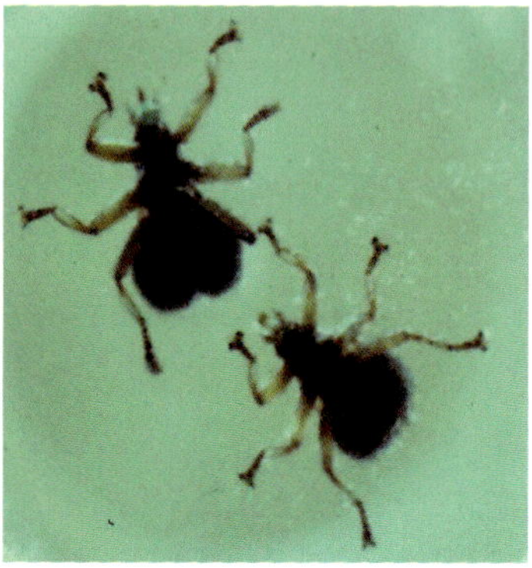

Plate No.21 Hippoboscides (flat flies or louse flies)

Overall, including the various sub-families, there are over 200 different species of Hippoboscides. As well as sheep, some flat flies are also found on cattle, camels and horses as well as some deer.

The bird blood parasites already mentioned, including Heamaproteous, Leucocytozoon and the trypanosomes, are all passed from one bird to another by the Hippoboscides, as well as being transmitted by mosquitos, because the flat flies just like mosquitos, do bite all their hosts.

Although the Hippoboscides may not, on first appearance, look like flies they are true flies and are related to the more familiar housefly. They are not particularly host specific but do vary in size according to their various host species, from the quite large to minute species found on hummingbirds.

C. Mosquitos and gnats

There are at least 3,500 species in this important family of insects, the Culicidae. The most ancient, have an anatomy similar to modern species of mosquito, and preserved specimens have been found in Canadian amber dated as being from 79 million years ago. However, more ancient types of mosquito go back at least until 90-100 million years ago. Consequently, we know that the mosquitoes had evolved by the time of the dinosaurs (the forerunners of the birds), and long before modern humans had evolved 200,000 years ago.

Amongst the different groups of mosquitoes, there is the genus of anopheline mosquitoes with, at present, well over 400 species, and new species have been discovered as recently as 2009. Anopheline mosquitos transmit many human and animal diseases such as malaria, West Nile virus and dengue fever. However, it must be remembered that not all species of mosquitoes transmit malaria.

Not all mosquitoes bite humans and some only bite birds, but some bird-biting mosquitoes are capable of changing their habits. This was illustrated by the interesting case of the London Underground mosquito. This was first reported in the London Times in August 1998 after extensive research by Kate Byrne and Richard Nichols of Queen Mary and Westfield College London (103).

This particular species of mosquito, *Culex pipiens*, evolved typically feeding on birds, but possibly some time in the past, when the London underground was being constructed, this species of mosquito became adapted to the subterranean environment and started feeding on humans, particularly the workers constructing the underground system. Intensive study by Byrne and Nichols and others has shown that this mosquito has now become a separate new species from its ancestor, which is still found living above ground biting birds. The underground species has been named *Culex pipiens molestus*, whilst the original above ground species has retained its name *Culex pipiens*. The DNA of the two species is different, the two species cannot be made to breed together and the above ground species still does not bite humans. Besides humans, the underground species also feeds on rats and mice. There is no indication yet that this underground species carries and transmits human malaria.

The name *Culex pipiens molestus* was given to this species of mosquito because it caused such a painful bite to Londoners sheltering from the London Blitz during the Second World War. The author, having slept in the Underground as an air cadet at the end of the War was fortunate not to have been bitten.

What is important to note is that the London Underground mosquito has evolved from the above ground species in a relatively short space of time, approximately a hundred years; such an evolutionary change would normally take considerably longer.

Interestingly, there was a suggestion from America by Spielman et al (104) in 1999, regarding the New York Underground, that a similar species of Culex mosquitos in the USA may feed on **both** birds and humans and be responsible for spreading the virus of West Nile fever.

It is not generally realised that normally both male and female mosquitoes feed on nectar. It is only the female mosquito which bites and then drinks from the pool of blood she has created by puncturing the host's skin, be it human or animal, and at the same time adding anti coagulants to stop the blood from clotting. The female mosquito needs the protein and iron in the blood to mature her eggs.

There are no flowers in the underground, so perhaps both sexes, male and female, of *Culex pipens molestus* feed on blood?

So where did the mosquitoes obtain their nectar from before the evolution of the flowering plants? Many evergreen gymnosperm trees such as the pines (for example the Scots Pine, *Pinus sylvestris*), the fir trees (like the Silver Fir, *Abies alba*) and the spruce trees (such as the Norway Spruce, *Picea abies*), all produce the sugary solution called honey dew. This could have been a source of nectar for ancient insects.

D. The Midges

This is a miscellaneous group of small biting insects, which includes the smaller, related versions of the mosquitoes that feed on amphibians and reptiles as well as the more advanced vertebrates.

Because of the importance of mosquitoes in transmitting many serious human diseases, ways are now being developed by scientists to genetically manipulate some of the more important species of mosquito in order to disrupt their breeding cycles. This work is described by Dean Thomas and his colleagues in a paper entitled 'Insect Population Control Using a Dominant, Repressible, Lethal Genetic System' (112).

Using this system of genetic manipulation, the male mosquito is genetically modified so that it carries a gene which, after mating with the female to produce fertilised eggs, those eggs which were due to develop into females, fail to produce fully mature females. The genetically modified males will go on mating with normal wild females, but because the eggs produced after fertilisation don't produce viable wild females, the number of normal females is gradually reduced. This could, in time, result in the extinction of this particular species of mosquito.

E. The 'true bugs' (classed as the Hemiptera)

These include the cicadas, aphids and the irritating bed bug, as well as some bugs already described like the Triatominae or assassin bugs, which transmit the Trypanosomes in South America.

The Arachnids (biological class Arachnida)

Apart from the insects, the arachnids are an important group of Arthropods, included amongst which are the scorpions, spiders, ticks and mites. A few scorpions can of course produce a potent venom which is potentially fatal not only to humans, but also to lizards and snakes and so potentially to birds. However, this venom is usually administered accidentally or defensively so they cannot be considered to be true pathogens.

Some spiders, such as the group of American black widow spiders (included in the genus *Latrodectus*), can bite and produce a poison fatal to humans. However, this again is a defensive mechanism and so they are not really pathogens.

There are also the large so-called bird eating spiders such as the red-kneed tarantula (*Brachypelma smithii*), which, like other tarantulas are sometimes kept as pets and which vets are sometimes asked to examine.

Plate No.22 Tarantula spider - one of the author's patients, held on a gloved hand

The so-called bird eating spiders probably do not catch many, if any, birds but subsist mainly on very small mammals, small reptiles and invertebrates such as crickets. Altogether, around 20,000 species of spider have been identified but because the spiders are much more obvious than mites and are seen more easily, there are probably many more species of mites not yet identified.

The Mites (class Arachnida, subclass Acari)

Unlike fleas and lice, the mites appear to have evolved independently from their hosts in the environment, from their original arthropod ancestors. Mites have exploited a multiplicity of environments including house dust (much of which is human shed scales of skin), and are easily seen swarming over any spilled grain in warehouses or in farm buildings. It is estimated that there are over 48,000 species of mites.

The mites have evolved parasitism of both plants and animals in several ways and on many independent occasions. They are sometimes even seen on the tarantulas mentioned above. Only secondarily have they parasitised birds. Also, apart from the air sac mites, they don't appear to be particularly host specific. The blood sucking mites can transmit viral, rickettsial and protozoan pathogens amongst birds.

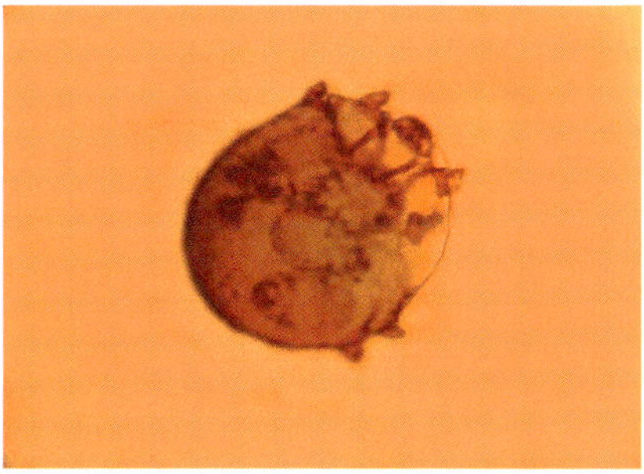

Plate No.23 The Avian mange mite (Cnemidocoptes pilae) greatly magnified. In life, it is not much bigger than two pinheads in size.

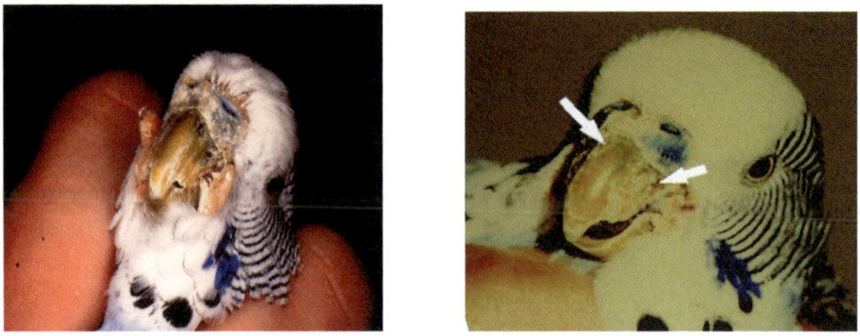

Plate No.24 Two budgerigars infected with mange mites (cnemidocoptes pilae).

In plate 24 above, can be seen the scaly appearance around the top of the beak which is caused by small tunnels made by the mites (indicated by the white arrows in the right hand picture), and also the growths of excessive horn on either side of the beak in the left hand picture, which are due to stimulation of the tissues by the mites. The avian mange mite, *Cnemidocoptes pilae*, is seen very commonly in pet budgerigars.

Epizootics of the Cnemidocoptic mange mites have been recorded in the American robin (*Turdus migratorius*), the red-winged blackbird (*Agelaius phoeniceus*), the common grackle (*Quiscalus quiscula*), the brown-headed cowbird (*Molothrus ater*), the evening grosbeak (*Coccothraustes vespertinus*), the chaffinch (*Fringilla coelebs*), the sedge warbler (*Acrocephalus schoenobaenus*) and many other birds.

Most of the above-mentioned birds are Passeriformes, which are mostly small perching birds. The chicks of many passerine birds once hatched, are reared by their parents in a typical closed 'hole' or semi-closed nest, rather than the more open type of nest used by birds of prey or waterfowl. The semi-closed nest necessarily favours infection, because of the close contact between the chicks and their siblings in the nest.

Plate No.25 A Zebra finch (Taeniopygia guttata) showing an area of crustiness at the top of the beak due to mange mites.

Mange mites also infect dogs, but these are not the same species as those seen in birds. In dogs, mange mite infection, also known as canine scabies, is a highly contagious infestation of *Sarcoptes scabiei canis*. The canine sarcoptic mite can also infest humans, causing a condition similar to typical human scabies, which itself is caused by a close cousin, *Sarcoptes scabiei*. Other types of mange mites can also infest cats, pigs, horses, sheep and various other species.

So far, at least 2,500 species of mites have been associated with birds, and no bird group is free from them, even penguins, which have body mites but not feather mites. This is possibly because penguins often dive to great depths when feeding, and the feather mites are unable to withstand the water pressure placed upon them.

Mites have been reported on the abdomens of Hippoboscid flies mentioned above, but that may be because they are just 'hitching a ride.' Also, apart from the air sac mites which are found internally in birds, mites do not appear to be particularly host specific.

Whilst some mites are detrimental, others are benign or even beneficial. Some mite species are parasitic upon other mites, and will attack other species of mites on the same host. Other species of mites are relatives of the household dust mites feeding on dermal dust, (skin scales constantly being shed by humans), or bird nest mites, feeding on feather dust collecting in the nest. These are distinct from the pathogenic red mites (Dermanyssus gallinae) which are parasitic on a variety of birds including poultry and cage birds.

The red mites can occur in very large numbers; as many as half a million have been recorded as being extracted from one nest. These mites can get onto human contacts, as experienced by the author, when handling several casualty wild owls and a sparrow hawk. These mites do not usually bite humans, but do cause skin irritation.

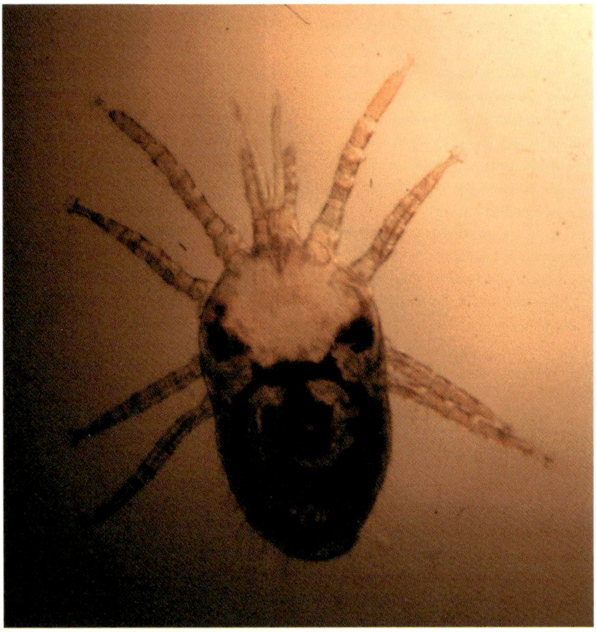

Plate No.26 Red mite (Accipiter nisus), taken from an injured sparrow hawk magnified many times. In life, they would be about 2mm. in size

The air sac and nasal mites (family *Rhinonyssidae*).

There are approximately 510 species so far described. However, few neo-tropical birds have been examined for these mites, so there may be as many as 5 -10,000 different species.

Some Rhinonyssid mites do penetrate the nasal mucosa of waterfowl with their claws in order to suck blood and feed on body tissues. Although confined to the nasal passages in waterfowl, they can cause enlargement and thickening of the tissues, resulting in chronic inflammation, and producing quite severe disease.

It is well known that the blood sucking mites, the red mite and the similar northern fowl mite, can have a detrimental effect on hatchlings in the nest. This is because they cause severe anaemia and so affect the survival of the chicks.

The air sac/nasal mites are believed to have evolved from free living soil mites, which are thought to have become secondarily endoparasitic, at least in some of the dinosaurs (the forerunners of the birds). The air sac mites, having first entered the original animal's air sacs through the nasal passages, would then have passed on the mites down the generations, from parent to offspring whilst feeding their nestlings. In consequence, they are only reported to occur in omnivorous or herbivorous species. They are not reported as being found in carnivorous birds.

In hummingbirds, some species of mites use the nostrils of these birds as a means of transport from one 'hummingbird flower' to the next, and at the same time, the mites are competing with the bird for the food resource obtained from the plant's nectar.

Genetic studies by Greg Spicer and others, indicate that each species of bird appears to have its own species of parasitic air sac mite, which is being passed from parent to offspring. However, host prevalence varies from one geographic region to another. The air sac mites are blood sucking and possibly they transmit infectious diseases like their relatives, the red mites. However, this transmission would have to take place in the air *passages* leading to and from the air sacs, since a bird's internal air sacs are practically bloodless.

In captive canaries and goldfinches, air sac mites can cause severe inflammation of both the airways and the air sacs, resulting in a fatal pneumonia.

As far as the author is aware, air sac mites do not *commonly* occur in other types of vertebrates. Possibly this is because in birds the air sac provides a safe, warm, internal environment away from most of the bird's immune system. Nevertheless, all the great apes *except* humans, do have air sacs, and chimpanzees are reported to harbour air sac mites. They are also reported to occur in lion-tailed macaque monkeys.

Incidentally, there is a small air sac mite which invades the respiratory system of the honey bee. In the honey bee, as in all insects, respiration is carried out by diffusion through a network of minute air, or tracheal, tubes, which open via small holes (spiracles) along the sides of the insect's abdomen.

Apart from the types of mites already mentioned, there are the feather mites. Concurrently with the evolution of the feathered dinosaurs a multiplicity of feather mites and lice gradually evolved from their ancestors, to exploit the great diversity of habitats provided by numerous and different types of newly and gradually evolving feathers. As Sarah Bush (42) and her colleagues, already mentioned in the previous chapter, has shown when researching the relative size of feather lice in relation to different species of pigeons, these insects adapt to the different sizes of feather.

Plate No.27 Feather mites on a cockatiel's plumage, seen with a magnifying lens.

Mironov (51), has stated that "feather mites belong to a morphologically diverse and abundant group that live permanently on the skin and feathers of birds." They have been recorded from all avian species except some of the ratites (emus, rheas and cassowaries.)

The feather mites probably evolved after the evolution of the ratites which had themselves evolved after the early evolving birds. Currently, approximately 2,400 species of feather mites have been identified.

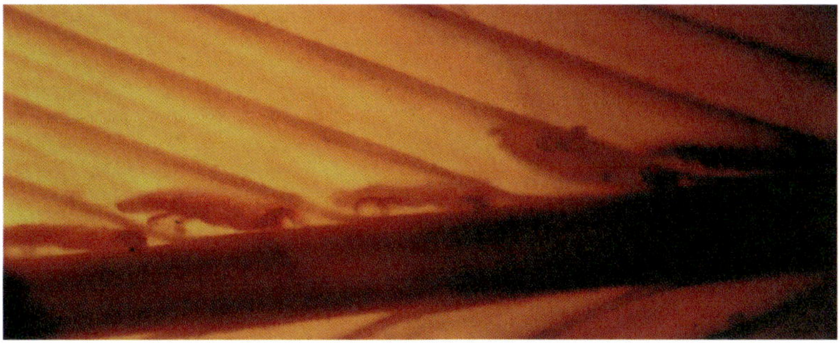

Plate No.28 The same feather as above in plate No.27, this time viewed with a microscope.

The various species of feather mites found on different birds, are morphologically diverse because the feathers of the different species of birds are also morphologically diverse. As an example, there are differences found in both the size and structure of feathers on the same bird, such as between the covert feathers, compared with the flight feathers. Also, the structure of feathers varies between different avian species. For example, those on the birds of paradise are quite different from those on marine birds. Again, the stiff flight feathers of pheasants are quite different when compared to the small, softer and more pliable feathers of small garden birds. A new species of specific feather mite, only found on one species or genus of birds, is continually being described and is a favourite subject of study for those scientists who research the classification of birds and their parasites.

Fortunately, from the disease producing perspective, the feather mites are mostly saprophytes, feeding on dead material. They feed on feather debris, feather oils, pollen and the fungi surviving on the oil secreted by the oil glands of the bird. It has been suggested that some feather mites might even be beneficial to the bird, by acting to control the growth of fungi and bacteria. Harper (49), found a negative correlation between the load of feather mites and a bird's bodily condition (*more* feather mites equated to a *better* bodily condition.) Moreover, he observed that the plumage was brighter in several small passerine birds carrying a high number of feather mites. In this case, the mites were probably cleaning the feathers of dust and fungal growth.

Péter Lászió Pap et al (87), came to the conclusion that, as the feather mites were neither harmful nor beneficial to the bird, they were simply commensals, living in harmony with their host.

In birds, there is in fact little immune defence against most kinds of mite infestation. The only defence used by birds against such external parasites is behavioural, such as preening, bathing, dust bathing, and 'anting' (that is, squatting in an ants' nest to cover themselves in ants and so make use of the formic acid secreted by the ants.) The formic acid kills both bacteria and fungi.

Nevertheless, in some birds which become infested with mites these can provoke a severe inflammatory reaction, such as has already been mentioned as affecting the goldfinch and canary.

Both ticks and mites belong to the taxonomic sub-order the Acari and the ticks are little more than large mites.

Ticks

There are approximately 900 recorded species of tick, but it may well be that many have not yet been recovered and identified. The ticks are a serious threat to all animals, including birds and humans, which they parasitize and to which they transmit a variety of other pathogens. This is particularly the case in tropical climates, which favour the ticks' reproduction and survival.

This is likely to become an increasingly serious problem in today's temperate regions because of climate change, as such regions are likely to experience periods of hotter and wetter weather which favour tick reproduction.

The tick, *Ixodes uriae,* is a common external parasite of more than fifty species of seabirds, from both the north and south polar regions. These ticks may attack other vertebrate animals besides marine birds, including passerine birds, seals, river otters, sheep, voles, foxes and even humans.

The causal organism of Lyme disease which affects humans, is one of those bacteria belonging to the genus *Borrelia,* which is carried by ticks. Humans become infected through irritating, but often not painful, bites, caused by several species of ticks, all of which belong to the genus *Ixodes*. Early symptoms of Lyme disease in humans, can include flu like signs with a high temperature, headache, tiredness, aching of the joints and mental depression. The tick bite leaves a characteristic circular "bulls-eye" skin rash (many illustrations of which can be found on the internet.)

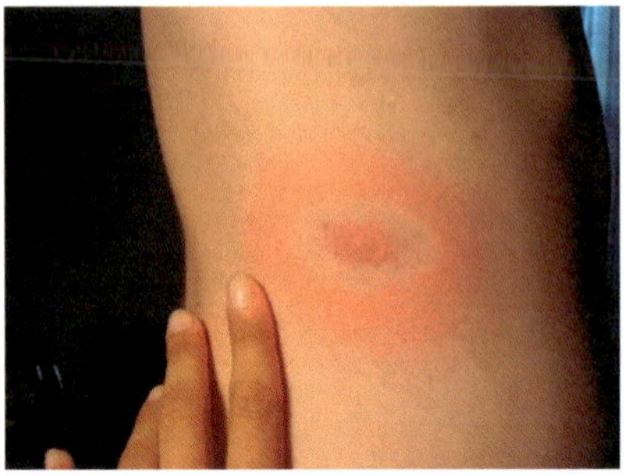

Plate No.29 Characteristic circular "bulls-eye" skin rash

Left untreated, symptoms of infection can occur anything up to two or three months later. These may involve the joints, the heart and the nervous system. A late, delayed, or inadequate treatment can result in more serious disease, such as arthritis or heart problems. However, tick bites without any subsequent symptoms are more common in Europe than in North America.

Unfortunately, the condition can be misdiagnosed by doctors. A case reported in the Daily Telegraph newspaper dated 19th June 2013, concerned a woman who had been bitten by a tick in local woodland and she had later been misdiagnosed with multiple sclerosis. She was not making any kind of recovery, and decided to carry out her own research. She remembered the tick bite, asked to be tested for Lyme disease and tested positive. A course of appropriate antibiotics resulted in her full recovery.

A colleague of the author picked up a tick and subsequently, Lyme disease, whilst bird watching in North America, and he described it as a very painful and debilitating condition. His eleven year old son, who had accompanied him on the trip, also had a tick on him but did not develop any symptoms.

Another colleague, a fellow vet, was bitten whilst on holiday with her family in the Isle of Wight. She developed Lyme disease and her GP failed to recognise the seriousness of the condition.

In the UK, tick bites are most often picked up in forested and heathland areas during the summer months. However, they could also be picked up by people walking in any habitat where there are numbers of nesting sea birds, such as the Farne Islands, off the northeast coast of England, or in the Shetland Isles. Some of these ticks could be carrying *Borrelia.*

In the author's personal experience as a vet, many British doctors in general practice do not recognise the potential seriousness of tick bites. In several instances when a client has brought a dog or cat to the author with a tick on it, and at the same time has mentioned that their child had also picked up a tick. The parent, having taken the child to their family doctor, was told not to worry about it because it will just fall off.

For anyone worried about Lyme disease in the UK, a good source of information is www.lymediseasaction.org.uk. There are also many other websites on the internet, some of which are well illustrated and worth researching. Also see Lyme disease in Wikipedia, the free encyclopaedia on the internet.

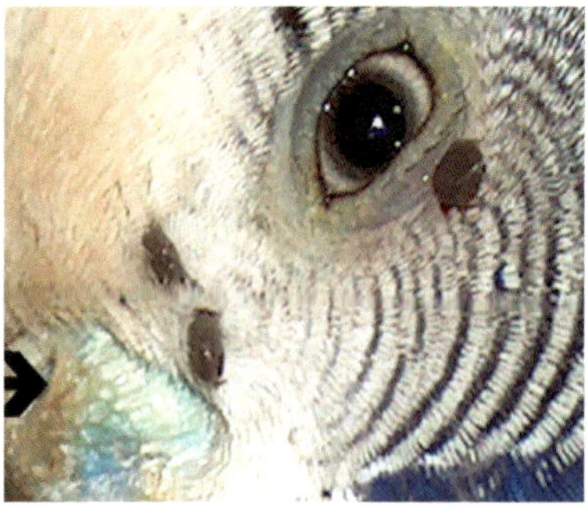

Plates No. 30a & 30b The head of a budgerigar showing three ticks, one just to the right and below the eye and two other ticks just above the cere, or the top of the beak. The right-hand photograph shows the ticks enlarged.

This bird was a casualty stray bird found in a wood in Holland and taken to a veterinary colleague, Vet. Dr. Jan Hoomeiyer. Although these ticks would not normally be able to parasitize a budgerigar, this is a good illustration of how many pathogens will exploit the opportunity to attack any potential victim offered to them.

There is a prevalence of *Borrelia burgdorferi* (the Lyme disease pathogen) antibodies in the king penguin, *(Aptenodytes patagonicus),* in the Crozet islands, a subantarctic archipelago in the southern Indian Ocean, Gauthier-Clerc et al 1999 (47). This seems a little odd, taking into account the climate.

It has also been suggested that sea birds and migratory passerine birds, particularly blackbirds, dunnocks (hedge sparrows), and the American robin *(Turdus migratorius)*, may transport the *Borrelia* organism between the Northern and Southern hemispheres accompanying the ticks, rather than just carrying the ticks themselves. Comstedt P et al (45) and (46).

Recent intensive studies, mainly in the USA, have indicated that the causal organism of Lyme disease, *Borrelia,* has been around for thousands of years. The oldest case of Lyme disease was discovered in the genome of a man called Ötzi the Iceman. Ötzi died around 3,300 B.C., and his remains were discovered in the Eastern Alps, on the border between Austria and Italy, in September 1991.

In North America, changes in farming practices, resulting in the clearance of some forests, and the reduction in the numbers of the deer tick (Ixodes scapularis), have resulted in an increase of the other species of Ixodes ticks carried by small rodents such the white-footed mouse (Peromyscus leucopus), which can also carry and spread Lyme disease.

The Centers for Disease Control and Prevention in North America, say that 30,000 cases of Lyme disease are recorded each year, but because many cases are unrecorded the actual number may be as many as 300,000.

An investigation into the behaviour and lifestyle of the *Ixodes* ticks and their hosts, and how this has had an influence on genetic mutation in ticks was carried out by Karen McCoy and her colleagues (58). They compared the ticks *(Ixodes uriae),* also known as the seabird tick, hosted by both Atlantic puffins *(Fratercula arctica)* and by black-legged kittiwakes *(Rissa tridactyla.)* These ticks are sympatric races of the same tick species.

The puffin breeds in burrows on moderate cliff slopes. Visiting puffins move around the colony, and may even visit a burrow occupied by another puffin, so there is plenty of opportunity for the ticks to switch hosts, both between individual birds and onto rabbits, which are also found in the burrows.

Plate No.31 Puffins cohabiting with rabbits in burrows in the Shetland Isles.

Switching hosts happens if the tick has just had a blood meal, after which the tick drops off the bird onto the ground to digest its meal of blood. The tick then moults, and climbs up any neighbouring vegetation to catch another passing animal onto which it will cling and start feeding again.

In contrast, the kittiwake nests on the narrow ledges of vertical cliffs. Moreover, the kittiwakes vigorously defend their nesting site from other birds, even of the same species. Consequently, there is much less chance of ticks switching from one kittiwake to another in a neighbouring nest site.

Plate No. 32 Kittiwakes at nest site with young.

Karen McCoy and her colleagues, surveyed 13 different colonies of these sea birds over the North Atlantic, including those in France, the UK, Norway and Canada. The ticks were all sampled for DNA.

The results were interesting. Whereas the puffins were found to move between colonies for distances of up to about 100 km, kittiwakes only tend to visit other colonies less than 50 km. away. Thus, the extent of tick dispersal was greater for ticks which exploit puffins than for those that that were hosted by the kittiwakes. Subsequently it was found that the genetic variation amongst ticks found on kittiwakes was almost twice that as those of the puffin tick populations. Consequently, the gene pool for the ticks on the puffins will be much smaller than that for those on the kittiwakes.

When mutant genes become diluted there is much less overall variation in the population. It is generally recognised that island populations of any species tend to have smaller gene pools and so are much more subject to adverse conditions because they cannot so readily adapt to changed circumstances, such as climate change. In this case, there is the possibility, in the long term, of the extinction of the sub-type of tick which is found on the puffin, together with any pathogen it may be carrying.

Another aspect of this situation is, if the effectiveness of the immune system of the host should, for any reason, be compromised (for example because of lower food intake), the ticks, and any micro-pathogens carried by them, would normally be able to take advantage of their host. However, before the implications of these findings are considered there is another complicating factor that must be taken in to account.

The main diet of the puffin is the sand eel *(Ammodytes tobianus)*. However, the supply of these fish is declining, and what is left tends to be of poor quality. Consequently, puffins tend to catch other food, such as pipe fish (a relative of the seahorse), which have a tough skin and are of lower nutritional value to the birds.

Plates No.33a and 33b

On the left is a puffin with a pipe fish in its beak, whilst on the right is a puffin holding in its beak a normal catch of sand eels.

Both the reduced supply, and the poor quality,(meaning they are immature), of sand eels is almost certainly due to two factors: -

1) Over fishing. These fish have been harvested intensively from parts of the North Sea, and used not only as a food resource but also as fish meal fertiliser. In 2005 as much as 300,000 tonnes were taken in this way by Danish fisheries (their un-reached EU quota was 800,000 tonnes!)

2) Global warming may be increasing the temperature of the North Sea by as much as 0.4°C per decade. This has happened since the 1980s, and the temperature is likely to go on rising. Because of this, more warm water fish, such as the huge, but harmless, basking shark *(Cetorhinus maximus)*, and some turtles such as the leatherback sea turtle *(Dermochelys coriacea),* have been seen more frequently in UK waters in the summers of recent decades.

Sea temperature change has resulted in changes to the zooplankton, at the bottom of the food chain, on which the sand eels feed. Sand eels burrow in sand at a depth of 30 metres, but swim near the surface in huge shoals on which the larger, predatory fish and sea birds feed.

It therefore follows that, because their poor-quality diet is likely to have an effect on the puffins by reducing their immunity to infection from tick borne disease, the whole parasite/host relationship will be changed. However, the ticks are unlikely to become genetically more virulent because of their reduced gene pool, and so the eventual outcome is equivocal. This all serves to illustrate the complex web of interaction involving some types of infectious disease.

The lice

Lice have almost certainly evolved in parallel with their hosts, both birds and mammals. In fact, *all* the warm-blooded animals, except bats and the marine mammals, such as whales. Additionally, lice are not found on pangolins (scaly anteaters), which are covered in scales instead of hair or feathers.

There are approximately 3,000 species of lice. These wingless insects spend the whole of their life cycle on one animal, attaching their eggs to the shaft of either hair or feather. Consequently, they tend to be host specific.

David Grimaldi and Michael S. Engle (41), recently reviewed a number of articles dealing with the early evolution of lice. Most avian species which have been checked, have lice. Ostriches have their own lice which can easily get onto their keepers' clothing when handling these birds in captivity. Even the stately swan, gliding down the river or across a lake, will have its own louse passengers.

*Plates No.34a & 34b_*

On the right, a louse taken from a wild casualty swan

The gannets (boobies), a large seabird, known for catching fish by plunge-diving, have their own lice. Quite how these parasites hang on when this sea bird makes its plunge dive into the sea is astounding!

Other marine birds also have chewing lice, and these are often host specific. For example, the two species of common, (Sterna hirundo) and Arctic, terns (Sterna paradisaea) each carry their own different species.

Species of lice may be restricted to a specific geographic region. They feed on dead skin, feathers and feather products, which they digest with the aid of endo-symbiotic bacteria in their gut. In wild birds, lice are relatively benign although in large numbers they can be debilitating and cause holes in the plumage of the bird, which is caused by chewing.

Plate No.35

A biting louse seen on the plumage of a captive cockatiel

Some lice suck blood and act as vectors for other pathogens, for example filarial worms causing Filariasis and also bacterial disease. Filariasis is caused by a type of nematode, or roundworm, which inhabits the blood circulation of many species of animals, including birds and humans. In humans, the larvae (microfilariae) of the adult worm causes river blindness (see glossary), due to gradual damage to the cornea. The author has seen similar microfilariae in the anterior chamber of the eye of a grey parrot.

All those researchers listed below have found that the ectoparasitic louse gradually adapts, by mutation or epigenesis, to a size applicable to their host. As the host gradually evolves into another large or smaller sized species, in parallel with it, so does the parasitic louse.

Sarah Bush and her colleagues (42), K.P.Johnson (43) and D.H.Clayton (44). In the case of the wing lice of birds, this enables the various species of Columbicola wing lice found on pigeons to fit more snugly between the feather barbs of the host and so to remain attached to their host during flight.

Sarah Bush and colleagues compared the size of Columbicola wing lice in the 30g common ground dove *(Columbina passerina),* with those on the very much larger 2,400g Victoria crowned pigeon *(Goura Victoria.)* They concluded that direct host switching of external parasites between closely related species was most likely to occur between hosts of a similar size.

Fleas

Fleas are another type of wingless insect. Many different species, but particularly the moorhen flea, *Dasypsyllus gallinulae*, are found on many birds, particularly ground nesting birds.

As already discussed, lice spend the whole of their life cycle on a single individual host. The female louse lays her eggs and attaches these to the feathers (or hairs) of the host animal. In contrast, fleas deposit their eggs in the surrounding environment. After the flea eggs hatch, they can become attached to a different host animal. In consequence, any infectious organisms, such as bacteria, that the fleas happen to be carrying, can easily be transferred to a different individual host.

Fleas can act as vectors for a variety of viral, bacterial and Rickettsia diseases. In humans, these include the bacteria causing typhus and bubonic plague and can be transferred by the fleas on rats or other small rodents. The myxoma virus, causing myxomatosis in rabbits, is passed between rabbits by the rabbit flea.

CHAPTER 10

The Dinosaurs

The evolution of the dinosaurs is important for this account, dealing with the evolution of infectious disease, because dinosaur evolution indicates just how the birds evolved from the dinosaurs in parallel with some of the infectious diseases that they were carrying.

Many avian infectious diseases have been carried over from their ancestors, the dinosaurs. Certainly, by the time the dinosaurs had evolved, most pathogen-vector relationships, such as that carried by the mosquitoes, which transmitted the blood parasites causing malarial-like diseases, were well established.

Long before most of the dinosaurs became extinct around 65 million years ago, many of the early birds, including the well known Archaeopteryx, were living alongside the dinosaurs and sharing their infectious diseases with them.

In fact, the ancestral mosquitoes were not only biting dinosaurs, but simultaneously biting those early birds which had evolved by this time.

To quote Colin Tudge (36), "The birds are little more than modified dinosaurs." Clearly, many of the characteristics, as well as the infectious diseases, developed in the dinosaurs have been carried on to their descendants, the birds.

We tend to think, in awe, of dinosaurs being huge animals, due to the popularisation of Tyrannosaurus rex (meaning "the tyrant lizard king".)

Fig.No.15 Comparative sizes of the Indian elephant and Tyrannosaurus rex

Indeed, this animal, which may have been about the same size, or slightly taller, than an elephant, particularly when standing up on its hind legs, was very large.

Plate No.36 A model of Tyrannosaurus rex exhibited at Chester Zoo.

However, the dinosaurs were a very diverse group of animals, not only in relation to their size and lifestyle, but also in their physiology.

Some were quite small, the size of pheasants or dogs. One of these smaller dinosaurs, which stood about half the height of a man and with a total length of about two meters, was named Oviraptor. This dinosaur was toothless and had a beak rather like a modern parrot. The creature was originally named Oviraptor (the name in Latin for "egg taker"), because a fossil of the dinosaur was found on top of a group of eggs and it was assumed at that time, that this creature was an egg thief. However, this assumption has since been shown to be incorrect. The dinosaur was probably incubating its own eggs, rather than eating them. It is noteworthy that Oviraptor had a rigid head crest rather like today's cassowaries, which are large non-flying birds inhabiting the tropical rainforests of northern Australia and New Guinea.

Plate No.37a Citipati osmolskae, a relative of Oviraptor, although somewhat larger than Oviraptor.

The plate above is a model photographed at Chester Zoo. As detailed below, like many of the more advanced dinosaurs, this animal had feathers which acted as body insulation, but it was not able to fly.

Plate No.37 A double-wattled cassowary (Casuarius casuarius)

(The red double wattle can be seen hanging down from the upper part of the neck.)

The head crest of the double-wattled cassowary is used by the bird for pushing its way through the dense undergrowth of the tropical rainforest in which it lives. It is possible that Oviraptor used its' head crest in the same way.

A much smaller dinosaur was Microraptor, which weighed only about one kilogram, about the weight of a common pheasant. It had wings, with a wingspan of just under one meter, but Microraptor had *four* wings, one on each of its two fore limbs as well as one on each of its two hind limbs. Stephen Czerkas hypothesizes that the wings were positioned rather like the wings of a biplane. It is supposed that, with large claws on the inside of its hind legs, Microraptor could easily climb up a tree and, with its well-developed eyes, scout around for prey below it on the ground, and could then glide down onto its victim.

The birds evolved from the sub group called the therapod dinosaurs. These dinosaurs walked on their hind legs, so they were in fact, bipedal three toed dinosaurs, with a foot rather like many of today's birds, such as the farmyard chicken.

Plate No.38 The hind foot, with three large toes, of Tyrannosaurus rex, from the model at Chester Zoo.

The two small digits with attached claws, seen hanging down from the top left-hand corner of the illustration, are from the fore limb, which in the therapod dinosaurs, is much smaller than the hind limb. Compare with Plate No.36.

The therapod dinosaurs were mostly fearsome carnivorous predators. However, some were omnivorous, whilst others were purely insectivorous. The smaller dinosaurs often hunted in packs.

Another main group of dinosaurs were the sauropods, which were much larger (up to 120 tonnes), they walked on four legs, were slower moving and were mainly herbivores. Such was Argentinosaurus huiculensis, one of the heaviest creatures ever to walk the earth, with a total length of 33-35 metres (98-115 feet). Fossil remains of this animal were found in Patagonia, South America in 1988. At least half of this animal's total length was its' neck. We can compare this to the size of the average giraffe, which is only about 5-6 metres high at the shoulder, and with a neck length of 6 feet. This titanosaur giant, would have been able to reach treetops such as the giant Araucaria conifers, which can reach a height of up to 80 metres. This sauropod was two and a half times as high as the giraffe when extending its neck *and* standing on its hind legs and when balanced by its tail.

Plate No.39 Brachiosaurus, a sauropod dinosaur model at Chester Zoo.

Fig No.16 Giraffe, compared with the size of one of the smaller saurapod dinosaurs.

In both cases the long necks have evolved to enable these animals to reach the foliage at the top of the tallest trees, so that they would not be competing for food resources with other smaller, herbivorous animals.

Probably trillions of dinosaurs lived and died during the time when these creatures were the dominant land animals, a period of over 160 million years. This was from the late Triassic period (about 230 million years ago), until the end of the Cretaceous period (about 65 million years ago.) Steve Wang and Peter Dodson (91), consider that, although dinosaur fossils representing 527 genera of dinosaurs have already been described, it is estimated that there are, at least, another 71% of dinosaur fossils still to be discovered.

Research indicates that *some* dinosaurs were warm blooded and had a body chemistry able to produce energy at a rate closer to that of today's warm-blooded mammals and birds. This contrasts with the ancient cold-blooded reptiles (Archosaurs), from which the dinosaurs are believed to have evolved.

John R. Horner, Kevin Padian and Armand de Ricqlès (59), have studied the long bones of dinosaurs and have shown that they have growth lines similar to the annual growth rings of trees. Examination of these growth lines has enabled, not only the age of the animal but also its rate of growth, to be estimated. The indications are that even the largest dinosaurs had rates of growth comparable to that of today's birds. To achieve this, they must have had similar high rates of metabolism and body chemistry. Accordingly, their bodies must have been able to regulate their body temperature.

However, in contrast, some other types of dinosaurs may have been cold-blooded, rather like today's reptiles. All cold-blooded animals are dependent on the early morning sun's rays to increase their body temperature before they can become active.

Cold-blooded animals, such as lizards and snakes, can be seen to bask in the morning sun, and the same is true of many insects. Using the sun's rays to raise their body temperature, the creature's warmth then enables the body chemistry to speed up, and the animal can become active.

There is now little doubt that birds did originally evolve from a small, bipedal, Therapod dinosaur. Even before 1861, when the first fossil of Archaeopteryx was found, Thomas Henry Huxley, an eminent biologist of his day, and a friend of Charles Darwin, was suggesting that the birds had probably evolved from the dinosaurs.

Since that time, it has been shown that the dinosaurs are like the birds in having the following characteristics: -

1) Hollow, thin-walled bones, except for the females during that period prior to the time of egg laying.

Before laying and during the formation of the eggs in a bird or a dinosaur, the females had the centre of the long bones (the medulla) "filled in" with extra medullary bone. This additional bone was used for storing the calcium needed for the formation of the eggshells. After egg laying, the medullary bone disappears and the bone returns to its usual thinner walled, hollow form. The same process still occurs in today's birds. The hollow, thin-walled dinosaur bones, helped to reduce the overall weight of these huge animals, and the reduced weight would have helped these creatures to eventually become airborne and fly like birds.

Thin-walled long bones are no more liable to fracture than the more solid bone of mammals, because the thin-walled bone is braced internally by a series of "struts" or trabeculae, each of which is so orientated to counteract the forces imposed on the bone at the point of attachment of muscles and the like. This engineering principle of internal bracing is similarly used in some modern aircraft wings.

2) Gastroliths, formed like polished stones, have been found in parts of some sauropod dinosaur fossils. These are similar to those found in the gizzard, or fore stomach, of most of today's grain eating birds. Many of these birds take in grit of appropriate size, to grind up food such as seeds and grain, just like the way in which grain is ground in a corn mill. The grinding action of the gastroliths is carried out by the action of powerful stomach muscles.

3) Therapod dinosaurs walked on two hind legs, supported by three main weight bearing digits or toes (see plates 36 and 38), as do many of today's birds. The great body weight of many dinosaurs balanced by the large tail.

4) Using CT scans of the fossils of some smaller dinosaurs, it has been demonstrated that some dinosaurs at least, had an air sac system similar to that found in the birds.

Moreover, the research carried out by Richard J. Butler and his colleagues (76), and others, looking into the air cavities of the bones of the spine, has also indicated that some primitive dinosaur-like reptiles, such as the flying pterosaurs (with a wingspan of up to 15 metres, larger even than a Second World War Spitfire), may have had air sacs and had a lung system similar to today's birds.

Furthermore, like today's birds, the dinosaurs had backward pointing, uncinate processes on the ribs. These would give more rigidity to the rib cage during breathing. According to Peter Ward (60), levels of atmospheric oxygen were probably lower than today, during the early dinosaur period (225-100 million years ago). An efficient respiratory system, enabling the maximum amount of oxygen to be extracted from the atmosphere, would have enabled the dinosaurs to reach much larger sizes and to become a much more active group of animals than their forebears, the first reptiles (which originated about 320 – 310 million years ago.) Furthermore, it has been suggested by Dave Unwin of the University of Leicester in the UK, that the air sacs of the pterosaurs may have had inflatable, subcutaneous, air-filled compartments, helping to adjust the shape of their wings.

Fig. No. 17 The air sacs of a therapod dinosaur

In figure 17 above, the top diagram shows the air sacs of a duck, coloured blue. The bottom diagram shows the air sacs of a dinosaur, also coloured in blue.

The birds of today have kept this type of respiratory system developed by the dinosaurs. The air sac system operates by having large bloodless air sacs filling most of the space between the body's organs. When the animal inhales it expands the air sacs, pulling in a large volume of fresh air through the windpipe and then through the relatively small lungs, (when compared with those of a mammal.) When exhaling, the air sacs are contracted by all of the body’s muscles, not just those of the chest, (as is the case in mammals), pushing out the contained air in the air sacs. Again, this exhaled air passes through the relatively small lungs.

Because the air sacs have a greater capacity than the mammalian lungs, this enables the bird to make use of a far greater volume of air from which to extract oxygen. The air sac type of respiratory system is therefore a much more efficient respiratory system for the exchange of the atmospheric oxygen for carbon dioxide than that of mammals, including man. This is why migrating birds, such as the bar-headed goose (Anser indicus), are able to fly well in excess of the height of Mount Everest (with a peak at 8,848 metres or 29,029 feet), during its' migration flight. At this altitude, most humans need supplementary oxygen.

The efficient avian respiratory system can also rapidly absorb into the body any atmospheric gasses, whether noxious or otherwise. This is the reason why canaries were at one time used in mines to detect a dangerous build-up of poisonous gas such as methane and carbon monoxide. In this instance, the birds would die before those dangerous gasses could affect the miners.

This also calls to the mind of the author, an instance which happened some years ago in the industrial heart of England. A large number of wild birds such as starlings, blackbirds and house sparrows were found dead, together with some domesticated and captive budgerigars housed in two outside aviaries. The dead birds were found along the path of a smoke plume, directly downwind of a factory manufacturing plastic covered metal plates. The industrial process involved coating the metal plates with a layer of plastic material. The continuous process took place in an electronically controlled oven. Unfortunately, the electronic control was subsequently found to be faulty, so that the oven was not set at the correct temperature and noxious gasses were being emitted from the factory's smoke stack. It was fortunate that the level of harmful gasses was not fatal to humans, although many people in the affected area did develop sore throats and coughing, due to laryngitis.

A further effect of the efficient "dino/avian" respiratory system, was to enable the dinosaurs to speed up their rate of metabolism. They were able to quickly process the large quantities of food they consumed and so could develop into large land animals. Furthermore, the Dino/avian lung overall, is relatively smaller in size and weight than the mammalian lung, which helped reduce the total bodyweight of the animal.

It is estimated that Tyrannosaurus rex took approximately 15-18 years to reach full size; standing 10 feet at the hips, it was 34 feet (12.4 m) long and weighed 5-8,000 kilograms, or five to eight metric tonnes. We can compare this with what we know of some of the huge extinct reptiles, such as the giant crocodile Deinosuchus, living at the same time as the dinosaurs, during the Cretaceous period (75-80 million years ago), and which was 10-11 meters long. This reptile took 50 years to reach adult size. Being reptiles, they were cold-blooded and their rates of metabolism, body chemistry and growth was much slower. Moreover, they were not able to extract oxygen from the atmosphere so efficiently.

The dinosaurs and the reptiles undoubtedly had a common ancestor in the amphibians, and were evolving in parallel as distinctly separate branches of the 'evolutionary tree.'

As a result of the investigations of bone growth in the dinosaurs by John R Hunter (59) and his colleagues, it has been demonstrated that in the dinosaurs there was typically a juvenile burst of bone growth, after which the animal grew at a normal rate. This rapid early growth was also exhibited in some of the early birds such as Confuciusornis, many fossils of which have been found in China. This bird had evolved slightly after the better-known Archaeopteryx, and was the size of a magpie. In the early evolving birds, the initial burst of growth became truncated (that is, the animal stopped growing after the early spurt in growth.) This enabled the early birds to become miniaturised, when compared with their ancestral dinosaurs. This feature was important, because with the feathers developing at the same time, the reduced weight and smaller size enabled the birds to become airborne.

There may also have been a "trade-off" between the extra energy required for the muscles used during flight, and other nutritional resources, such the extra requirement for protein used for the growth of feathers. Compare this with the energy and nutritional resources needed for the continued growth of more skeletal bone to support a larger animal. Put another way, the huge dinosaurs had to grow fast to reach adult size in around 15-18yrs, but those ultimately evolving into birds had to put a check on this period of initial rapid growth, to remain small and use more of their nutritional resources to grow feathers and become flying animals.

All of this indicates that the dinosaurs must have developed an efficient body insulation system. This was necessary to conserve the increased heat being generated by a higher rate of metabolism. Better body insulation would appear to have evolved in some of the smaller dinosaurs. Those which were ultimately to become birds, achieved this by their development of feathers. The primary purpose of the development of feathers was therefore insulation, and not to enable these creatures to fly. Flying had already been achieved by their relatives the pterosaurs, by developing wing membranes, rather like those seen in bats.

All the early plumulaceous, or downy feather-bearing, dinosaurs were relatively small. This is possibly because, as the ratio of the body surface area increases in relation to decreasing body volume, more body heat would be lost as the creature became smaller. In consequence, the indications are, that the plumage became much more dense as the evolving creature got smaller, and the feathers acted as a means of thermal insulation. This is rather like the function they serve today in the downy feathers of newly hatched chicks of domestic fowl, ducklings or any small bird.

More advanced and more complex feathers developed much later, so that they could then be used in flight. It is a remarkable fact that the flight feathers emerge from their feather follicles at exactly the same time on each side of the bird (that is, it is bilaterally symmetrical.) If this did not occur, the bird would be unbalanced when it attempted to fly. This also occurs each time the bird moults - the corresponding old flight feathers are dropped at *exactly* the same time on each side of the bird. This mechanism is under genetic control.

The early downy feathers were probably developing in the allosauroid therapod dinosaurs about 170 million years ago. The more advanced and complex feathers were not seen until about 120 million years ago, at the time of Microraptor. Consequently, the complexity of feathering in dinosaurs was gradually evolving over a period of about 50 million years. The small Microraptorians were possibly only a little larger that a modern pheasant. These creatures had long tail feathers and it is possible that they could fly, or at least glide.

Incidentally, the very large dinosaurs had the opposite problem of regulating body temperature. As their bodies got larger, the proportion of body surface to get rid of their body heat in relation to total body volume got smaller. Possibly, these large creatures may have been able to pant like a dog to get rid of the excess heat. Some of today's larger birds, such as storks and herons, get rid of their excess body heat by panting or "gular fluttering." This is vibration of the skin of the guttural pouch, situated below and between the two halves of the lower jaw, in the region of the throat.

As the small-bodied, energy-conserving dinosaurs evolved, they became much more active than their cousins, the typical very large ancestral dinosaurs. Also, some of the small dinosaurs hunted in packs, and so, overall, they became a much more successful group of animals than their larger relatives.

A comparatively recent finding, during 1998 and since, in the quarries of Liaoning province in northern China, is that by Ji Qiang (69) and colleagues from China and others from the USA and Canada. They firstly discovered two turkey-sized partial skeletons of feathered dinosaurs. These fossils date from about 145 million years ago. Since then, other investigators, led by Xu Xing from the Chinese Academy of Sciences (70), have found and named more than a dozen species of feather-bearing dinosaurs, totalling more than one thousand individual specimens, in the Xinjiang region of China. Many of these feathered dinosaurs had feathers on their legs. This indicates, as in the case of Microraptor mentioned above, that there was a four-winged stage in the early evolution of the dinosaur and birds. However, these earlier creatures were probably not able to fly with the same degree of skill as the birds of today.

Richard O. Prum and Alan H. Brush (50), have studied the evolution of feathers in the dinosaurs.

Feathers started evolving in a series of linked stages, with each stage of feather formation getting more and more complex. This started with a single filament gradually developing into the typical pennaceous veined flight feather, with interlocking barbs and barbules. This took place over a period of 25 million years as the early therapod dinosaurs evolved, 25 million years *before* the evolution of the first true birds.

It has also been suggested that the feathers in some dinosaurs may have played a part in sexual selection or other display purposes. Jakob Vinther of Yale University, working with Li Quanguo of the Beijing Museum of Natural History (118), have together discovered that by examining the shape of the pigment melanosomes (organelles found in animal cells), in fossilised feathers, it can be demonstrated that the feathers of avi/dinosaurs had various colour patterns. These were sometimes blue, green, orange, red or grey. Even amongst the reptiles, colour variation of the scales plays an important part in communication between individuals.

INFECTIOUS DISEASES OF DINOSAURS

During the period in evolution of both the dinosaurs and the reptiles, each was carrying with them representatives of the majority of the pathogenic organisms (that is, bacteria, protozoans, worms and arthropods), which had already evolved and been acquired by their common ancestors amongst the Amphibia.

Furthermore, examination of fossilized dinosaur dung indicates this contained the fossilized eggs of similar helminth parasites to those found in today's birds.

Some of the infectious diseases of the dinosaurs have been elegantly illustrated by George and Roberta Poinar (53, 54), in their book 'What Bugged the Dinosaurs.' These biologists have based much of their research on the examination of the various pathogens preserved in fossilised resin or amber.

Resin was copiously produced and flowed down the trunks of the many species of the ancient coniferous Araucaria trees, and, in the process, trapped many species of flying insects which were carrying the pathogens. Some of the remaining examples of these ancient conifers can be seen in the Northern Hemisphere, in parks and gardens, and are commonly called 'monkey puzzle trees'. Overall, about a dozen species of Araucaria trees survive today in the Southern Hemisphere, often in small woodlands. *Araucaria araucana* is the hardiest species in the genus and is native to central and southern Chile, western Argentina and South East Brazil. It is also the national tree of Chile. These trees are also found throughout the pacific islands and in Australia.

Araucaria trees are dioecious, meaning there are both male and female trees. Specimens of these species of tree have survived since the time of the dinosaurs. The trees originally grew to a height of 30–80 metres (98–260 feet), although most of those seen in domestic gardens today are often only half this height. Once established, these trees can live possibly as long as a thousand years.

Plates No.40a and 40b A particularly tall specimen of a present day representative of the ancient Araucaria trees can be seen in the left photograph. The detail in the right photograph shows the female cones bearing seed at the end of the branch.

In the past, these huge conifers occupied much of the primeval forests of the Cretaceous period, C.145-65 million years ago, extending over both the Northern and Southern hemispheres. Araucaria trees were the dominant trees in the Cretaceous forest, mostly at that time reaching heights of up to, and sometimes even over, two hundred feet. Possibly the sauropod dinosaurs evolved their long necks so that they could feed on such tall trees.

Other vegetation in the forests of that time were additional types of conifer, ginkgo trees (which are now particularly evident in New York's Central Park), cycads, liverworts and equisetums (horsetails) dominating the understory of the forest, and also some mosses. There were <u>no</u> flowering plants, which had not evolved by this time.

The resin which the trees produced, trapped a variety of creatures which were either crawling up the trunk of the tree or were flying insects landing on the resin covering the conifer trees' trunks. Well over 200 species of insects trapped in the amber (fossilized resin), have been identified. These insects include biting flies, such as some midges and mosquitoes, which could have been transmitting malarial parasites, viruses and other pathogens to the dinosaurs. In fact, with increased magnification, some large virus particles and flagellates can be identified within the bodies of the insects trapped in the amber.

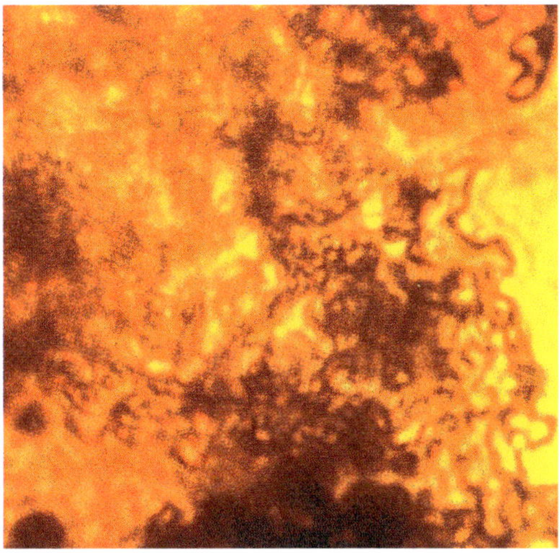

Plate 41 A magnified image of the polyhedral capsid form of a large cytoplasmic polyhedrosis virus in the midgut wall of a biting midge, trapped in amber

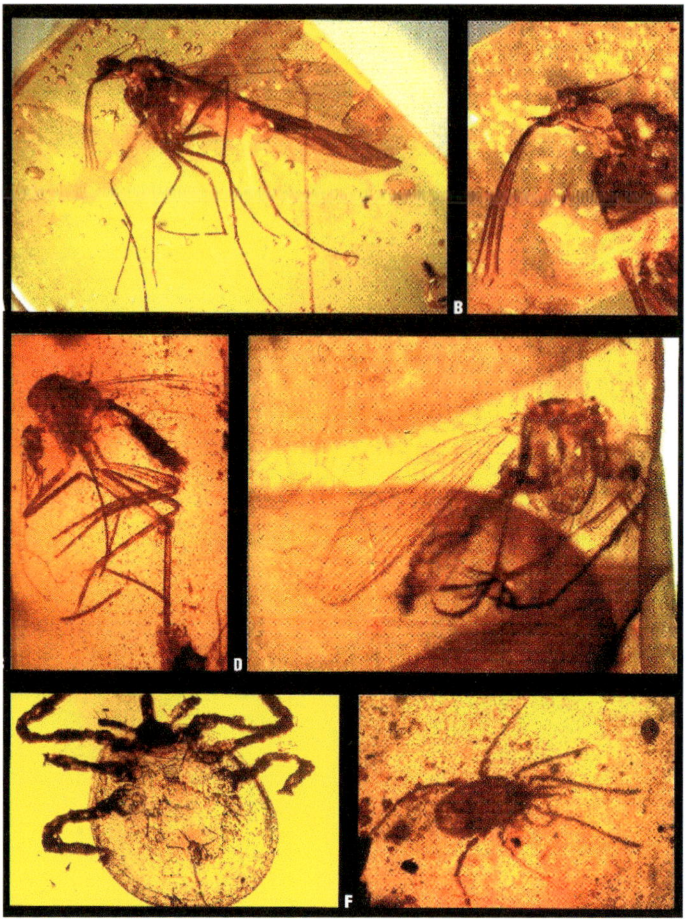

Plate No. 42 Biting arthropods, trapped in both Canadian and Burmese amber.

(Both Plates 41 & 42, copied from 'What Bugged the Dinosaurs' by George and Roberta Poinar.)

The tick illustrated in the bottom left picture, could have transmitted a pathogenic species of bacteria from the genus Borrelia, the present day causal organism of Lyme disease in humans, as mention in the previous chapter. To quote the Poinars (53) *"When the first dinosaurs walked the earth, they came with pathogens carried over from their ancestors."*

Those ancestors, were the amphibians, such as the frogs, toads, newts and salamanders, and the reptiles, such as the lizards, snakes and tortoises. In their book, George and Roberta Poinar have stressed the same theme that is being discussed throughout this book. *All* animals, including birds and humans, are in contact with microbes from the day they are born, and with which they have evolved together in parallel, from their own related ancestors. Each of us, the birds and all the other living creatures, are living, breathing, ecosystems, carrying around with us thousands of organisms both on our surfaces, and internally, within our bodies. As has been previously pointed out in the chapter on bacteria, the overwhelming majority of microorganisms, (bacteria and protozoa), are not harmful, but in fact co-operate with us and with the other creatures with whom they co-exist. They are, in truth, *essential* to the survival of all the highly developed animals.

Not only did the resin of the ancient conifers trap and preserve insects and other arthropod specimens at the moment of their death, but the chemicals in the resin (terpenes), also helped to fix the specimen. This prevented biodegradation of the invertebrate's body by decomposing bacteria, fungi or other biological means.

The resin flowed copiously from holes in the Araucaria (monkey puzzle) trees, because the trees themselves were continually being punctured by numerous wood boring beetles or weevils which were feeding on the tree's sap.

The trees were contributors to the warm, moist tropical forests, composed not only of Araucaria trees but also, as mentioned above, other early types of vegetation. Amongst these were a few smaller, shrubby, angiosperm plants, bearing a type of flower, which had not yet evolved to their present-day magnificence. The insects in the ancient forests were probably quite large and were abundant, as tends to be the case today. This is very evident to anyone visiting a tropical rainforest. The author noted this when visiting the tropical rainforests of Sumatra in 1982, where not only were the insects observed to be more numerous, but they were generally also proportionally much larger than in more temperate regions, clearly benefiting from the warm and moist environment.

On entering a forest of pine trees, there is a noticeable smell emanating from the trees, something which make the trees very popular in some countries at Christmas time. This is due to terpenes which are the main constituents of essential oils. Terpenes are derived from turpentine contained within the sap of the trees. A similar substance is crystalline frankincense, obtained from several species of desert trees of the genus Boswellia. Sometimes this is used to produce incense in churches, and in medicine, as an anti-inflammatory drug. This substance has been used for at least five thousand years in ancient Ayurvedic medicine, the traditional Hindu system of medicine. Many essential oils, which have been used in various cultures for thousands of years, are antimicrobial. By way of an example, the salts of benzoic acid, which occurs naturally in many plants, is used as a food preservative because it inhibits fungal growth and is also active against some bacteria, together with being an insect repellent.

In conclusion, although today's molecular scientists may not have got quite as far as the predictions portrayed in 1990 by Michael Crichton in his science fiction novel "Jurassic Park", it has been possible to show that most of the major types of *infectious pathogens* affecting both birds and humans today, were present during the time of the dinosaurs, some 250-65 million years ago.

CHAPTER 11

The demise of the dinosaurs and the early evolution of the birds

The dinosaurs are believed by many biologists to have become extinct as a result of a catastrophic event which happened to the earth about 65.5 million years ago, around the time of the Cretaceous–Paleogene (K–Pg) boundary, formerly known as the Cretaceous–Tertiary (K–T) boundary. At that time a huge asteroid, which has been calculated to have been about 6.2 miles in diameter and travelling at least at one thousand miles an hour, more than the speed of a bullet, collided with the earth. The impact was calculated to have had the energy of approximately 100 trillion tons of TNT.

The collision took place at Chicxulub on the end of the Yucatan Peninsula in the Gulf of Mexico, resulted in a crater calculated to have been 110 miles in diameter, and had the energy many times greater than several atomic, or hydrogen, bombs. The collision itself created a massive, suffocating wind shock, together with an ash and dust cloud blocking out sunlight and inhibiting the photosynthesis of all plants for several years. There would also have been extensive global forest fires. This resulted in the death of probably half of all plant species.

Despite this catastrophic event, some plants, particularly the coniferous podocarps survived. Their robust coniferous seeds were protected in fir cones, and before the explosion, some had become buried in the soil. Also, the magnolia plants, still seen in some gardens today, and evolving to be fertilised by beetles before the evolution of bees, were known to have evolved before the K-Pg catastrophe, circa 95-100 million years ago, and they survived.

At the same time, because of the perpetual darkness, there was a considerable drop in atmospheric temperature. The result was a global nuclear winter, lasting perhaps for two years or more, when there was no photosynthesis at all.

The catastrophic event also caused gigantic tsunamis 150 meters high, together with landslides on the areas impacted by the sea. All those animals living within the immediate area of ground zero (or hypocentre), would obviously not have survived the impact.

Nevertheless, some small animals, including some birds and their ancestors the small avi-dinosaurs, stood a better chance of survival, further away from the explosion. Some survivors were living at higher altitudes far away from the explosion, on the other side of the globe or were inside their burrows or in caves.

The large herbivorous dinosaurs like Brontosaurus and Diplodocus were the first to be affected by the disastrous event. These animals, being very large (up to 16 tonnes) plant eating creatures, probably required up to a tonne of vegetation per day, all of which had disappeared. Next affected, were the somewhat smaller carnivorous predators, such as Tyrannosaurus rex (6.4 tonnes). To make things worse for these carnivorous animals, with a reduced number of living prey, they were probably also scavenging on the carcasses of the dead herbivores. The carcasses would have been infected with maggots, hatching from the eggs laid by the flesh eating carrion flies scavenging on dead animals. These would act as vectors for the bacteria Clostridium botulinum (see Chapter 5), resulting in botulism poisoning, and death, of the carnivorous dinosaurs.

Consequently, immediately after the time of the K-Pg catastrophe, because of their direct and indirect dependence on plants, the majority of the dinosaurs became extinct, except for the very small avi-dinosaurs, living on the other side of the world or in sheltered valleys and the like. These would have survived on invertebrates or small reptiles, hidden in burrows at the time of the explosion, or on fish in the seas.

An hypothesis recently put forward by Dr. Daryl Codron and his colleague, Dr. Marcus Class, of the University of Zurich, concerning the result of the K-Pg catastrophe, is that because all the dinosaurs laid eggs, their relatively small hatchlings during the period of growth to their huge adult size, had occupied an ecological niche, which after the K-Pg catastrophe was rapidly filled by medium sized mammals evolving from smaller ground dwelling creatures. The early mammals were starting to evolve about 160 million years ago, long before the extinction of the dinosaurs and they were giving birth to bigger live babies than the smaller dinosaur hatchlings. As the mammals evolved and diversified, their young started to occupy a great range of ecological niches suitable for medium sized animals. The very small avi-dinosaurs took to the air and conquered new ecological niches not suitable for the evolving ground dwelling mammals.

However, the K-Pg explosion occurred at about the same time as some other global events, consequently the K-Pg catastrophe may not be wholly responsible for the complete extinction of the dinosaurs.

The other factors involved were environmental changes during the Cretaceous period such as (1) a global drought, (2) a massive increase in toxic blue-green algae in parts of the oceans, and (3) increased volcanic activity over a large area of the Indian Ocean. All may have been factors contributing to the demise of the dinosaurs.

It is also possible that infectious disease, apart from botulism, may also have played a part in the extinction of the dinosaurs. Decreased food intake, due to the reduction in vegetation resulting from the global drought, would have made it more difficult for an animal to mount an effective immune response to infection from bacteria and viruses. Also, there would have been an increased infestation of parasites in such weakened animals, with many of those parasites acting as vectors to spread bacteria, protozoa and viruses, and so the noxious situation, particularly for the large dinosaurs, would have been exacerbated.

However, despite all the above hypotheses regarding the *seemingly* sudden disappearance of the dinosaurs, recent research by Dr. Larry Heaman's team at the University of Alberta, Canada, has indicated otherwise. Using a new radioactive method of dating the age of the fossilised bone of the plant eating, duck–billed, medium sized dinosaur, the Hadrosaur, their research has indicated that this animal may have been alive after the K-Pg catastrophe.

The Avi-dinosaurs

Apart from all the above, the small avi-dinosaurs were probably able to climb trees and rocks, like some present-day goannas, or monitor lizards, found in Australia and Southeast Asia. They would have been feeding on insects and larvae, and other invertebrate prey, which would not have been wiped out by the K-Pg explosion. Some present-day monitor lizards are quite small, being only 20cm in length.

In addition, recent discoveries of fossils found in Hebei province of northern China, indicate the existence of a type of feathered wading bird *(Archaeornithura meemannae),* living about 130 million years ago, well before the extinction of the dinosaurs.

An important factor influencing the early evolution of the birds was that of plate tectonics, which gradually altered the relative position of the earth's continents.

The surface of planet earth is composed of several segments, or plates, (tectonic plates), each forming a continent and separated from one another by the oceans. Those plates forming the floor of the oceans lie at a lower level than the terrestrial plates, and consequently the water of the oceans collects in the depressed areas, just as rain water collects in puddles in the rutted parts of a road. All the earth's tectonic plates are floating on the underlying semi-fluid molten rock of the planet, called magma, and forming the central core of the planet. The magma occasionally pierces the surface as lava, such as happens when a volcano erupts and discharges red hot molten rock.

When planet Earth was first formed as a white-hot chunk of solid matter detached from its parent star, the sun, a single land mass coagulated on the surface of the gradually cooling planet. The first distinct land mass or "supercontinent" was Pangea.

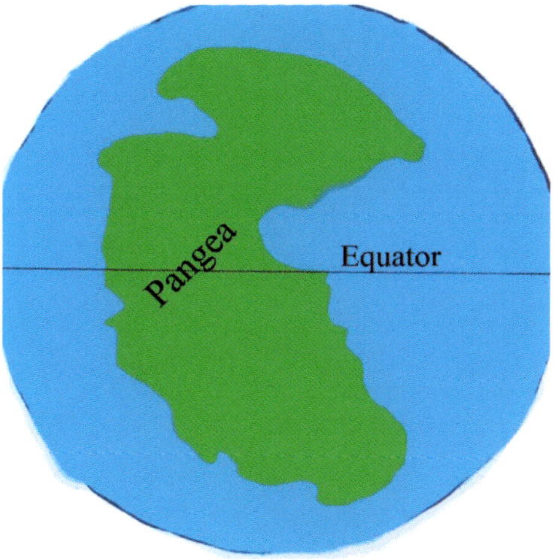

Plate No. 43 Plate Tectonics.

A very rough guide to show how the continents of the earth were formed by plate tectonics.

By about 155 million years ago Pangea had separated into two supercontinents known as Gondwana in the Southern Hemisphere, and Laurasia (also named Laurentia by some authorities) in the Northern Hemisphere. By this time, the dinosaurs had already evolved and the early birds, such as Archaeopteryx and Archaeornithura, had begun to evolve from the small feathered therapod dinosaurs.

Gondwana later separated into the major continents of the Southern Hemisphere. However, before this occurred, the first major group of extant birds were evolving around this time. These were the large flightless birds known as ratites (ostriches, emus, rheas, cassowaries and kiwis), which had evolved in Gondwana, and some were travelling on the drifting land masses which went on to form the different continents of the Southern Hemisphere: South America, Africa, Antarctica and greater Australia (then including New Zealand). Consequently, the fossils of those ratite birds are found in all of these emerging continents; even in Antarctica there are fossils of the ostrich.

In due course, part of the African land mass split off to drift across the Indian Ocean. This drifting land mass later collided with the southern part of Asia, pushing up land to form the Himalayas, and so formed the Indian continent (today's Pakistan, India and Bangladesh).

Lastly, as illustrated above, the supercontinent of Laurasia subsequently separated into the continents of North America and the supercontinent of Eurasia, eventually to form Europe and Asia.

The above explanation is only a very rough outline, to place the discussions within this book into some type of context; if the reader wants more exact information, an easily accessible source is Wikipedia, the internet encyclopaedia. The theory of continental drift is important in relation to the evolution of the birds because it was taking place both during, and before, the time when the birds were starting to evolve from the dinosaurs.

It should be remembered that the various continents were not all formed at precisely the same time. Most early birds probably evolved in Gondwanaland around 100 million years ago, but a few species may have evolved in Gondwanaland in the south, and then subscquently populated the northern land mass of Laurasia after its formation, because they could fly or swim. Moreover, some birds may have established migration patterns, as illustrated in Plate 14 in Chapter 4, before the supercontinents drifted apart. It is to be noted that the general direction of these migratory patterns is north to south and vice versa, following the alternating seasonal weather patterns between north and south parts of the globe. The ancestors of the migrating birds such as terns, Manx shearwater, geese, swifts, storks and others, were originally nesting and rearing their young in those regions of the supercontinent during the summer months when these places had a plentiful food supply of insects and their larvae and newly growing plants. After the gradual continental separation, the birds continued to migrate (possibly across dry land), to a more equitable region of the vast land masses in those parts which had a milder climate during the winter. The annual migration of many bird species is, in fact, what they continue to carry out today, long after the continents separated.

It is significant that the Southern Hemisphere has far more extant taxonomic bird families than the Northern Hemisphere, a fact evident to all birdwatchers traveling to different parts of the world. This would indicate that most birds probably evolved in the Southern Hemisphere, in Gondwanaland, after this supercontinent had separated from the northern supercontinent, Laurasia.

Most species of birds, whether in the Northern or Southern Hemispheres, carry the same groups (genera) of parasites and other pathogens, because they were all acquired from their dinosaur ancestors before the major land masses split up.

Some of the prehistoric birds.

Amongst the early birds is the well-known *Archaeopteryx lithographica*, the fossil remains of which were first found in a limestone quarry at Solnhofen in Bavaria, southern Germany in 1860. When the fine-grained limestone was split into thin plates it opened rather like a book, to reveal the fossil of Archaeopteryx encased within its folds.

Since that first discovery, a number of other species within the genus Archaeopteryx, have been found. This bird lived around 150–145 million years ago and was about the size of a modern raven. When examining the fossils of this bird, it has been found to have more features in common with a small Therapod dinosaur than with modern birds. However, the fossils of Archaeopteryx do show definite imprints of flight feathers in the rock in which they were fossilised.

Angela Milner and Stig Walsh (146) have researched the anatomy of the brains of these archaic birds by using endocranial casts and computed tomography (serial X-ray slices.) Their research indicates the presence of a large brain, showing those regions of the inner ear which control balance and which would have been necessary for controlled flight, were well developed. Moreover, Archaeopteryx had excellent eyesight which was important, since, being a carnivore like its ancestors, the animal probably spent most of its time searching for small invertebrate prey on the ground. From examination of the archaeological remains, Archaeopteryx is thought to have been a glider rather than a bird capable of powered flight. It probably spent much of its time perched safely in trees, scanning the ground for suitable prey.

Plate No. 44 An imaginary reconstructed drawing of what Archaeopteryx was thought to have been like in life

The claws the artist has drawn, sticking out from the upper edge of the wing, should be noted. These claws are extensions of the separate 'fingers' of the fore limb which have disappeared through lack of use in modern birds. Like Archaeopteryx, the newly hatched fledglings of today's hoatzin (Opisthocomus hoazin), also known as the stinkbird and a favourite bird of taxonomists, living today in parts of the north east of South America, still retain claws on their wrist bones (carpo-metacarpals.)

Recent research into Archaeopteryx using x-ray spectroscopy, has indicated that the feathers were actually pigmented black near the edges, since black pigment strengthens the feather and that is where most wear takes place, Phillip L. Manning et al (127).

In 2009, Palaeontologists examining the fossil remains of extinct birds in China, discovered 31 distinct genera, Zhonghe Zhou (78). One of these was Gansus, described as a Pterodactyl by Roger Highfield (55). This was a waterfowl-like creature which lived around 120 million years ago, much later than Archaeopteryx. Altogether, five well preserved fossils of this species were discovered in 2006, in the Gansu province of western China. This prehistoric bird could fly, and had webbed feet with a well-developed cnemial crest on the front of the tibia, indicating that it was a foot-propelled diver, rather like today's loon or grebe.

Somewhat later to evolve was Ichthyornis (meaning "fish bird") living 95-85 million years ago, fossils of which have been found in several areas of North America. Since it had a prominent breast bone for the attachment of flight muscles, this bird probably could fly and it was possibly rather like a modern gull, except that it had teeth.

Plate No.45 An artist's impression of Ichthyornis, chasing another prehistoric bird, Apatornis

After these birds had evolved, there came several species of quite large sea birds. An example of these is Hesperornis, which was about two meters in length. The fossils of nine species of these prehistoric birds have been found, which were living in the Late Cretaceous period (83.5–78 million years ago.) They were flightless sea birds without wings, which looked rather like today's Galapagos cormorant. Hesperornis had teeth, rather like some modern sea ducks, the mergansers *(Mergus merganser)*. They also had webbed feet, placed at the back of the body like modern diving birds such as the loons (divers) and the grebes. Consequently, this prehistoric bird dived for fish rather like today's penguins and gannets. The fossils of these birds were found along the shorelines of the seas of the Northern Hemisphere, in modern day Russia and Canada.

Plate No.46 An artist's impression of what Hesperornis may have looked like

Most of the early birds would have perished during the time of the K-Pg catastrophe which was believed to have wiped out most of the dinosaurs. However, at least thirteen of today's classified *orders* of birds evolved *before* the K-Pg catastrophe.

The fish-eating birds would have had a food supply, so they were living together with the dinosaurs and would have been subject to the same parasites and infectious diseases as were the dinosaurs. All these infectious pathogens would have been passed on to today's birds.

When considering the number of different families of birds living today, as has been stated above, the majority are to be found in the Southern Hemisphere. It follows, therefore, that the ancestors of these birds must have found some way to have survived the global winter, caused by the collision of the asteroid with the earth. It should be remembered that not all the dinosaurs were large, some were quite small, and it may have been the case that many of the small dinosaurs did not survive as such, because they could not compete with the evolution of the carnivorous mammals: the dinosaur hatchlings would not be able to compete with the evolving, more active, mammalian young. However, clearly *some* of the very small dinosaurs *did* escape the emerging carnivorous mammals, by evolving into birds and either taking to the trees, or by being able to run faster than the less athletic mammals of that time.

By way of contrast, an emerging branch of very large, carnivorous, flightless birds started to evolve in what is now, South America, about 62 million years ago, just after the K-Pg boundary. These birds were the Phorusrhacids, or terror birds, and were for some time top predators, with some standing nearly 9ft tall, and able to search and devour some smaller, developing mammals such as the very early, dog-sized, forest-dwelling ancestors of the modern horse, Eohippus.

Marcel van Tuinen and S. Blair Hedges (52), using molecular clock techniques, estimate the very earliest ancestors of the birds evolved about 125 million years ago, well before the extinction of the dinosaurs during the late Cretaceous period.

Today's ratites comprise the ostriches and their relatives, the Australian emus, three species of cassowary, two species of South American rhea and five species of the smaller kiwi. Kiwis are found only in New Zealand and all are approximately the size of domestic chickens, or smaller, together with the related volant tinamous. Tinamous are a family of birds found in Mexico, Central and South America. Molecular and other studies indicate that the tinamous are most closely related to the extinct moas of New Zealand.

The ratites, except for the kiwis and tinamous, generally tend to look rather like some of the smaller therapod dinosaurs (ornithomimosaurs), with long legs and a long neck. Also, the crest on the head of the cassowary (see Plate No.37), tends to resemble that of some of the dinosaurs, like Oviraptor.

Thc ratites are so called because they have a breastbone which is flat, or raft like. The breastbone, or sternum, is so formed because these flightless birds do not have extensive flight muscles covering their breast. The breast muscles in other birds which do fly, are well developed, with a more extensive surface area for muscle attachment onto the keel of the breastbone. In birds, the muscles enabling the bird to fly, stretch between the breast bone and the bones of the upper part of the wing, which is hinged around the shoulder joint, enabling the bird to flap its' wings and so become airborne.

It is thought that the common ancestor of the ratites may possibly have had wings. However, these were not developed because the birds, being running creatures, did not use them to fly. Because they were not used, these particular muscles, and their bony attachments, became redundant and were eventually lost. This is an evolutionary process rather like that which has happened to some island species of birds, such as the flightless Galapagos cormorant and a number of species of island rails, many of which have now become extinct. The well-known extinct island pigeon, the dodo, which lived on the island of Mauritius, is another example of this phenomenon of atrophy of a body appendage through lack of use.

Most of the different species of ratites are thought to have moved via plate tectonics, drifting on their respective tectonic plates rather like shipwrecked sailors carried on a raft, and they were carried to the different geographical areas in which they are found today. They walked on dry land long before the continents drifted apart. Their fossils are even found in Antarctica, which at one time was connected to the continent of South America and was also, at that time, covered in tropical rainforest. In essence, the continental separation of the different species of today's ratites was a direct result of continental drift. There is however, an alternative theory which suggests that some ratite ancestors, related to the volant tinamous, may have flown to different locations and become secondarily flightless, like the moas of New Zealand.

Today, the ratites are only found in the Southern Hemisphere where they originally evolved. A relatively recently extinct group of large ratites, the elephant birds *(Aepyornis maximus),* which were about 3 metres tall and were heavily built, weighing about half a tonne, lived in North Africa and Madagascar, and were last seen there in about 1650. Similarly, there were the moas of New Zealand. These ratites were about 10ft tall, and probably became extinct about 1500 AD, following the arrival of the Maori people from eastern Polynesia, who arrived on the islands of New Zealand from about 1250 AD. The Maori hunted the moa birds for food, until they became extinct.

Plate No. 47 Model of the extinct Elephant bird (Aepyornis maximus)

Plate No 48 The comparative sizes of three eggs. The egg on the left is a model of an elephant bird's egg, the middle egg is an ostrich egg and the small egg on the right is a typical hen's egg.

Although the plumage of the ostrich is more like (but not the same as), that of other birds, the feathers of some of today's ratite birds, namely the cassowary and the emu, are more like coarse hair, as is that of the kiwi, the much smaller ratite.

Although the ratites are an ancient group of birds, evolving long before all other birds and quite distinct from them, they are still subject to all the same types of infectious organisms and parasites as other birds. This indicates that the organisms causing infectious and parasitic diseases in today's birds, have travelled with the prehistoric birds during their evolution. In fact, as discussed in the previous chapter, all these diseases were present in the dinosaurs. Nevertheless, *some* of the infectious parasites with which the dinosaurs would have been infected, will have been eliminated, along with their hosts, at the time of the K-Pg catastrophe. Other species of parasites however, would have persisted in the smaller birds which had survived, so enabling the pathogens to change and to develop their type of parasitism in the newly evolving birds.

Galloanserae (Fowl)

After the ratites, the next group of evolving birds were the Galloanserae. This group is what Colin Tudge likes to call the 'barnyard birds.' They are rather distantly related to, and distinct from, all other birds. The Galloanserae emerged somewhat later than the ratites from a common ancestor, about 105 million years ago and then split from each other about 87 million years ago, all of which happened before the extinction of the dinosaurs.

Until the emergence of the Galloanserae, all the birds up to that time, namely the ratites and the prehistoric birds, had the palatine bones forming the roof of the mouth and part of the upper jaw, and which were fused to the adjacent parts of the skull. After the time of ratite evolution, the junctions between the bones of the upper jaw and the rest of the skull bones became hinged and more flexible. This evolutionary development was important because the bird was then able to pick up and manipulate smaller pieces of food much more easily.

EPILOGUE

"Prediction is very difficult, especially about the future."

Niels Bohr, Danish Nobel prize winning physicist and philosopher.

Having reached the end of this book, it is to be hoped that the reader has seen that infectious disease of all creatures is just one aspect of life on Earth. All life is constantly evolving, ***so what does the future hold?***

Bacteria, viruses and *some* of the arthropods can change their genomes quite rapidly, so that they can become more, or indeed less, virile. This is because of the rapidity of their reproduction, combined with possible mutation each time they reproduce. However, the more slowly reproducing organisms, which are often neither vectors nor causes of infectious disease, are unlikely to change so rapidly. Consequently, humans, birds and other vertebrate animals are unlikely to see any *entirely new types* of infectious disease affecting them. Despite this, it is predicted that at least two new pathological viruses may emerge *each year* from the many thousands yet to be identified.

As referred to briefly in Chapter 4, an extremely large virus, at least 30% larger than any previously found, and referred to as "Megavirus," was identified by Chantal Abergel et al. in 2011. *Megavirus chilensus* was isolated from a water sample collected in April 2010 off the coast of Chile, near the marine station in Las

Cruces. The researchers baited their culture with a type of amoeba which large viruses are known to invade, and when cultured, the virus infected the amoeba. This virus was large enough to be seen with a normal microscope. Since the discovery of Megavirus, these workers have added further discoveries; the Pandoravirus genus was first announced in a paper in 2013. The Pandoraviruses are twice as large as Megavirus. *Pithovirus sibericum* soon joined the family of giant viruses, in 2014. The 2014 discovery was made when a viable specimen was found in a 30,000-year-old ice core harvested from permafrost in Siberia, Russia. In principle, these viruses do not present any threat to humans, but the search for other viruses, which could also be preserved in the permafrost and some of which could be pathogenic, continues (145), remembering that the first large virus to be found was Mimivirus (Plate No.11 in Chapter 4), it was found in an amoeba and it was pathogenic to humans.

The birds and most other wild animals which evolved long before humans, have, for the most part, been able to "call a truce" in the so called 'arms race' between host and pathogen. That is, animals in general have learned to live with the pathogens. This truce has only been broken when Man has chosen to interfere with the animals' environment, particularly in the case of poultry or intensively farmed cattle and pigs, and especially when the use of antibiotics as growth promoters, has occurred.

We humans, with our superior intelligence, have perhaps been 'too clever by half' or, in other words, as expressed in Aleksandr Ostrovsky's play, there is 'Enough Stupidity in Every Wise Man.'

Doctor Albert Einstein has been quoted as saying "*The world is a dangerous place, not because of those who do evil, but because of those who look on and do nothing.*" It is imperative that the human species recognises that it is privileged to live within an immense ecosystem which supports incalculable biodiversity, that we are relative newcomers to that environment, and as well as our abilities to do tremendous good, we also have the power to do catastrophic damage to that environment. That damage could ultimately not only signal the end of numerous species, as we are already seeing, but indeed the end of our own species, and life on Earth as we know it.

We have been able to develop the wonder drugs we know as antibiotics, together with an increasing variety of antiseptics, agricultural insecticides and selective weed killers. We inject ourselves with an alarming, and growing, number and variety of vaccines, in our efforts to avoid succumbing to infectious disease, despite there being both long-standing, and indeed new, evidence that most vaccines are both ineffective and unsafe.

Because of our increasing desire to "control" our environment, we have *irreversibly* polluted it with a multitude of unforeseen hormone and metabolic modulators. Amongst these are phthalates which are employed in the manufacture of, amongst other things, adhesives and glues, detergents, agricultural adjuvants, building materials, personal-care products and medical devices, including those used in hospital baby units. Phthalates are released into the environment and, due to the ubiquity of plastics in modern life, the vast majority of people are exposed to some level of phthalates. There is also Bisphenol A (BPA), one of the highest volume chemicals produced worldwide, which amongst other uses, is employed in the manufacture of compact discs, drinking water bottles and for lining food beverage cans. BPA can act as an endocrine disruptor by chemically copying the hormone oestrogen, as well as having other harmful effects on the human body. Both chemicals are employed widely in the plastics business, which itself dominates many areas of manufacturing industry today.

In addition, some industrial chemicals may act not only as toxins but *may also have unforeseen epigenetic effects.*

Much of this was predicted by Rachel Carson in her book "Silent Spring" published in 1962. Miss Carson's thesis was mainly aimed at the extensive use of the insecticide DDT, which at the time did extensive environmental damage, being toxic to a wide range of living organisms, not just the insects upon which the birds feed. DDT, or Dichlorodiphenyltrichloroethane, is also toxic to marine animals such as crayfish, water Daphnia, the small crustaceans commonly called fresh water shrimps, and also to marine shrimps, all of which are at the bottom of the food chain. Similarly, DDT is toxic to many species of fish. Birds of prey such as the American bald eagle, the peregrine falcon and the osprey, as well as the brown pelican, all being at the top of the food chain, and feeding mainly on fish, are thus also at great risk from such toxins. The DDT metabolite, DDE, which is fat-soluble and therefore is rarely excreted from the body except in breast milk, acts as an antiandrogen, or blocker of male hormones, in all vertebrates, including humans.

Rachel Carson's theories were subject to a good deal of criticism, particularly from the chemical and pharmaceutical industries, at the time of publication in 1962. The American industrial biochemist Robert White-Stevens, was amongst the most aggressive critics of her work, especially her analysis of DDT. He said that "if man were to follow the teachings of Miss Carson, we would return to the Dark Ages, and the insects and diseases and vermin would once again inherit the earth." Others argued that by helping to restrict the use of DDT, Carson was responsible for many deaths caused by malaria. In fact, far from calling for an outright ban on useful pesticides, she advocated simply for their controlled use, with advice for spraying as little as possible in order to limit the development of resistance.

Although she died in 1964, Rachel Carson's "Silent Spring" is credited with helping to raise public awareness of the consequences of the indiscriminate and excessive use of pesticides, and with the development of the environmental movement. There is no doubt that the effect of her work was profound, and continues to provoke controversy today. Now of course, other methods of tackling malaria have been, and continue to be, developed. The mass spraying of

DDT had to be abandoned, not through environmental concerns, but because the insecticide has lost its ability to kill the mosquitoes. Agricultural spraying of pesticides, it would seem, produces resistance to the pesticide in *as little as seven to ten years*.

Unfortunately, in the 50 or so years since 1962, although the use of DDT is now significantly more restricted, in many other respects the pollution of our environment has got much worse. The vultures in southern Asia, mainly in India and Nepal can be used as a case in point, having declined dramatically in just the last 10–15 years. It has been shown that this may be due to the residues of the veterinary drug Diclofenac in animal carcasses. The farmers in these areas have been using this drug for treating their cattle suffering with mastitis and other inflammatory conditions. Diclofenac is an anti-inflammatory drug, used to reduce swelling and treat pain. In the event that the animals die, their carcasses are habitually left out by the farmers, to be scavenged by vultures, who act as nature's "garbage disposal team." The vultures have then been poisoned by the Diclofenac in the dead animals' tissues.

The decline in numbers of vultures has a further consequence; because the cattle carcasses are not being eaten by the vultures they are then being scavenged by feral dogs, which are known to carry the viral disease rabies. This rise in available food, leads to increased numbers of feral dogs and thus an increased risk of rabies passing to the local human population. More than 95% of human deaths caused by rabies occur in Africa and Asia and there were about 17,400 deaths from this disease worldwide in 2015.

Diclofenac has also been shown to harm freshwater fish species, such as rainbow trout. It seems obvious that this chemical has wide ranging adverse effects on many biological organisms.

In the Western world, Diclofenac is marketed under a large number of trade names (over 100) for human use, some of which do mention a warning of *occasional* side effects. The drug is also still sold for veterinary use in some European countries such as Spain, where there are still vultures feeding on the carcasses of farm animals which die, and are left, outside. To the mind of the author this demonstrates a totally irresponsible attitude on the part of the legislature and the pharmaceutical companies. However, there has lately been a move to have the whole procedure of carcass disposal brought under the control of a registered veterinarian.

Another extensively used chemical, and quite possibly a far more serious problem, is the organophosphorus herbicide glyphosate, the principle active ingredient of the well-known range of weed killers known by the trade name Roundup. Records show that worldwide 9.4 million tons of the chemical has been sprayed on fields – enough to spray nearly half a pound of Roundup on every cultivated acre of land in the world. Globally, glyphosate use has risen almost 15-fold since so-called "Roundup Ready," genetically engineered glyphosate-tolerant crops were introduced in 1996.

This chemical is widely available for purchase and is used not only in agriculture where it is sprayed onto food crops and in orchards, but also quite liberally by some local authorities wishing to control weeds on grass verges, along highways and in other public spaces. It *may* be carcinogenic in humans, a fact highlighted by the International Agency for Research on Cancer, a branch of the World Health Organisation. In August 2018 a jury in the United States found that the chemical had contributed "substantially" to the terminal cancer of a groundskeeper named Dewayne Johnson.

In 2016, several countries such as France, the Netherlands, Denmark and Sweden banned the sale of Roundup for use in gardens and nurseries. Some countries such as El Salvador, Bermuda, Sri Lanka and Colombia have banned the use of glyphosate altogether. The risks posed by this chemical may be very far reaching indeed.

One of the detrimental effects of this chemical might already be becoming clear. The human species faces one of its most serious challenges yet, in the continuing and exponential rise in the numbers of children diagnosed with autism spectrum disorders (ASD), which for many people can mean significant, and lifelong, disability. In 2014 the figures released by the U.S. Centers for Disease Control and Prevention stated that 1 in 59 U.S. children had an autism spectrum disorder, a 15% increase from 1 in 68 two years previously, and a huge increase since 2000, when the figure reported wsa 1 in 150. If the numbers continue to increase at their present rate, according to Doctor Stephanie Seneff, a Senior Research Scientist at the Massachusetts Institute of Technology Computer Science and Artificial Intelligence Laboratory, by 2025 *one in every two* children born in the United States will be diagnosed with ASD, and *80%* of the boys. Of course, the rising numbers of individuals diagnosed with ASD is not just a problem in America, but globally.

It is now largely acknowledged that glyphosate has a serious adverse effect on normal human gut flora, the microbiome, as evidenced by Doctor Stephanie Seneff and her colleagues in numerous scientific papers in peer reviewed journals, by Dr. Thierry Vrain, a former genetic engineer and soil biologist with Agriculture Canada, and many other scientists and medical doctors.

Dr Vrain further states "studies show that proteins produced by engineered plants are different than what they should be. Inserting a gene in a genome using this technology can and does result in damaged proteins. The scientific literature is full of studies showing that engineered corn and soya contain toxic or allergenic proteins."

It would seem that humans continue to use their knowledge and skills to "adjust" nature, in a way that better suits the needs of humans, without properly testing, or worse, even bothering to consider, the potential harm this may do to the biodiversity of our natural world, and to our own species.

Human nature, and human attitudes to the world around us, haven't changed that much. Conservation and rewilding of the environment is a growing force, but is not always viewed positively by those working in industry or even by all politicians. Whilst individuals working for a company may have reservations about that company's policies, it is the company's policies that ensure a profit is made in a competitive market, and which drives the company forward, and keeps those employees in work. Regrettably, the company's chief executives often have little, or no, knowledge of basic biology.

We have been busy destroying tropical rainforests to plant oil palm trees, palm oil being a profitable product used extensively in the cosmetics and food industry, and now the Bank of England has backed the use of palm oil in its new £20 notes, due to be introduced in 2020. In addition, tropical hardwoods are used widely in the Western world as materials in the building and furniture industries.

'Civilised' man, by venturing further into these relatively unexplored and undeveloped habitats of tropical rainforest, has helped to release the viruses of Ebola and other tropical diseases. The cutting down of the rainforests and the construction of roads for logging, has allowed human access deeper into parts of previously untouched areas of rainforest, which support abundant wildlife including chimpanzee and gorilla populations, as well as various kinds of monkeys, bats, pangolins, rodents, and deer. Ebola is introduced into the human population through close contact with the blood, secretions, organs or other bodily fluids of infected animals such as these, found ill or dead in the rainforest. The hunting, butchering and processing of this "bushmeat," which is an essential protein source for many rural West Africans, and is also considered part of their cultural heritage, has been blamed by some for the Ebola virus outbreak and epidemic in 2013-16. There is evidence to show that the better off occupants of the areas affected continued their consumption of bushmeat during the outbreak, whilst those with fewer resources significantly reduced theirs. "Eco tourism" and people illegally bringing home to Western countries, dried bushmeat acquired whilst in Africa and Asia, have also been blamed for spreading disease.

We are becoming increasingly aware of the damaging pollution of our seas and oceans with the tons of plastic which humans produce, use and then discard. A recent study estimated that around **eight million** metric tons of our plastic waste enter the oceans from land each year, and this is in addition to the other land based sources of pollution, which include oil and runoff flowing into the sea from the land, containing agricultural pesticides and fertilizers. Over 90% of all seabirds have plastic pieces in their stomachs, and micro and nanoparticles of plastic are being found in the oceans' fish, and are thereby entering the human food chain. A recent report also stated that not only are the overall total numbers of fish in the seas declining, but the numbers of *old* fish are also falling disproportionately: this is important because older fish tend to be larger, produce more offspring and are more flexible in their behaviour and so can adapt to changes in their environment more quickly.

These potentially harmful consequences of our complex modern industrial technology are driven, not by altruistic motives, but mostly by the profit motives of capitalism and the enterprise economy.

Formalised medical knowledge, which started in ancient times in Babylon, then passed to Egypt, India and China, all began with close observation of the patient. Medical wisdom has changed significantly over time, and not merely with regard to the types of treatment available. The original desire to heal the sick was accompanied by both a keen investigation into the immediate history of the patient and close observation of their symptoms, followed by the application of first principles in order to achieve a successful outcome, and recovery. There were the Ancient Greeks, such as Hippocrates, the "father of modern medicine," and after whom the Hippocratic oath, which is taken by all doctors of human medicine, was named. Whilst the phrase "do no harm" does not actually appear in the original oath, the Latin equivalent of the phrase "I will utterly reject harm" does, and it is arguable whether this remains one of the major principles of modern medicine today.

Galen, another Greek, working within the Roman Empire and spending four years as physician to the gladiators, correctly recognised that observation is key, and that there is a methodological difference between taking account of the patient in front of you, in all of the patient's particularity, and viewing the patient in front of you as simply representing an *instance* of a general rule of biomedical science. The term "galenicals" is still used, to mean a medicine made of natural, rather than synthetic components.

During the Middle Ages, Paracelsus was a Swiss physician and a pioneer in several aspects of the "medical revolution" of the Renaissance, emphasizing the value of observation when used in combination with received wisdom.

In the more recent past some of the great advances in medicine were made by scientists conducting and *observing* the results of experiments, such as Louis Pasteur, and Robert Koch, both of whom advanced our knowledge of bacteriology.

These discoveries, together with those of penicillin by Alexander Fleming and, much more recently, DNA by Francis Crick and Robert Watson, were carried out in academic institutions, such as universities. Nowadays, the universities have tended to become largely commercial businesses, needing to demonstrate their newsworthy research in order to attract investment and funds to build 'factories' for turning out ever increasing numbers of graduates.

Moreover, modern medical students, and to some extent veterinary students, leave university having been trained systematically *not* to think for themselves from first principles, but to act more like cogs in a machine, "matching" the symptoms described by their patients, or the owners of their patients in the case of veterinary practice, to the latest pharmaceutical drugs listed in their computer programmes. This is something which Suzanne Humphries M.D. discusses at length in her book "Rising from the Dead." In fact, the current British General Medical Council's Good Medical Practice contains only the rather general requirement "where necessary, examine the patient."

However, there are many, more positive, aspects of our modern world. Homo sapiens' intelligence has enabled us to develop computer algorithms to more accurately predict the diagnosis of most infectious disease. Since both bacteria and viruses have smaller genomes than humans and other animals, it is now possible for medical technicians using traditional culture methods for bacteria, to rapidly identify the most appropriate antibiotics and other anti-pathogenic drugs. There are now automated overnight desktop DNA sequencing machines and even miniature machines using solar energy concentrated by a lens for use in the field, both of which can rapidly detect the specific genomes of pathogenic bacteria and viruses.

More recently, fluorescent paper-based synthetic materials, acting rather like the long-established litmus paper, have also been developed for the much quicker diagnosis and differentiation of groups of micro pathogens, Keith Pardee et al (141).

Information technology has greatly increased global communication between scientists. The Bioinformatics Resource Centers (BRCs) are a group of five internet-based research centres established in 2004 and funded by NIAID, the USA's National Institute of Allergy and Infectious Diseases, which monitors the emergence of outbreaks of global infectious disease.

During the lifetime of the author, all medicine, both human and veterinary, has made huge advances in the understanding of the nature of disease both infectious and genetic. As Winston Churchill said, in a worldwide broadcast on February 9th 1941, when asking for the support of the United States in the Second World War, "give us the tools, and we will finish the job." With all the great advances in knowledge, we do now have the tools to deal with infectious disease, *but will the human race use these tools wisely?*

Humans have not changed their basic human nature which seems to be hard wired into their brains. As Desmond Morris, has said "the human species is still an aggressive, violent animal capable of extraordinary brutality." However, the fast-developing science of epigenetics may enable the human race to adjust personalities, possibly using suitably designed 'pills' or even vaccines. However, there continues to be considerable opposition to anything which would be considered genetic engineering, and perhaps we should be cautious, because who would be the "right" humans to make decisions about how other humans behave, think and feel? So, can we survive on this planet and not commit virtual suicide?

We are a very specialized species of animal, distinct from all other animals because of the development of our brains. This has enabled us to think and to explore the universe around us, so that humans are now developing methods of travelling in space, with man landing on the moon in 1969, and then achieving the first successful landing of a module onto a comet over 300 million miles away, in 2014.

Another feature of the human brain is that humans have become very creative creatures, able to produce fascinating and inspiring works of art, literature and music.

Many religious leaders, gurus, sages, imams, mullahs and prophets have tried, and still try, to encourage us to accept a particular religious belief system. Sometimes this is an attempt to guide us along a path of tolerance, with less aggression, less acquisitiveness and the ability to live together. Unfortunately, their proselytizing sometimes becomes so twisted that some attempt to create a theocracy, controlled by those same holy men (and they are mostly men) and their particular beliefs, to the exclusion of all other belief systems. Often it would seem that these extreme religious teachings adversely influence the maturing brains of the susceptible young male (and occasionally female) Homo sapiens, ultimately resulting in increased aggression between members of differing belief systems.

This point of view has been elegantly illustrated by several authors amongst whom are HRH Prince Salma bin Hamad Al-Khalifa Crown Prince of Bahrain, writing in the Daily Telegraph, in February 2016 when he declared that "it is only through a concerted, collective and fundamental review of the nature of our threat that we will help refine the focus of our challenge and thereby bring us closer to achieving our shared goal. We can then strategically use our combined resources to hold accountable these criminal ideologues who place themselves above other ordinary human beings and claim divine authority for misrule." The 1993 book "Islamic Fundamentalism: The New Global Threat" by Mohammad Mohaddessin, traces the history of this religious movement in Iran, and explains how the basic tenets of Islam were distorted by the leaders of that country, and the dire effects of fundamentalism fed by the frenzy of the ayatollahs. Other authors, coming to similar conclusions include Karen Armstrong (once a catholic nun) in her book "Fields of Blood: Religion and the History of Violence," where she examines the impulse toward violence in each of the world's great religions. Also, Jonathan Sacks, the former Chief Rabbi, and author of "Not in God's Name: Confronting Religious Violence" and Jared Diamond, writing in his two books "Guns, Germs and Steel: The Fates of Human Societies" and "The Third Chimpanzee: The Evolution and Future of the Human Animal", provide further food for thought on this wide subject.

If the human species is to survive, it is clear that the time for these types of tribalism has passed, and that moves towards greater cooperation, which are slowly taking place, need to progress, urgently. The threat to our survival as a species, and the survival of all other living creatures, will come, not as people seem to fear, from new viruses and other infectious organisms causing pandemics, but from Man himself, the most dangerous of all the animals.

APPENDIX

Taxonomy chart:

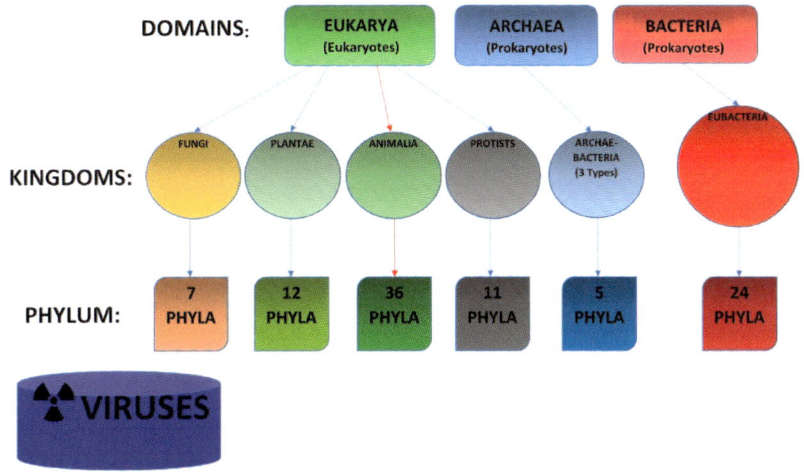

Taxonomy diagram – how the Red Kite is classified:

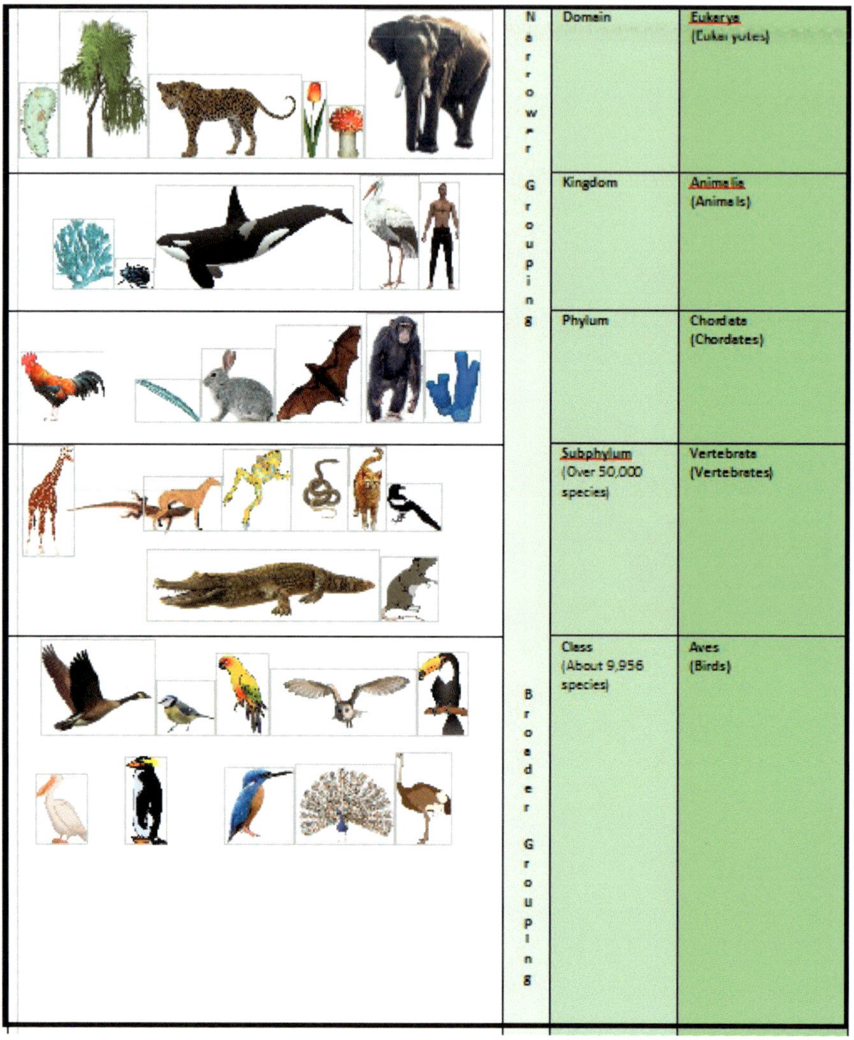

Narrower Grouping
Broader Grouping
Domain
Eukarya
(Eukaryotes)
Kingdom
Animalia
(Animals)
Phylum
Chordata
(Chordates)
Subphylum
(Over 50,000 species)
Vertebrata
(Vertebrates)
Class
(About 9,956 species)
Aves
(Birds)

		Order (About 265 species)	Accipitriformes (Most of the diurnal birds of prey)
		Family (255 species)	Accipitradae (Eagles, hawks and kites)
		Genus (3 or 4 species)	Milvus (Kites)
		Species	Milvus (Red kite)

GLOSSARY

Aids: A human viral disease causing **A**cquired **I**mmune **D**eficiency to many infectious diseases. The virus reduces the effectiveness of the patient's immune defences.

Algae: A general term describing a group of single or multicellular photosynthetic organisms. The multicellular algae include some giant seaweeds. Algae are often aquatic and, unlike typical plants they are simple in structure in not having well defined parts such as leaves, a stem or roots.

Allopatric: Species of organisms occurring in separate, non-overlapping geographic areas.

Amino Acid: A complex organic molecule containing an amine group (NH2) attached to an acid carboxyl group (COOH); [amine +acid]. They also have a side chain of atoms that varies with different amino acids. Amino acids contain the key basic elements of carbon, hydrogen, oxygen, and nitrogen. They are important biological precursors of proteins and other biological chemicals such as histamine, thyroxine, adrenalin, serotonin and the purines.

Amphibia: A class of vertebrate animals comprising frogs, toads, newts, salamanders and the caecilians (the smaller species of the caecilians look rather like worms, whilst the larger species look like snakes.) Some amphibians spend time on land but all return to water to breed. They all have a moist skin permeable to water and gases, such as oxygen.

Angiosperms: The seed-bearing flowering plants. Their reproductive organs are formed in their flowers, which attract insects and birds acting as the plant's pollinators. After pollination of the ovary, which goes on to form the seeds, sometimes the fleshy outer covering of the seeds develops into a fruit such as an apple or a plum.

Appendix: A small, blind ended tube or pouch attached to the caecum at the junction between the small and large intestine in humans. Almost a vestigial organ in humans but is important and larger in many other vertebrate animals. In all animals, it is possibly a depot of beneficial organisms ("good bugs.")

Archaea: A group of single-celled micro-organisms which have no cell nucleus or any other membrane-bound internal structures. They were originally called archaebacteria since they are similar in size, and also look like, the true bacteria or prokaryotes. Archaea were not recognised as a distinct group until 1977.

Archosauria/Archosaurs: The common ancestor of the dinosaurs, the birds and the crocodiles.

Arthropods: A very diverse group of animals without a vertebral column of back bones i.e. they are invertebrates. They include such creatures as insects, mites, ticks, spiders and crustaceans including crabs and barnacles.

They have an external skeleton made of chitin (a rigid polysaccharide), to support the body tissues which is jointed, rather like a suit of plate armour used by medieval knights.

ATP: energy transport system: Adenosine triphosphate is the main energy -carrying chemical intermediate molecule for many metabolic reactions taking place within all biological cell systems. It is involved in muscle cell contraction, in the transmission of nervous impulses, in the production of digestive enzymes, for example. Energy is released when the ATP molecule is converted back into one of its precursors, such as Adenosine diphosphate (ADP) or further back into Adenosine monophosphate (AMP).

Biochemical Bases: Bases, in physical chemistry terms, are chemicals such as alkalis which neutralize acids. Biochemical bases are more complex molecules which form heterocyclic rings containing nitrogen, and are classified into two types of chemicals called purines and pyrimidines. Both of these are used in the formation of the nucleotide bases and nitrogenous bases respectively, which form the essential parts of DNA and RNA. The four main nucleotide bases are cytosine, guanine, adenine (these three are found in both DNA and RNA) and thymine. Thymine is found only in DNA, and in RNA the thymine is replaced by uracil. The above nucleotide bases are abbreviated as C, G, A, T, and U, respectively. They are usually simply called bases in the context of genetics.

Biomass: The total amount of life or living organisms, both plant and animal within a defined region, for example the mud of an estuary, or a defined area of forest.

Biota: The total collection of animal and plant life of a geographic region.

Binary fission: Often spoken of as prokaryotic fission, the process results in the production of two living prokaryotic cells by the division of the original cell into two daughter cells. Each of the daughter cells contains a complete copy of the original chromosome, and thus has the potential to grow to the size of the original cell.

Bipolar disorder: Manic–depressive disorder of the human mind in which an elevated "excited" stage, which is known as mania, swings back to an opposite mood of depression. The signs and symptoms vary greatly between individuals. This mental abnormality should not be confused with schizophrenia or split personality. This is a serious psychiatric condition.

Bumblefoot: The formation of an abscess in the 'ball' of the foot of a bird often causing the whole foot, and sometimes the leg, to swell.

Burgess Shale: A scree slope in the Canadian Rocky Mountains in British Columbia composed of mud stone (geologically compressed mud). In this shale, an American palaeontologist Charles Walcott found, in 1909, a great variety of fossils, being the imprints of soft bodied creatures dating from the Cambrian geological period. Altogether, some 65,000 specimens of extinct creatures have now been found in this geological formation.

Cambrian (the): The geological period lasting from 540-488 million years ago. During this time, many of the phyla of the multicellular animals first evolved. This was made evident by the large number of fossils found in the rocks of this geological period.

CD4 Helper T Lymphocytes: These are a subgroup of those white blood cells known as lymphocytes, which are an important part of an animal's immune system. Helper T lymphocytes cannot themselves kill pathogens such as bacteria, but they do help other white blood cells, such as the phagocytes and the macrophages, to do this. The helper T cells do this via their CD4 proteins on their cell surface.

Chitin: A long chain polysaccharide molecule made from repeated subunits and derived from glucose. Chitin is tough, rather leathery and often strengthened with a mineral such as calcium carbonate. Found widely as a skeletal material in the animal and fungal kingdoms.

Chordates: That group (Phylum) of animals which have a cartilaginous semi-rigid skeletal rod, the notochord. This encloses the main trunk nerve from the brain, situated at the front (anterior) end of the animal, running along the dorsal (back) of the animal's body. The chordates include the vertebrates, in which the cartilage has become mineralised and changed into bone. All chordates have, at least at some stage of their development, pharyngeal gill clefts or slits.

Clade: A group of organisms which share common characteristics and all originate from a common ancestor (the most recent common ancestor), for example, all birds have feathers. In other words, a clade is a single "branch" on the "tree of life". The whole array can be set out as a cladogram.

Cladistics: The classification of organisms which makes use of lines of descent only.

Chloroplast: These are biochemical organelles found in green plants (often but not exclusively, in the leaves) and are also found in algae. Chloroplasts capture solar energy as photons (packets of solar energy) that carry out photosynthesis. This is a chemical process in which carbon dioxide in the atmosphere is taken in by the plant, as well as water from the roots and, together with other chemicals in solution, produces sugars and other food storage substances. Chloroplasts act rather like solar panels.

Classification (biological): See Taxonomy below

Cnemial crest: A ridge of bone found projecting from the upper end and running down the front surface of the tibia or shin bone. It occurs in mammals, birds, some reptiles and the dinosaurs. To it are attached the muscles for extending or straightening the knee joint.

Covert feathers: Those feathers which cover the quill of other feathers such as the flight feathers and other body covering feathers. Covert feathers help to smooth the air flow over the body of a bird in flight.

Cretaceous/Tertiary (K/T) or K-Pg boundary: A geological time line, dated to circa.65.5 ± 0.3 million years ago. K is the traditional abbreviation for the Cretaceous period (142-65.5 million years ago), and T is the abbreviation for the Tertiary period (65-2.6 million years ago.) The term "Tertiary period" is now a rather defunct term, used in past geological terminology. However the term "(K/T) boundary" or "K-Pg catastrophe" is still used when referring to the actual time of the mass extinction of most of the earth's living creatures. Most importantly this was the time when most of the dinosaurs were wiped out.

Commensalism: The association of two organisms of different species living together, where only one of the two partners benefit. (Commensal: a non- harmful coexistence.)

Computed tomography: X-ray computed tomography (CT). This is a method of X-ray photography using a computer to generate a series of layered images, or slices, around a single axis so as to produce a final, three dimensional, image and so 'see inside' the patient.

Coprophagia: To eat faeces or "dung."

Cyanobacteria: A phylum of bacteria known as blue green bacteria. Sometimes also known as blue green algae, however they are not algae but bacteria. They are believed to have been responsible for the conversion of the earth's ancient atmosphere, which was dominated by carbon dioxide, to become oxygenated. After this, the present day oxygenated atmosphere was able to support life as we know it today. Oxygenation occurred when the cyanobacteria entered the plants to form chloroplasts, thereby enabling the plants to carry out photosynthesis. However, some species of cyanobacteria can form part of an 'algal bloom' on expanses of eutrophic water when there is an increased nutrient content caused by run off, often from fertilised agricultural land. The increased nutrient is often phosphate-containing, and results in an extensive area of the static water becoming covered with a continuous, usually green, but occasionally brown or red, film of the 'algae.' At the same time, these blue green bacteria produce a variety of poisons (often neurotoxins) which result in the poisoning of animals, sometimes causing death.

Cyto: A prefix used in biological terms referring to the cell or cells.

Cytoplasm: The cytoplasm is that gel-like part of a cell containing all the organelles e.g. mitochondria, chloroplasts and Golgi apparatus, plus other intra structures of the cell, and in which the whole is enclosed, like the contents of a plastic bag, within the cell membrane. In prokaryote organisms such as bacteria (which lack a cell nucleus), the whole of the organism is contained within the cytoplasm. In the cells of the more advanced eukaryote organisms, which have a nuclear membrane, the contents of the cell nucleus, referred to as the nucleoplasm, are separated from the cytoplasm.

DNA: This comprises a very long double chain of molecules which are formed into a spiral. Each twist of this spiral is made of pairs of molecules called nucleotides. Each member of the pair is linked to its partner by a hydrogen atom. The backbone holding the chain together and forming the twist of the helix is composed of the sugar-phosphate molecules of deoxyribonucleic acid (DNA.)

Dorsal root ganglion: A nodule of nerve cells, or neurons, which are situated at the sides of the spinal cord, where the sensory nerves from the rest of the body enter the spinal cord.

Ediacaran: A geological period named after the Ediacaran hills of South Australia. It is the last geological period 630-542 million years ago immediately preceding the Cambrian period.

Endosymbiosis: The process by which a living organism (usually a prokaryote) comes to live within the cells of another living organism to the mutual advantage of both organisms. This is Illustrated by blue-green bacteria entering plant cells to become chloroplasts, and by mitochondria entering animal cells to become energy generators, both of which were originally free living. Another example is the nitrogen fixing bacteria, called Rhizobia, which live in root nodules of leguminous plants such as peas, beans, lupins and clovers.

Eosinophilic meningitis: A type of meningitis, or inflammation of the membranes covering the brain, showing a predominance of eosinophils (a type of white blood cell) in the cerebral spinal fluid. This type of meningitis is often caused by a parasitic infection.

Epizootic: An outbreak of infectious disease among animals, as distinct from an epidemic which is an outbreak of disease amongst humans.

Epiornitic: An outbreak of infectious disease confined to birds.

Era of geological time: An **Era** is measured in periods of about two hundred million years. Each Era is again divided into shorter **Periods** of geological time of several tens of millions of years, and these again are subdivided into **epochs** of about 10 million years each. For further information the reader is directed to the International Commission on Stratigraphy (www.stratigraphy.org)

Enzyme: A biological catalyst which helps or guides a biological reaction between two molecules, or helps a biochemical reaction to increase or decrease its' rate of reaction.

Eukaryotes : One of the four domains or super kingdoms within which all living organisms are classified These are; (1) the Eukaryotes, (2) the Bacteria (c.f. Prokaryotes) (3) the Fungi and (4) the Archaea.

The Eukaryotes have a cyto (within the cytoplasm) skeleton of microtubes and they have membrane bound organelles, such as mitochondria, chloroplasts and Golgi apparatus. Moreover Eukaryotes have a membrane-bound nucleus containing their DNA. This is compacted by histones into chromosomes. The histones act as spools around which DNA winds. The compaction enables the large genomes of the Eukaryotes to fit inside cell nuclei. The compacted molecule of DNA is 40,000 times shorter than an unpacked molecule.

Facultive anaerobe (eg. bacteria): an organism that makes ATP by **aerobic** respiration if oxygen is present, but is capable of switching to fermentation or **anaerobic** respiration if oxygen is absent. An obligate **aerobe**, by contrast, cannot make ATP in the absence of oxygen, and obligate **anaerobes** die in the presence of oxygen.

Family (regarding classification): A taxonomic Family is a group of related genera.

Flagella: A whip-like extension of the cellular membrane of either a prokaryotic cell (bacterium) or a eukaryotic cell (such as trypanosomes) which is used to move the cell forward.

Filial worms: A type of parasitic nematode (roundworm), the larvae of which are called microfilariae, which lives in the bloodstream of the host. They are transmitted by black flies and mosquitoes. They are found in many animals including humans and birds.

Galliformes: This a taxonomic group of birds containing turkeys, chickens, grouse, quails and pheasants. Also commonly referred to as the gallinaceous birds.

Gamete (formed from a gametocyte): A reproductive cell, either male (e.g. sperm) or female (e.g. egg), which contains half the (haploid) number of chromosomes, so containing only half the genetic information of a mature individual organism. When two gametes combine they fuse to form a zygote, which then contains the diploid or complete number of chromosomes.

Genome: This is the entirety of an organism's hereditary information. It is encoded either in the genes formed from DNA or alternatively, for many types of virus, in RNA.

Genus: A taxonomic group of organisms grouped together as closely related species which have common characteristics, such as a similar body form, and are distinct from those species in other genera. This relationship is rather like human cousins, as distinct from siblings. Sometimes members of a genus can breed together but they do not produce fertile offspring, e.g. lions and tigers can breed together to produce ligers (male lion combined with female tiger) or tigons (male tiger mated with a female lion) both of which are infertile. However dogs, wolves, coyotes and jackals all belong to the genus Canis, can interbreed and can produce fertile offspring.

Gland: A single cell or an organised group of cells formed into a structure to produce and secrete such substances as hormones, digestive juices containing enzymes, mucus or saliva.

Gymnosperms: The early evolved seed-bearing woody plants in which the seeds are not enclosed within an ovary but are typically borne on the surface of specialised leaves called sporophylls. These combine together to form the typical fir cone. Sporophylls carry on their surface the sporangia producing spores for reproduction. Such trees are the various species of conifers, the cyclades and the ginkgo or maidenhair trees.

Helminth: A parasitic worm.

Heterozygote/homozygote: A homozygous individual has the two alleles or genes controlling a certain trait such as shape e.g. erect or floppy ears (one from each of the gametes that fuse during fertilization.) In the heterozygous individual the two genes are not the same, but are alternatives. One such gene of the alternatives, for instance black, may be dominant over the gene expressing white or red colour.

Histopathology: The microscopic examination of tissue looking for the manifestation of disease.

HIV: Human **I**mmunodeficiency **V**irus. See AIDS above.

Horizontal gene transfer: Also called lateral gene transfer. This usually, but not exclusively, occurs amongst the more lowly evolved organisms such as bacteria or other prokaryotes. It is the incorporation of genetic material into the genome from one individual creature into that of another individual to which it may not be related. This type of transfer of the genetic material takes place other than by the normal processes of vertical reproduction from parent to offspring. It is usually carried out by plasmids, distinct small collections of genes. It is best illustrated by antibiotic resistance being passed from one bacterium such as E.coli to another, unrelated, bacterium such as salmonella via a plasmid, carrying the necessary genes, passing straight through adjacent cell walls of the two different bacteria.

Hydrogen Sulphide: Chemically signified as H2S, this is produced by the sulphur-reducing bacteria which get their sources of energy by combining elemental sulphur with hydrogen, to produce hydrogen sulphide which is characterised by its rotten egg smell.

ICTV: The International Committee for the taxonomy of viruses.

Immuno–compromised: An individual in which their immune system is unable to efficiently combat the organisms of an infectious disease.

Ion (Chemical): An atom or molecule in which the total number of electrons surrounding the nucleus does not equal the number of protons in the nucleus and so the ion may be positively or negatively charged.

Kingdom: A term used at one time in the classification of living organisms, such as the kingdom of animals or the kingdom of plants.This was replaced in the 1990's by the evolutionary biologist Carl Woese who introduced the three-domain system of taxonomy in which the term kingdom is subordinated to the term Domain

K-Pg catastrophe: See above under Cretaceous.

Lymphocytes: See above under CD4 Helper Lymphocytes

Magma: Magma is a mixture of molten rock, composed of both solids and gasses, which wells up from a rupture in the Earth's crust, exposing and releasing the semi-solid mantle surrounding the centre of Planet earth as larva, during a volcanic eruption.

Macrophage: (Greek: big eater) A type of white blood cell that engulfs and digests cellular debris, foreign substances and microbes.

Meiosis: This a particular type of cell division which takes place in those cells of the reproductive organs which are producing reproductive cells or Gametes. This type of cell division only takes places in eukaryotes such as multicellular animals, plants and fungi.

Melanosomes: Specialized parts of animal cells which manufacture and store the dark coloured pigment melanin. This is a common light absorbing substance which helps protect the rest of the skin from ultraviolet light and sunburn. They are also contained in the retina of the mammalian eye. In some lower animals such as fish, melanosomes are involved in colour changes of the skin.

Metabolism, metabolic rate: This is the sum total of all of the chemical processes fundamental to all living organisms. These chemical reactions produce heat and energy which is needed to maintain life and the living processes such as growth, respiration and reproduction. The metabolic rate, or speed at which these chemical reactions take place, differs amongst different species and different organisms. It may even differ amongst individual members of the same species. There are warm blooded animals such as mammals and birds, and cold blooded animals such as reptiles, frogs and insects. The latter have a slower metabolic rate and so are generating less heat within their bodies, consequently these creatures often have to warm up in sunlight before they can become active.

Metabolites: These are the individual chemical substances involved in the process of metabolism.

Metamorphosis: In biological terms, the change from one body form into another. This occurs in pupation when a caterpillar turns into a butterfly, or a maggot changes into a fly. Also, metamorphosis takes place when the tadpole of a frog changes into a frog.

Metazoan: These are the multicellular animal creatures. Their many cells are organised into groups which go to form tissues, and these then group together to form specific organs.

Molecular clock: A method of estimating how long it has taken two distinct species to separate from their common ancestor. The technique depends on measuring the number of mutations in a defined length of DNA. This method depends on knowing that the rate of unselected nucleotide change (i.e. mutations), is directly proportional to the time elapsed if the measurements are restricted to specific sections of DNA; a bit like comparing two similar bar codes and seeing how these have changed over a specific period of time. Consequently, counting the number of mutations in a particular section of DNA in two allied creatures, gives an estimate of the rate of speciation; that is, how their genomes have come to differ from each other in order for them to have become separate species, and incompatible breeders.

Molecular (DNA) taxonomy: The comparison of different living creatures by seeing how their DNA is sequentially arranged along the length of each particular gene. This sequential arrangement will differ between each gene, occurring at the same location in each chromosome, so that the changes occurring by mutation will result in a slightly different living organism, or, in other words, a different species. The technique is also known as molecular phylogenetics or molecular systematics. It is the analysis of DNA sequences, to gain information on an organism's evolutionary relationships.

Mya: An acronym for millions of years ago.

MRSA: Methicillin-resistant Staphylococcus aureus. This is, in fact, a 'strain' of Staphyloccus aureus bacteria which has developed a resistance, by mutation, to the beta-lactam group of antibiotics, which are the more advanced penicillins and also the cephalospsorins.

Mucosal surface or lining: The surface layer of cells of many tubular organs in the animal body such as the gut, the respiratory or the urinary tracks which is composed of cells some of which secrete mucus.

Nucleic acid: A very large linear molecule containing the chemical elements of carbon, hydrogen, nitrogen and phosphorus which, on hydrolysis, break down yielding nucleotides and nucleosides. Nucleic acid is an essential component of all living things.

Nucleoid: In a prokaryote organism (e.g. bacterium) this is the genetic material, rather like a single chromosome of the more advanced creatures, but it is not enclosed within a nuclear membrane.

Neuron: A nerve cell.

Obligate parasite: These parasites cannot reproduce independently of their host: they are "obliged" to their host for their reproduction. Intracellular obligate parasites are parasitic microorganisms that are only able to grow and reproduce inside the cells of their host. Examples are the viruses and some bacteria, such as Chlamydophila (causing psittacosis), Rickettsia and the malarial organisms. An example in a larger organism is the cuckoo, which lays its eggs in the nest of another bird, and the cuckoo's eggs are incubated, and their fledgings reared, in the nest of the bird they parasitize.

Ontogeny: The study of the stage by stage development of the fertilised egg, through the development of the embryo to the adult organism.

Passerines; birds of the taxonomic order, or rank, of birds called Passeriformes, containing more than half of all living species of birds. These small to medium sized perching birds have their grasping feet adapted for clinging onto branches, reeds and the like. The feet have three toes pointing forward and one toe pointing backward. The group includes all those birds with an ability to communicate with each other by singing, and consequently are sometimes called songbirds. They are mostly seed-eating birds but the shrikes, crows, magpies and ravens are also included in this order although they do not communicate with each other by singing.

PCBs (polychlorinated biphenyls): Industrial chemicals or products, widely used as dielectric (insulating) material and coolant fluids, in transformers, capacitors, and electric motors. A persistent environmental pollutant and endocrine disruptor, also causing types of cancer and acute die-off in some birds.

Periods of Geological time: From the time when the planet Earth was first formed, layers of rock have condensed and sequentially been eroded by water and the weather from the earliest times until today. Each of these layers (stratigraphically) has been found to have been formed at a particular period of time and provides a system of chronological measurement used as a reference by geologists and palaeontologists. By way of example, the Cambrian period corresponds to the geological time period from 542 $\pm$ 0.3 mya (million years ago) to 488.3 $\pm$ 1.7 mya, when early life on earth was first recognised as fossils.

Phenotype: The visible, or otherwise measurable, physical (morphological), or biochemical and physiological characteristics or traits of a particular organism. This results from the organism's interaction between its genotype and the environment, and is what distinguishes it from other organisms.

Phylum (plur. phyla) : Related to the classification of animal and plant organisms and forming a large group or rank of organisms, all constructed on a common plan. For example, the Chordates, The Platyhelminthes and the Arthropods. Phylum is the taxonomic rank subordinate to a Kingdom of living organisms, which in turn is now subordinated to Domain. See **Taxonomy** below.

Physiology: How an animal or plant works. How the heart, liver, kidneys, reproductive organs or immune system functions.

Plasmid: A small, separate length of DNA which replicates independently of the single nucleoid chromosome in prokaryotic organisms, such as bacteria and yeasts. They sometimes carry genes which provide resistance to antibiotics.

Polymer: A large molecule (a macromolecule), often composed of repeating structural units.

Polymerase: An enzyme, the primary function of which is the polymerization, or building of complex molecules called polymers, from the less complex molecules. In biology, the more simple molecules are the nucleotides (building blocks of life), which are formed into new lengths of DNA or RNA by using an existing DNA or RNA template. The enzyme adds extra deoxyribonucleotides (each one a single unit of DNA) to the 3' end of a strand of DNA. The polymerase chain reaction (PCR) is widely used in many branches of biological science including forensics.

Precambrian: The geological period of time (before the Cambrian geological period), that extends from about 4.6 billion years ago (the point at which Earth began to form) to the beginning of the Cambrian Period, 541 million years ago.

Prokaryotes: The early evolved unicellular micro-organisms which had not yet collected their chromosomes into a nucleus to be surrounded by a nuclear membrane; (the word prokaryote comes from the Greek 'pro' meaning 'before' and 'karyon' meaning 'nut' or 'kernel.') This subsequently took place in the more complex evolved eukaryotes. Moreover, prokaryotes lack mitochondria and other membrane-bound intracellular organelles. Their DNA is in the form of a singular length rather like a ball of wool, and is not compacted by histones. Prokaryotes form two kingdoms of living organisms, Bacteria and Archaea.

Protozoa: Unicellular microscopic primitive organisms. They are non-photosynthetic and aquatic eukaryotes which do not have true cell walls but their surrounding cell membrane is supported by a protein pedicle or small stalk-like structure. Some protozoa have a lash-like flagellum. Some protozoa are various species of amoebae,and some are parasitic such as the species of Eimeria living in the gut of cattle, sheep and poultry and causing coccidiosis, whilst others are the malarial parasites, living in the blood of the host.

Phthalates: Substances very widely used in the chemical industry as plasticizers (substances added to plastics to increase their flexibility and transparency.) They are used in adhesives and glues, in electronics, in the agricultural industry, in personal-care products, medical devices, detergents and in children's toys, in paints, printing inks, pharmaceuticals, food products, and textiles. Most Americans tested by the USA Centre for Disease Control and Prevention have metabolites of multiple phthalates in their urine. These substances interfere with the normal action of hormones, particularly those relevant to reproduction, both in humans and animals.

Pupation of insect larva: A pupa is the resting stage during the life cycle of some insects, after which metamorphosis is completed and the larval insect changes into a fully formed adult insect. Pupae are enclosed in a protective case, while the tissues of the insect undergo reorganisation. In some insects such as butterflies and moths, the pupa is called a chrysalis.

Quorum sensing: This is a method of communication within a population of living organisms, often bacteria but sometimes insects. The mechanism is related to population density and may influence how the individuals within the particular population coordinate the expression of their genes in response to their environment.

Ratite birds: Literally 'raft like' birds because their breast bone (sternum) is flat, like a raft. It has no central sternal keel, as these birds do not fly, consequently they do not have well developed breast muscles for powered flight (which in flying birds are attached to the sternum.) Ratites are classified in a separate taxonomic order.

Ribosome: A complex piece of molecular machinery involved in linking amino acid molecules together to form protein molecules.

This process is carried out following the instructions of messenger RNA (mRNA.)

River Blindness: This progressive blindness in humans mostly occurs in sub-Saharan Africa but occasionally in South America. It is caused by a gradual thickening of the cornea of the eye from irritation by microfilaria (the pre-larval form of any filarial worm), resulting in gradual blindness. The nematode parasite is transmitted by a black fly and not by a louse as indicated in the text.

RNA: Ribonucleic acid. This is single stranded and similar to one half of DNA. See **DNA** above.

Saprophytes: Those plant, fungi or bacteria which derive their nourishment from dead or decaying organic matter.

Schizophrenia: A severe long-term mental health disorder that causes a range of different psychological symptoms and may lead people to have hallucinations, delusions and other confusing thoughts and behaviours which distort their view of reality.

See **Bipolar disorder** above.

'Sense' of a single strand of DNA:

This may be either positive or negative. A positive sensed strand can be laid alongside a length of mRNA and is shown to be an exact copy of it. A negative sense strand can be thought of as having to be turned around the other way so that the two ends have to be reversed in order to match the mRNA strand. DNA in its usual form of a double strand has two separate strands which are complementary, one strand being positive whilst the other is negative.

Serovar or serotype: Refers to distinct mutations within various subspecies of bacteria or viruses, based on their cell surface antigens. These surface antigens react with a host organism's immune system, so effectively allowing a pathogen to enter or be rejected by a host.

Bacteria or viruses within a particular genus, such as the bacterial genus Salmonella, may have many serovars. Salmonella has over 4,000 subspecies. By this mechanism, the organism's immune cells recognise other cells as 'self' or 'non self.' Some serovars may be more pathogenic than others in the same genus.

Strandedness (of the viral genome): Viruses may have a single or a double strand of either DNA or RNA, rather like a ball of knitting wool, forming their genome. See above for **sense** of a single strand of DNA.

Species: A group of living creatures which are almost identical and which are able to breed together and produce fertile offspring. They are not usually able to breed with other similar species and produce fertile offspring. See definition of **Genus.**

Spore: (a) Asexual spores are small, usually unicellular, bodies. From such spores a new organism is formed after division of the initial single cell. Being very small, they are adapted for dispersal but in spite of the fact that they have little food supply, they can survive in adverse conditions in the environment.

(b) Sexual spores are also unicellular but they only have the haploid (half) number of chromosomes of the mature cell, which has the complete or diploid number of chromosomes.They are produced by meiosis from the reproductive cells in either plants or animals. The Sexual spore is in fact a gamete, which after finding and fusing with a gamete of the opposite sex (formed by another member of the same species), will fuse to form a zygote, later maturing into the adult or mature animal or plant.

Sporozoites: A spore released from the sporocyst of a plant or, in the case of the malarial parasite plasmodium, it is the stage in the parasite's life cycle which takes place in the salivary glands of the mosquito. It is this form of the parasite which is transmitted to the final host (i.e.human or bird, when the mosquito bites this host, human or animal.

Symbiosis: The living together of two dissimilar organisms for their mutual benefit, a condition which may also be called mutualism. An example is the case of lichens commonly seen growing on rocks or old wooden posts. A lichen is not a single organism; it is a stable symbiotic association between a fungus and algae and/or cyanobacteria. Also the rhizobia nitrogen-fixing bacteria that live in special root nodules of leguminous plants, such as peas and beans.

Sympatric: This refers to two similar species inhabiting the same, or overlapping, geographical areas, so that they come into contact with each other. This is in contrast to allopatric species, where similar species occupy non-overlapping ranges,

Taxonomy: The science and practice of classification; i.e. the systematics of living organisms. Taxonomy uses taxonomic units, known as taxa (singular; taxon). This involves the visual and other characteristics (genotype) of an organism so that these signs can be compared and contrasted with another organism. Traditionally, this system has been based on that initially devised by Carolus Linnaeus (Carl von Linné) who, in 1738, classified organisms according to shared physical characteristics. The whole of the animal *kingdom* (as distinct from the plant kingdom) is subdivided firstly into *phyla*. These are then divided into *classes* which are in turn, sub-divided into different *orders*. The orders are then sub-divided into *families*, these into various *genera* which are lastly divided into *species*. There may also be a further division into *subspecies*.

See also **Molecular taxonomy** and **Phylum** above.

Thrips: This is the common name for an order of small, slender, sap-sucking insects named Thysanoptera, containing over 5,000 species. They are often considered as pests by commercial plant growers but some species do feed on other insects, mites and fungi.

Tinamous: A taxonomic family of early evolved ground-dwelling birds consisting of 47 species. They look rather similar to grouse and quail but are related to the ratite birds.

Triassic: A geological period circa 250-200 mya.

Uncinate process (in birds): These are backward extensions projecting from the upper part of each rib of most birds. They overlap the rib behind and serve to strengthen the rib cage and chest.

Vector: An unrelated species (often an insect) which transfers a non-contagious pathogen (eg. the malarial organism) from an infected animal to an uninfected animal e.g.the mosquito. Also ticks transfer Lyme Disease by biting an uninfected human or animal after having drawn blood from an infected person or infected animal.

Vertebrates: All those animals with a backbone enclosing the main trunk nerve, the spinal cord, from the brain enclosed within the skull, down the body to the trunk. The vertebrates include all fish, birds, reptiles, amphibians and mammals.

Viron: An individual virus particle.

Zooplankton: Plankton is the total amount of living organisms, both plant and animal, living and drifting in the oceans, seas and bodies of fresh water. Zooplankton is the animal part of the plankton, including small protozoans, crustaceans, and the eggs and larvae of larger animals. Zooplankton is distinct from phytoplankton, the plant material, and also from bacterioplankton made up of bacteria and archaea.

Zygote: A cell formed by the union of two gametes, one from the male (eg. sperm) and one from the female (eg. ovum) which is called fertilisation. The zygotic cell then divides into two cells which repeatedly divide, thus commencing the formation of a complete living multicellular organism.

REFERENCES

(1) Miller S.L. (1953) A Production of Amino Acids under Primitive Earth Conditions. Science 117:528. (www.sciencemag.org) DOI:10.1126/science./117.3046.528.

(2) Miller S.L., and Urey H.C. (1959) Organic Compound Synthesis on the Primitive Earth. Science 130:245. DOI:10.1126/science.130.3370.245.

(3) Johnson Adam P. et al (2008) The Miller Volcanic Spark Discharge Experiment. Science 17 Oct. 2008, Vol. 322, Issue 5900, p. 404.

DOI: 10.1126/science.1161527.

(4) Stuart A. Kaufman. (1995) What is Life: Was Schrodinger Right? in What is Life: The Next Fifty Years. Cambridge University Press, eds. Michael P. Murphy and Luke A.J. O'Neil.

(5) Woese, Carl & Pace, Norman (2000) The Variety of Life p.126, ed. Colin Tudge, pub. Oxford University Press.

(6) Nadell C.D., Xavier J.B., Levin S.A., Foster K.R. (2008) The Evolution of Quorum Sensing in Bacterial Biofilms. PLOS 6(1): e14 DOI.org/10.1371/journal.pbio.0060014.

(7) Colin Tudge (2000) The Variety of Life pp.114-119, pub. Oxford University Press.

(8) Turgeon Steven & Creaser Robert, (2008) Nature, Vol. 454 p.323.

(9) Pass, D.A. and Perry, R.A. (1984) The Pathology of Psittacine Beak and Feather Disease. Aust. Vet. J., 61, 69-74.

(10) Waters A.P., Higgins D.G., McCutchan T.F. (1991), Proc. Nat.

Acad. Sci. USA, Vol.88, pp.3140-3144.

(11) Joyce Filer, (1995) Disease, in Egyptian Bookshelf series pp. 14 & 81, Pub. British Museum Press.

(12) Desser S., Fallis A.M., & Garnham P.C.C. (1968) Relapse in ducks chronically infected with *Leucocytozoon simondi* and *Paraheamoproteus nettionis.* Can. J. Zoo. 46, 281-5.

(13) Siegmund O.H. and Fraser C.H. (eds.) (1973) The Merk Veterinary Manual, 4th edition, Rahway, New Jersey: Merk.

(14) Colin Tudge (2000) The Variety of Life pp.160-163 pub. Oxford University Press.

(15) Bowman B., Taylor J. W. and White T.J. (1992) Molecular Evolution of Human Pathogens. Molecular Biology and Evolution Vol. 9, pp.893-904.

(16) Medawar P.B. and Medawar, J.S. (1993) Aristotle to Zoos: A Philosophical dictionary of biology, Harvard University Press, Cambridge, Massachusetts, USA.

(17) Ackermann Hans-W, Berthiaume Laurent and Tremblay Michel (1998) Virus Life in Diagrams p.1. Pub. CRC Press, Boca Raton, London, Washington D.C.

(18) La Scola B. et al (2003) A Giant Virus in Amoebae Science [Journal] Mar.28; 299 (5615):2033 PMID 12663918. New Scientist Mar 23, 2006.

(19) La Scola B. et al (2005) Mimivirus in pneumonia patients. Emerg. Infect. Dis. Mar:11(3):449-52. PMID 15757563.

(20) Seshadri R. et al (2007) CAMERA: A community Resource for Metagenomics. PLOS Biology Vol.5, No.3, e75 DOI: 10.1371/journal.pbio. 0050075.

(21) Hamilton G. (2008) New Scientist 30 August pp.38-41.

(22) Ryan Frank (2010) New Scientist 30 January pp.32-35, Virolution 2009, pub. Collins pp 49-50.

(23) Koonin E.V., Senkevich T.G. and Dolja V.V., The ancient Virus World and evolution of cells, Biology Direct Sept. 2006, 1:29. DOI:10.1186/1745-6150-1-29.

(24) Forterre Patrick (2005). Proceedings of the National Academy of Sciences, Vol.103, p.3669.

(25) Nettelbeck Dirk M., Alvarez Ronald D. and Curiel David T. Tumor- Busting Viruses' Virotherapy, Scientific American, New Answers for Cancer Volume 18, Number 3, 2008 p.74.

(26) Crawford Dorothy, H. (2007) Deadly Companions, how microbes shaped our history, p. 63, Pub. Oxford University Press.

(27) Roelke-Parker, M.E. et al (1996) A canine distemper virus epidemic in Serengeti lions (*Panthera leo*). Nature, Feb.1;379(6564):441-5.

(28) Tudge, Colin (2000), The Variety of Life, A Survey and a Celebration of all the Creatures that Have Ever Lived, p.202. Pub. Oxford University Press. ISBN 0-19-860426-2

(29) Ostrowski S., Dorrestein G.M. et al (1996) Cross-protection of an avian poxvirus isolated from Houbara bustard. Avian Diseases 1996: 40, 762-79.

(30) Gerlach H. (1994) Chapter on Viruses, Avian Medicine: Principles and Application pp. 862-948. (Eds) Ritchie, Harrison and Harrison, Wingers, Florida.

(31) Jarmin Susan et al (2006) Avipox phylogenics: identification of a PCR length polymorphism that discriminates between the two major clades. Journal of General Virology 87: 2191-2201. 1 August 2006.

DOI: 10.1099/vir.0.81738-0.

(32) Karabatsos N. (1985) International Catalogue of Arboviruses.

(33) Robert G. McLean and Sonya R. Ubico, Arboviruses in Birds, Chapter 2 of Infectious Diseases of Wild Birds. Eds. Nancy J. Thomas, D. Bruce Hunter, and Carter T. Atkinson. Pub. Blackwell Publishing.

(34) Bendinelli et al (2001) Molecular properties, biology, and clinical implications of TT virus, a recently identified widespread infectious agent of humans. Clinical Microbiology Reviews 2001 Jan: 14(1):98-113. PMID 11148004.

(35) Dawkins R. (2004) The Ancestor's Tale pp.449-462. Pub. Phoenix, London.

(36) Tudge Colin, (2000) The Variety of Life, A Survey and a Celebration of all the Creatures that Have Ever Lived, p.202. Pub. Oxford University Press. ISBN 0-19-860426-2.

(37) Monks D. J., Carlisle M.S., Carrigan M. et al (2005) Angiostrongylus cantonensis as a cause of cerebrospinal disease in a yellow-tailed black cockatoo *(Calyptorhynchus funereus)* and two tawny frogmouths (*Podargus strigoides.*) Journal of Avian Medicine and Surgery, 9(4).

(38) Rosemary Drisdelle (2007) Water birds & Trematodes. Last accessed at http://wild-birds suite E-101.com/article.cfm/water_birds_and_trematodes.

(39) Jamie Voyles et al, Pathogenesis of Chytridiomycosis, a Cause of Catastrophic Amphibian Declines. Science 23 Oct. 2009: Vol. 326. Issue 5952, pp. 582 – 585. DOI: 10.1126/science.1176765.

(40) Richard Wrangham, (2009) Catching Fire, How Cooking made us Human, p.53. Pub. Profile Books Ltd. London.

(41) David Grimaldi and Michael S. Engel, (2006) Fossil Liposcelididae and the lice ages (Insecta: Psocodea.) DOI: 10.1098/rspb.2005.3337. Proc Biol Sci. 2006 Mar 7; 273(1586): 625–633.

(42) Bush Sarah E., Clayton Dale H. (2006) The role of body size in host specificity: reciprocal transfer experiments with feather lice. PMID:17133872. Evolution. 2006 Oct;60(10):2158-67.

(43) Johnson K.P., S. E. Bush, and D. H. Clayton (2005). Correlated evolution of host and parasite body size: Tests of Harrisons's rule using birds and lice. Evolution. 2005 Aug;59(8):1744-53. PMID:16329244.

(44) Clayton D.H. (1991) Coevolution of avian grooming and ectoparasite avoidance. Chapter in Bird-Parasite interactions: Ecology, Evolution, and Behaviour, pp.258-289. J.E. Loye and M. Zuk (eds.) Oxford Ornithology Series, Oxford University Press, Oxford, U.K.

(45) Comstedt P., Asokliene L., Eliasson I., Olsen B, Wallensten A., Bunikis J. and Bergström S. (2009.) Complex Population Structure of Lyme Borreliosis Group Spirochete Borrelia garinii in Subarctic Eurasia. PLOS ONE 4(6): e5841. DOI:10.1371/journal.pone.0005841.

(46) Comstedt P., Bergström S., Olsen B., Garpmo U., Marjavaara L., Mejlon H., Barbour A.G., Bunikis J. Migratory passerine birds as reservoirs of Lyme borreliosis in Europe (2006) Emerg. Infect. Dis. 2006 Jul;12(7):1087-95. PMID:16836825 PMCID:PMC3291064 DOI:10.3201/eid1207.060127.

(47) Gauthier-Clerc M. et al (1999) Prevalence of Borrelia burgdorferi (The Lyme Disease agent) antibodies in the king penguin *(Aptenodytes patagonicus)* in the Crozet Archipelago. Polar Biology, July 1999. Volume 22, Issue 2, pp. 141-143. Pub. Springer

International Publishing, Berlin / Heidelberg .

(48) A. Handa, B. Dickstein, N.S. Young and K.E. Brown. Prevalence of the newly described human circovirus, TTV, in United States blood donors. Transfusion, Volume 40, Issue 2, pp. 245 – 25. Published online: 24 Apr 2002. DOI 10.1046/j.1537-2995.2000.40020245.

(49) Harper, D. G. (1999) Feather mites, pectoral muscle condition, wing length and plumage coloration of passerines. Anim Behav. 1999 Sep;58(3):553-562. PMID:0479371 DOI:10.1006/anbe.1999.1154.

(50) Richard O. Prum and Alan H. Brush, (2003) Which Came First, the Feather or the Bird? Scientific American, March 2003, Volume 288, Issue 3 pp.60-69.

(51) Mironov S.V. and Palma R.L. (2006) Two new feather mite species (Acari: Analgoidea) from the Tuamotu sandpiper *Aechmorhynchus parvirostris* (Charadriiformes: Scolopacidae): Tuhinga 17: 49-59. Te Papa Tongarewa Museum of New Zealand.

(52) Marcel van Tuinen and S. Blair Hedges (2001) Calibration of Avian Molecular Clocks. Molecular Biology and Evolution, Volume 18, Issue 2, 1 Feb. 2001, pp. 206–213. https://doi.org/10.1093/oxfordjournals.molbev.a003794.

(53) & (54) Poinar George. Jr. and Poinar Roberta (2008) What Bugged the Dinosaurs?: Insects, Disease, and Death in the Cretaceous pp. 171-184. Princeton University Press and Oxford.

(55) Highfield Roger (2006) Peroducktyl. Daily Telegraph June 16, page 13.

(56) Sharon A. Huws, Anthony W. Smith, Mark C. Enright, Pauline J. Wood, Michael R.W. Brown, (2006) Amoebae promote persistence of epidemic strains of MRSA. Environmental

Microbiology 2006 Jun:8(6):1130-1133 DOI:10.1111/j.1462-2920.2006. 00991.x PMID:16689734..

(57) Unwin S. et al (2012) Renal trematode infection due to *Paratanaisia bragai* in zoo housed Columbiformes and a red bird-of-paradise (*Paradisaea rubra*). International Journal for Parasitology: Parasites and Wildlife Vol.2, (December 2013) 32-41.

(58) McCoy K.M. et al (2003) Host - Dependant genetic structure of parasite populations: Differential dispersal of seabird tick host races. Evolution 2003 Feb;57(2):288-96 Society for the Study of Evolution, Lawrence, USA.

PMID:12683525

(59) John R. Horner, Kevin Padian and Armand de Ricqlès (2005) How Dinosaurs Grew So Large-And So Small. Scientific American July 1, 2005, pp.46-53.

(60) Ward Peter D. (2006) Out of Thin Air: Dinosaurs, Birds, and Earth's Ancient Atmosphere. Pub. Joseph Henry Press. ISBN-10: 0309100615.

(61) Huws Sharon A. et al (2006) Amoebae promote persistence of epidemic strains of MRSA. Environmental Microbiology (2006) 8(6), 1130–1133 doi:10.1111/j.1462-2920.2006.00991.x

(62) Coles B. H. (1985) Avian Medicine and Surgery pp. 117. Pub. Blackwell Scientific Publications, Oxford.

(63) Ritchie, B. W. (Ed.) (1995): Avian viruses: function and control. Wingers Publishing, Inc., Lake Worth, FL.

(64) Scott Wilson, Conservation Biologist North of England Zoological Society 2010 pers. com.

(65) Marr J.S., Calisher C.H. (2003) Alexander the Great and West Nile Virus Encephalitis. Emerg. Infect Dis. 2003 Dec; 9(12): 1599–1603.

DOI: 10.3201/eid0912.030288

(66) Gerlach H. (1994) Chap. 33 in Bacteria in Avian Medicine and Surgery, p.978. Pub. Wingers Publishing Inc., Lake Worth, Florida.

(67) De Filippo Carlotta, Lionetti Paolo, et al (2010) Impact of diet in shaping gut microbiota revealed by a comparative study in children from Europe and rural Africa. Proceedings of the Natural Academy of Sciences, 14691–14696.
DOI:10.1073/pnas.1005963107.

(68) Martin W. and Müller M. (1998) The hydrogen hypothesis for the first eukaryote. Nature 1998 Mar 5;392(6671):37-41
PMID:9510246 DOI:10.1038/32096.

(69)Ji Qiang et al (1998) Two feathered dinosaurs from northeastern China, Natwe 393, 753-761 (25 June1998).

(70)Xu Xing (2010) Unearthing China's feathered fossils. New Scientist Volume 205, Issue 2747, 10 February 2010, Pages 26-2.
https://doi.org/10.1016/S0262-4079(10)60361-2

(71) Atkinson Steve and Williams Paul (2009) Quorum sensing and social networking in the microbial world. Journal of the Royal Society Interface 2009 6 959-
978; DOI: 10.1098/rsif.2009.0203. Published 25 September 2009.

(72) Chang Eugene B. et al (2007) The Bacillus subtilis Quorum-Sensing Molecule CSF Contributes to Intestinal Homeostasis via OCTN2, a Host Cell Membrane Transporter. Cell Host & Microbe, Volume 1, Issue 4, 14 June 2007, pp. 299-308.
https://doi.org/10.1016/j.chom.2007.05.004.

(73) Claverie Jean-Michel, Legendre M. et al (2010) mRNA deep sequencing reveals 75 new genes and a complex transcriptional landscape in Mimivirus. Pub. Genome Res. 2010 May;20(5):664-74. DOI: 10.1101/gr.102582.109. PMID:20360389 PMCID:PMC2860168.

(74) Peter Aldhous (2007) Why the long wait for gene-specific drugs? New Scientist, 27 October 2007, Volume 196, Issue 2627.

(75) Reid Harris and Kevin P. C. Minbiole (2008) Can Manipulations of Amphibians' Mutualistic Skin Bacteria Control a Lethal Skin Disease? Biocontrol News and information 30(2).

(76) Richard J. Butler, Paul M. Barrett, and David J. Gower (2009) Postcranial skeletal pneumaticity and air-sacs in the earliest pterosaurs. Biology Letters August 23; Vol. 5 issue 4: 557–560. Published online 2009 May 1. DOI:10.1098/rsbl.2009.0139.

(77) A.B. Osterhaus MSc & PhD. Personal Communication.

(78) Zhonghe Zhou and Fucheng Zhang Zhiheng Li. A New Lower Cretaceous bird from China and tooth reduction in early avian evolution. Proceedings of the Royal Society B, published online 8 July 2009 DOI:10.1098/rspb.2009.0885.

(79) Turton John A. (1976) IgE, Parasites and Allergy The Lancet, Vol. 308, No. 7987, p686 Published: September 25, 1976. https://doi.org/10.1016/S0140-6736(76)92492-2

(80) David Deamer (2006) Self-assembly processes in the prebiotic environment. Philos. Trans. R. Soc. Lond. B. Biol. Sci. 2006 Oct 29; 361(1474): 1809–1818. DOI:10.1098/rstb.2006.1905.

(81) Sanderson, Stephanie MA VetMB, MSc (WAH), MRCVS Head of Live Sciences, North of England Zoological Society (personal communication.)

(82) Weimin Liu, Hahn Beatrice H. et al (2010) Origin of the human malaria parasite *Plasmodium falciparum* in gorillas *Nature* 467, 420–425 (23 September 2010) DOI:10.1038/nature09442.

(83) O'Donoghue James (2007) How Trees Changed the World. New Scientist 21 November p.38.

(84) Pembrey, Marcus E. et al (2006) Sex-specific, male-line transgenerational responses in humans. European Journal of Human Genetics,(2006) 14, 159–166. DOI:10.1038/sj.ejhg.5201538; published online 14 December 2005.

(85) Damon R. Asher, Anna M. Cerny, and Robert W. Finberg (2005)

Proceedings of the National Academy of Sciences, Vol. 102, no. 36

12897–12902, DOI: 10.1073/pnas.0506211102.

(86) Ewan D. S. Wolff et al (2009) Common Avian Infection Plagued the Tyrant Dinosaurs. PLOS.

https://doi.org/10.1371/journal.pone.0007288.

(87) Péter Lászió Pap, Jácint Tökölyi, and Tibor Szép. (2005.) Host-symbiont relationship and the abundance of feather mites in relation to age and body condition of the barn swallow *(Hirundo rustica):* an experimental study. Can. J. Zool. 83(8):1059-1066(2005), DOI:10.1139/z05-100.

(88)Priya Shetty (2009) Six Diseases You Never Knew You Could Catch. New Scientist 14 October2009.

(89) Bethany L. Woodworth et al (2004.) Host population persistence in the face of introduced vector borne disease; Hawaii amakihi and avian malaria. Proceedings of the National Academy of Sciences of the United States of America. 2005, Feb. 1. 102:5, 1531-1536. Published online 2005 Jan 24. DOI:10.1073/pnas.0409454102

PMCID: PMC547860.

(90) André Lwoff, Robert Horne and Paul Tournier (1962) A system of Viruses. Cold Spring Harbor Symposia on Quantitative Biology 1962.27:51-55 DOI:10.1101/SQB.1962.027.001.008 PMID: 13931895.

(91) Steve C. Wang and Peter Dodson (2006) Estimating the Diversity of Dinosaurs. Proceedings of the National Academy of Sciences, September 12, 2006. Vol.103 no.37 pp.13601-13605. DOI: 10.1073/pnas.0606028103.

(92) Nick Lane. (2009) Was our oldest ancestor a proton-powered rock? New Scientist,14 October 2009.

(93) Mason OU, Nakagawa T, Rosner M, Van Nostrand JD, Zhou J, et al. (2010) First Investigation of the Microbiology of the Deepest Layer of Ocean Crust. Published: November 5, 2010. PLOS ONE 5(11): e15399. DOI:10.1371/journal.pone.0015399.

(94) Eamonn M. M. Quigley (2015) Probiotics in Gastrointestinal Disorders. Hospital Practice Volume: 38. Number: 4, Pages 122-129. Published online: 13 Mar 2015.
http://dx.doi.org/10.3810/hp.2010.11.349. Index: November 2010. *Clinical* Focus: Eur J Gastroenterol Hepatol. 2003;13(4):391–396. Delia P, Sansotta G., Donato V., et al. Grehan MJ1, Borody TJ, Leis SM, Campbell J, Mitchell H, Wettstein A. (2010) Durable alteration of the colonic microbiota by the administration of donor fecal flora. J. Clin. Gastroenterol. 2010 Sep;44(8):*551*–561. DOI: 10.1097/MCG.0b013e3181e5d06b. PMID:20716985. Borody TJ, Warren EF, Leis S, Surace R, Ashman O. Treatment of ulcerative colitis using fecal bacteriotherapy. J. Clin. Gastroenterol. 2003 Jul;37(1):42-7. PMID:12811208

(95) Anil Ananthaswamy (2010) Bugs VS Super Bug. New Scientist 18 December 2010,p.36.

(96) Jablonka Eva and Raz Gal (2009) Transgenerational Epigenetic Inheritance: Prevalence, Mechanisms, and Implications for the Study of Heredity and Evolution.The Quarterly Review of Biology, Vol.84, No.2, June 2009.

(97) Samour J.H. and Naldo J.L.(2003) Diagnosis and management of trichomoniasis in falcons in Saudi Arabia. Journal of Avian Medicine and Surgery 17(3):136-143.
2003. https://doi.org/10.1647/2001-047.

(98) Jon Lyall, et al (2011) Suppression of avian influenza transmission in genetically modified chickens. Science, Vol 331, no.6014, pp.223-226. DOI:10.1126/science.1198020 PMID:21233391.

(99) Keith Hamilton BVSc MSc MRCVS. Flu virus gene reassortment in poultry (personal comm.)

(100) Castrucci, M.R., Donatelli,I., Sidoli,L., Barigazzi,G., Kawaoka,Y. and Webster,R.G. (1993) Genetic reassortment between avian and human Influenza A viruses in Italian pigs. Virology 1993 Mar; 193(1):503-506 PMID:8438586 DOI:10.1006/viro.1993.1155.

(101) Tudge, Colin (2000) The Variety of Life, A Survey and a Celebration of all the Creatures that Have Ever Lived, p.172. Pub.Oxford University Press. ISBN 0-19-860426-2

(102) Horák P., Kolářova L., Adema C. M. (2002) Biology of the schistosoma genus *Trichobilharzia*. Advances in Parasitology Vol. 52, 2002, pp.155-233

Department of Parasitology, Charles University, Viničná 7, CZ-12844 Prague 2, Czech Republic. https://doi.org/10.1016/S0065-308X(02)52012-1.

(103)Byne K., Nichols R.A. (1999) Culex pipiens in London

Underground tunnels: differentiation between surface and subterranean populations Heredity (Edinb). 1999 Jan;82 (Pt 1):7-15. DOI:10.1038/sj.hdy6884120. PMID:10200079.

(104) Spielman A., Andreadis T.G., Apperson C.S. et al (2004) Outbreak of West Nile virus in North America Science 306 (5701);1473-5..

(105) Craddock N., Owen M.J. (2010) The Kraepelinian dichotomy - going, going... but still not gone. The British Journal of Psychiatry. Jan. 2010; 196 (2) 92–95. DOI:10.1192/bjp.bp.109.073429.

(106) T. Andrew Clayton, David Baker, John C. Lindon, Jeremy R. Everett and Jeremy K. Nicholson. Pharmacometabonomic identification of a significant host-microbiome metabolic interaction affecting human drug metabolism. Proceedings of the National Academy of Sciences U S A. 2009 August 25; Vol. 106 No.34: 14728–14733. Published online 2009 August 10. DOI:10.1073/pnas.0904489106

(107) Hughes A.L. and Piontkivska H. (2003) Phylogeny of Trypanosomatidae and Bodonidae (Kinetoplastida) based on 18S rRNA: evidence for paraphyly of Trypanosoma and six other genera. Molecular Biology and Evolution 2003 Apr;20(4):644-652. PMID:12679543. DOI:10.1093/molbev/msg062

(108) Simpson A.G.B., Stevens J.R. and Lukes J. (2006).The Evolution and diversity of kinetoplastid flagellates. Trends in Parasitology 2006 Apr;22(4):168-174. PMID:16504583. DOI:10.1016/j.pt.2006.02.006.

(109) Lieve Van Hoovels, Anne Vankeerberghen, An Boel, Kristien Van Vaerenbergh, and Hans De Beenhouwer (2006) The first case of *Staphylococcus pseudintermedius* infection in a human. Journal of Clinical Microbiology. December 2006, vol. 44, no.12, 4609-4612. DOI:10.1128/JCM.01308-06

(110) Sujata Gupta (2011) Reverse Evolution: Chicken revisits its dinosaur past. New Scientist, 20 August.

(111) David I. Pritchard and Alan Brown. April (2001) Is Necator americanus approaching a mutualistic symbiotic relationship with humans? Trends in Parasitology 1001 Apr; Vol. 17 No.4: 169-72. PMID:11282505

(112) Dean D. Thomas et al. March (2000) Insect Population Control Using a Dominant, Repressible, Lethal Genetic System. Science 31 March 2000: Vol. 287, Issue 5462, pp. 2474-2476 DOI: 10.1126/science.287.5462.2474.

(113) Mansour F., Hussein and Saud I. Al-Mufarrej (2004) Prion Diseases: A Review. Scientific Journal of King Faisal University (Basic and Applied Sciences) Vol.5 No.2 (2004):1425 139.

(114) Bob Holmes (2012) First Glimpse at the viral birth of DNA. New Scientist, 21 April 2012, p.10.

(115) Geoffrey S. Diemer and Kenneth M. Stedman (2012) A novel virus genome discovered in an extreme environment suggests recombination between unrelated groups of RNA and DNA viruses. Biology Direct 19th April 2012, 7:13 https://doi.org/10.1186/1745-6150-7-13

(116) Nick Lane (2012) Life: is it inevitable or just a fluke? New Scientist, June 23, 2012, p.33.

(117) Atkinson S. and Williams P. et al. (1999) A hierarchical quorum-sensing system in *Yersinia pseudotuberculosis* is involved in the regulation of motility and clumping. Molecular Microbiology September 1999 Volume 33,

Issue 6 pp. 1267–1277. Article first published online: 1 Mar 2002.

DOI: 10.1046/j.1365-2958.1999.01578.

(118) Quanguo Li, et al. (2010) Plumage Color Patterns of an Extinct Dinosaur. Science 12 March 2010 Vol. 327 no.5971, pp.1369-1372. DOI:10.1126/science.1186290.

(119) Gray J.S.et al. (2009) Effects of Climate Change on Ticks and Tick- Borne Diseases in Europe. Interdisciplinary Perspectives on Infectious Diseases, Vol. 2009 (2009), Article ID 593232, 12 pages. http://dx.doi.org/10.1155/2009/593232.

(120) Kenneth Nilsson, Karin Elfving and Carl Påhlson (2006) *Rickettsia helvetica* in a Patient with Meningitis, Sweden, 2006. Emerg. Infect. Dis. 2010; 16(3);490-492. https://dx.doi.org/10.3201/eid1603.090184.

(121) R. Ewan Fordyce and Daniel T. Ksepka (2012) Fossil Finds Trace the History of Penguins. Scientific American. November 1, 2012, Vol. 307, Number 5.

(122) Dr. Kannan Ganapathy DVM PhD MRCVS, University of Liverpool, Sch. of veterinary science. Personal communication.

(123) McMahon Teagan A. (2012) Chytrid fungus *Batrachochytrium dendrobatidis* has nonamphibian hosts and releases chemicals that cause pathology in the absence of infection. Proceedings of the National Academy of Sciences Jan. 2, 2013 vol. 110, no. 1. DOI:10.1073/pnas.1200592110.

(124) Chris D. Thomas et al (2004) Extinction risk from climate change. Nature 8 January 2004 Vol. 427, Number 6970 p.145.

doi:10.1038/nature02121.

(125) Marshall, Michael (2012) Deep Future: Will There be any Nature Left? New Scientist Issue 2854, 3 March 2012, p.44.

(126) Nathan Wolfe (2011) The Viral Storm: The Dawn of a New Pandemic Age. Penguin Books ISBN-10: 0141046511.

(127) Phillip. L. Manning et al. (2013) Synchrotron-based chemical imaging reveals plumage patterns in a 150 million year old early bird. Journal of Analytical Atomic Spectromotry (Paper) 2013, 28, 1024-1030 DOI: 10.1039/C3JA50077B

(128) Achtman Mark et al (1999) *Yersinia pestis*,the cause of plague, is a recently emerged clone of *Yersinia pseudotuberculosis*. Proceedings of the National Academy of Sciences Nov. 23 1999, vol. 96 no. 24 14043-14048. DOI:10.1073/pnas.96.24.14043

(129) Ravilious Kate, (2013) The Early Turd: Our History is Written in Poo. New Scientist, 27April 2013, p.44.

(130) McKenna Maryn, (2013) Rethinking Rabies. Scientific American, August 2013,Volume 309, Number 2.

(131) Lawrence A. David et al (2013) Diet rapidly and reproducibly alters the human gut microbiome. Nature **505**,559–563 (23 January 2014) Published online

11 December 2013 DOI:10.1038/nature 12820.

(132) Geddes Linda (2013) "Bubble kid" success puts gene therapy back on track. New Scientist, 30 October 2013.

(133) Pion Martin et al (2013) Bacterial farming by the fungus *Morchella crassipes*. Proceedings of the Royal Society B published 30 October 2013

DOI: 10.1098//rspb.2013.2242

(134) Timothy G. Dinan et al (2013) Psychobiotics: A Novel Class of Psychotropic. Biological Psychiatry, 15 November 2013 Volume 74, Issue 10 , Pages 720-726, DOI:10.1139/W08-039.

(135) Partial list of dieases categorised as zoonoses (those associated with fairs and petting zoos.) Wikipedia "Zoonosis."

(136) Chan B. K , Abedon S.T. and Loc-Carrillo C. (2013) Phage cocktails and the future of phage therapy. Future Microbiology 2013 Jun;8(6):769-83.

DOI 10.2217/fmb.13.47. PMID:23701332.

(137) Matthieu Legendre et al. (2014) Thirty-thousand-year-old distant relative of giant icosahedral DNA viruses with a pandoravirus morphology. PNAS,March 18, 2014 vol. 111 no. 11, 4274–4279.

DOI: 10.1073/pnas.1320670111

(138) David M Wagner et al (2014) *Yersinia pestis* and the Plague of Justinian 541-543 AD: a genomic analysis. The Lancet Infectious Diseases Volume 14, No. 4, p319–326, April 2014. DOI:10.1016/S1473-3099(13)70323-2

PMID:24480148.

(139) Bichai F., Payment P. and Barbeau B. (2008) Protection of waterborne pathogens by higher organisms in drinking water: a review. Canadian Journal of Microbiology, 2008 Jul;54(7):509-24. DOI: 10.1139/w08-039. PMID:18641697.

(140) Aurélien Trompette et al (2014) Microbiota metabolism of dietary fiber influences allergic airway disease and hematopoiesis. Nature Medicine, 20, 159 - 166. Published online 05 January 2014. DOI:10.1038/nm.3

(141) Keith Pardee et al (2014) Paper-Based Synthetic Gene Networks. Cell, Vol. 159, Issue 4, p940–954, 6 November 2014. Published online October 23, 2014. DOI: http://dx.doi.org/10.1016/j.cell.2014.10.004 444

(142) Jose Ramirez, Sarah M. Short et al (2014) *Chromobacterium Csp_P* Reduces Malaria and Dengue Infection in Vector Mosquitoes and Has Entomopathogenic and *In Vitro* Anti-pathogen Activities.

Published: October 23, 2014
https://doi.org/10.1371/journal.ppat.1004398

(143) Hopwood Nick (2006) Pictures of Evolution and Charges of Fraud: Ernst Haeckel's Embryological Illustrations. Isis: A Journal of the History of Science Society Vol.97, No. 2: 260-301 June 2006.

(144) Martin Blaser (2015) Missing Microbes: How Killing Bacteria Creates Modern Plagues. One World Publications 16th April 2015.

ISBN-13: 978-1780746883.

Image Credits

Plate No.1 Swifts in summer sky.

Author's own photograph.

Plate No.2 A skein of Hooper Swans in V-formation flight.

Author's own photograph.

Plate No.3 The Red Jungle fowl

Seen in a power point presentation given by Stephanie Sanderson MA VetMB, MSc (WAH), MRCVS, whilst she was the veterinary manager at Chester Zoo.

Plate No.4 Some Wading birds Little Stint [Calidris minuta] searching in the mud of shallow water at low tide.

Author's own photograph.

Fig. No. 1 An illustration of the Miller and Urey laboratory apparatus

Author's own drawing.

Plate No. 5 Jim Peaco, National Park Service - http://www.nps.gov/features/yell/slidefile/thermalfeatures/hotspringsterraces/midwaylower/Images/17708.jpg (public domain)

Plate No. 6 The Bubbling Rocks was copied from an illustration entitled 'The lost city vent field' on page 42 of the NewScientist, 17 October 2009, in an article by Nick Lane.

Fig.No 2 Schematic representation of the basic structure of DNA.

Author's own work

Fig. No.3 The Basic Concept of the Gene.

Gene, National Human Genome Research Institute, CC.

Fig.No.3a An outline of Mitosis

Based on Mysid - Vectorized in CorelDraw
by Mysid from https://www.ncbi.nlm.nih.gov/About/primer/genetics_cell.html. (public domain)

Plate No.7 The Siskin (Carduelis spinus).

Photograph by Mr John Drakely FRCS

Plate No.8 The American Ruddy Duck (Oxyura jamaicensis)

Photograph by Dr. Roger Wilkinson

Plate No.9 White-headed Duck (Oxyura leucocephala)

Author's own photograph.

Fig. No.4 Basic structure of a typical icosahedral virus.

Author's own drawing.

Plate No.10 Gouldian Finches

Obtained from Birds of the World, page 436. Published by Harper Collins Publishers, 77-85 Fulham Palace Road, London.

Plate No. 11 Mimivirus

Copied from New Scientist 25th March 2006, page 37.

Plate No 12 Female Common Crossbill (Loxia curvirostra) with signs of Avian Pox.

Author's own photograph.

Plate No.13 Pigeon with pigeon pox.

Author's own phograph.

Plate No,14 Major flyways of western migratory shore birds

Avian Flu OIE, FAO & Government Sources, Flyways, Wetlands International.

Plate No.15 Peach-faced lovebird.

Author's own photograph

Plate No.16 Badly affected sulphur crested cockatoo.

Author's own photograph

Plate No.17 Head of normal healthy lesser sulphur crested cockatoo.

Author's own photograph.

Plate No.18 William T Cooper.

Plate No. 19 Blackbird with abnormal plumage.

Author's own photograph.

Plate No. 20 Hand held common North American nighthawk (Chordeiles minor.)

Author's own photograph.

Fig. No.5 Various types of bacteria.

Author's own drawing.

Fig. No.6 Basic structure of a bacterium.

Author's own drawing.

Plate No.22 Capercaillie.

Author's own photograph.

Plate No. 23 Bearded reedling.

Author's own photograph.

Plate No.24 Young elephant eating the droppings of an adult elephant which it has just passed.

Author's own photograph.

Fig. No.6 A typical Amoeba.

Author's own drawing.

Plate No.25 The crested wood partridge (Rollulus rouloul.)

Author's own photograph.

Plate No.26 Palawan peacock-pheasant (Polyplectron napoleonis.)

Author's own photograph.

Fig. No. 7 Giardia.

Author's own drawing.

Fig No. 8 Euglena.

Author's own drawing.

Plate No.14 Hyrax.

Author's own photograph.

Fig No.9 Paramecium

Elizabeth Buchsbaum

Plate No.15 Hawai'i 'amakihi (Hemignathus virens).

Amakihi, James Brennan Molokai (CC)

Plate No.16 The head of a parrot grossly infected with Candida.

Author’s own photograph.

Plate No.17 Western European Hedgehog (Erinaceous europaeus) badly infected with ringworm type fungi.

Author's own photograph.

Plate No. 18 Body of a Bourk's parrot showing the gut impacted with nematode worms.

Author’s own photograph; previously published in Avian Medicine,by Brian H Coles, Maria E.Krautwald-Junghanns with contributions from Thomas J.Herrman.

Also used in another of the Author's books; Essentials of Avian Medicine and Surgery, by Brian H.Coles with contributions from Maria Krautwald-Junghanns, Susan E. Orosz & Thomas N. Tully.

Fig No. 10 Life cycle of gapeworm (Syngamous trachae.)

Author's own drawing.

Plate No.19 An endoscopic view of the gapeworm (Syngamous trachea.)

Author's own photograph.

Fig. No.11 Liver fluke (Fasciola Hepatica.)

Author's own drawing.

Plate No.20 Red bird-of-paradise (Paradisaea rubra.)

Photograph taken at Chester Zoo. Use by courtesy of Andrew Owen, Curator of birds, North of England Zoological Society..

Fig. No.12 The life cycle of Schistosoma japonicum.

The human blood fluke which causes the disease Bilharzia.

Elizabeth Buchsbaum.

Fig No.13 Life cycle of Echinostoma revolutum.

Copied from fig. 2/10, p.181 of Bird Diseases: An Introduction to the Study of Birds in Health and Disease by L Arnall & I.F.Keymer. Pub. Bailliere Tindal, 8 Henrietta Street, London WC2E 8QE, 1975.

Used by kind permission of Dr. I.F.Keymer.

Fig No.14 A typical tape worm. whole worm & proglotidd.

Elizabeth Buchsbaum.

Plate No.21 Hippoboscida (flat flies or louse flies.)

Author’s own photograph.

Plate No.22 Red knee tarantula.

Author’s own photograph.

Plate No.23 Avian mange mite.

Author’s own photograph.

Plate. No.24 Two budgerigars infected with mange mites (Cnemidocoptes pilae.)

Author's own photographs

Plate No. 25 Zebra finch infected with mange mites.

Author’s own photograph.

Plate No.26 Red mite.

Author’s own photograph.

Plate No.27 Feather mites. Hand lens view

Author’s own photograph.

Plate No.28 Feather mites as seen with a microscope.

Author's own photograph.

Plate No.29 Erythematous rash in the pattern of a "bull's-eye" from Lyme disease. Hannah Garrison. (CC)

Platc No.30 Hcad of a budgcrigar showing three ticks. Also an enlarged photograph of more ticks.

Photograph courtesy of Dr. Jan Hooimeijer, Vet practitioner in the Netherlands.

This photograph has been previously used by the author in two of his previous publications. (1) Published in Avian Medicine by Brian H. Coles, Maria E. Krautwald-Junghanns with contribution from Thomas J. Herrman. Pub. Mosby St Louis, Baltimore and London 1998.

(2) Essentials of Avian Medicine & Surgery, Brian H. Coles with contributions from Maria Krautwald-Junghanns, Susan E.Orosz & Thomas N.Tully.

Plate No.31 Puffins cohabiting with rabbits on the same cliff edge in the Shetland Isles.

Ms.Anne Meller, naturalist, Unst Isle, Shetland Isles, UK

Plate No. 32 Kittiwakes at nest site with young - source unknown.

Plate No. 33 Two puffins comparing catches of pipefish and sand eels. Photo of Puffin with pipefish, courtesy of Ms Anne Meller, Unst, Shetland Isles, UK. Other photograph of puffin with normal catch of sand eels, Mr John Drakely and used with his permission.

Plate No.34 Louse taken from a casualty wild swan.

Author's own photograph.

Plate 35 Biting louse seen on a captive cockatiel.

Author's own photograph.

Plate 36 Tyrannosaurus Rex.

Author's own photograph, taken of model at Chester Zoo.

Fig. No.15 Comparative sizes of the Indian elephant and Tyrannosaurus Rex.

Author's own drawing.

Plate No.37 Double-wattled Cassowary (Casuarius casuarius.)

Author's own photograph.

Plate No 38 The hind foot with three large toes of Tyrannosaurus Rex, from a model at Chester Zoo.

Author's own photograph.

Plate No.39 Brachiosaurus a sauropod dinosaur model at Chester Zoo.

Author's own photograph.

Fig. No.16 Giraffe compared with the size of a sauropod dinosaur.

Author's own drawing.

Fig. No. 17 The air sacs of a theropod dinosaur.

Leon P.A.M. Claessens

Plate No.40 A particularly tall specimen of a present day representative of the ancient Araucaria trees.

Author's own photograph.

Plate 41 The polyhedra of a large cytoplasmic polyhedrosis virus in the mid gut wall of a biting midge trapped in amber.

Plate No.42 Biting arthropods trapped in both Canadian and Burmese Amber.

Roberta Poinar.

Plate No. 43 Plate tectonics. A rough guide to show how the continents of the Earth were formed as a result of plate tectonics.

Author's own drawing.

Plate No.44 An imaginary reconstructed drawing of what Archaeopteryx was thought to have been like in life.

Plate No.45 An artist's impression of Ichthyornis. It is chasing another prehistoric bird, Apatornis,

Plate No.46. An artist's impression of what Hesperornis may have looked like.

A.D. Cameron.

Plate No.47 The elephant bird (Aepyornis maximus.)

A photograph taken at Zurich Zoo, Switzerland by the author.

Plate No.48 Three eggs. (Left) a model of of an elephant bird's egg, (middle) an ostrich egg (right) hen's egg.

Author's own photograph.

Every effort has been made to contact the copyright holders for permission to use the images featured in this publication and to provide due credit for every image used. For any enquiries with regard to the images featured herein, please contact the publisher in the first instance.

37760179R00209

Printed in Poland
by Amazon Fulfillment
Poland Sp. z o.o., Wrocław